ADVANCE PRAISE

"I am proud to say that I am now using these strategies in *The Seeker's Code* every day of my life. After fourteen years of playing in the NHL and a severe head injury, I have moved from a suffering state to an extraordinary state of being filled with love, happiness, and fulfillment beyond what I thought could ever be possible. Without Donny's teachings and what is in this book, I don't know what things would look like for me. This book will allow you to see everything differently and to know how to identify your true energetic nature, as well as the types and qualities of energy that are available for you to use and tap into for the rest of your life. You can expect instantaneous progress and impact once you learn the skills shared in this book!"

—DAVE SCATCHARD, FORMER NHL PLAYER, LIFE AND BUSINESS COACH WITH ALL-STAR COACHING, AND AUTHOR OF *THE COMEBACK: MY JOURNEY THROUGH HEAVEN AND HELL*

"When it comes to health, life, and impact upon humanity Donny Epstein is one of the greatest masters of energy I have had the honor to know. For nearly two decades, my family has shared his gifts, and now you can too, through *The Seeker's Code.*"

—TONY ROBBINS, *NEW YORK TIMES* BESTSELLING AUTHOR, ENTREPRENEUR, PHILANTHROPIST, AND THE WORLD'S TOP LIFE AND BUSINESS STRATEGIST

"*Donny Epstein, a globally recognized leader in the energetics of healing and transformation offers The Seeker's Code, a profoundly important guide in acquiring personal empowerment. Starting from a fundamental perspective of physics that recognizes energy is life, in a clear user-friendly process, Epstein reveals how we can identify the energetics that show up as limiting beliefs, limited manifestations and reduced impact. And, even more importantly, how we can actively align with the energetics that transcend them.*"

—BRUCE H. LIPTON, PHD, STEM CELL BIOLOGIST, EPIGENETIC SCIENCE PIONEER, AND AUTHOR OF THE BESTSELLING BOOKS *THE BIOLOGY OF BELIEF, SPONTANEOUS EVOLUTION* (WITH STEVE BHAERMAN), AND *THE HONEYMOON EFFECT.*

"*Dr. Donald Epstein's wizardry and teachings about energy states and our relationship with creation are truly extraordinary. By focusing on the energetics, I have led transformational change in my own life and in the governments, universities, corporations, and other organizations with which I have worked. I have been able to make connections between very different people, cultures, and ideas by helping to shift their perspectives and their relationships with the environment. This work is truly revolutionary!*"

—KIMBERLY D. OSBORNE, PHD, FORMER CHIEF STRATEGIC COMMUNICATION ADVISOR TO THE AFGHAN NATIONAL SECURITY FORCES WITH THE US DEPARTMENT OF DEFENSE

"*The planetary climate catastrophe humanity faces is essentially about energy, but not just fossil energy. A redeployment of positive personal energy, the free energy we each command that determines how we engage one another, how we connect our bodies and our emotions with the earth and the environment, how we come to recognize a unity, a oneness with creation—that is the transformative encounter that Donny Epstein invites and guides. Our family has experienced his gift for deepening human connections and spiritual growth, and it leads to an opening up, a discovery that humanity needs to experience to find the deep passion for life and for the earth that confronting climate change requires.*"

—WILLIAM K. REILLY, FORMER EPA ADMINISTRATOR, FORMER PRESIDENT AND CHAIRMAN OF THE WORLD WILDLIFE FUND, AND HEAD OF THE US DELEGATION TO THE EARTH SUMMIT

"According to theoretical physicist David Bohm, 'All matter is frozen light.' In other words, creation is the transformation of light into matter. But how does light become life, and how can life once again become light? In The Seeker's Code, Dr. Donald Epstein offers a portal into the womb of our maximum potential—the liminal space where the ordinary become extraordinary."

—DR. JACOB ISRAEL LIBERMAN, AUTHOR OF *LUMINOUS LIFE: HOW THE SCIENCE OF LIGHT UNLOCKS THE ART OF LIVING*

"Reach out and touch the cosmos through this book. Make nourishing change in your life by tapping the energies of creation."

—BEVERLY RUBIK, PHD, PRESIDENT AND FOUNDER OF THE INSTITUTE FOR FRONTIER SCIENCE

"Donny is a real genius! His innovative theories and protocols for people to optimally use their energy and maximize the application of their potential continues to positively impact countless people's lives, including mine and so many others I know. You will be the next if you read this book. And be sure to allocate time as you will want to experience more at his events!"

—ICHAK ADIZES, FOUNDER OF THE ADIZES INSTITUTE FOR ORGANIZATIONAL THERAPY AND DEVELOPMENT

"Donald Epstein is an inspiring genius enabling people to discover their soul's purpose and mobilize their energy fields toward fully realizing their divine purpose. Most amazing is that people who make use of Epstein's programs and methods can regularly connect with the Holographic Universe where humanity's wisdom and creativity resides—past, present, and future. I've had the good fortune to directly experience Epstein's work, and to my delight, those revolutionary programs have significantly enhanced the gifts I give to others."

—RALPH H. KILMANN, CO-AUTHOR OF THE THOMAS-KILMANN INSTRUMENT (TKI) AND AUTHOR OF *CREATING A QUANTUM ORGANIZATION*

THE SEEKER'S CODE

THE
SEEKER'S
CODE

YOUR ACCESS TO THE
UNREASONABLE AND EXTRAORDINARY

DONNY EPSTEIN

EPIENERGETICS®

THE SEEKER'S CODE
Your Access to the Unreasonable and Extraordinary

FIRST EDITION

ISBN   978-1-5445-4477-9 *Hardcover*
       978-1-5445-4476-2 *Paperback*
       978-1-5445-4475-5 *Ebook*
       978-1-5445-4478-6 *Audiobook*

For my other half, Jackie Louise,

My eternal gratitude for your choosing to be my muse, soul lover, wife—and so much more—on this crazy, unreasonable, and extraordinary journey we continue to share.

I acknowledge your brilliance, beauty, and elegance. I am so blessed by your years of love and dedication to whatever it takes to help me on my/our quest for a greater MORE for each and all of us.

Thank you for your tenacity in helping shape my ideas and the transmissions through these pages, honoring what we truly serve with your wisdom in our co-joined style. Your gentle and permeating energy adds its unique shaping and fragrance to and between the words, helping better articulate the energetics for making a new humanity a reality!

*Together we dedicate this book to this Next Tier of the human experience and instant access to humanity's collective unbound potential through one Field of magic and reverence for **Creation's Codes**.*

CONTENTS

CHAPTER 1

———

AN INVITATION

YOUR UNREASONABLE AND EXTRAORDINARY

This is *not* an ordinary book. These are not ordinary times. You are not ordinary.

You know this, and these pages will speak to you. They will call out to your non-ordinary and *extraordinary* self. You are far more than your-self, and you will realize here that there is no such thing as just *your-self*. Just as when you throw something away, there is really no such place as away, just...a way; so, too, will you throw your less resourceful self away in exchange for something of far greater value: your true way.

What we have been conditioned to believe about ourselves and others, our limits and our impact, the way we interact in the world and the amount of effort required to produce change, how we manifest and what to expect in life—all these beliefs are at best ordinary and in transition to something **MORE**, something so much **MORE**.

The way humans have gone about life and how we impact and are impacted by our world is going through the greatest change in human history.

And Seekers—for if this book has called to you, you are a Seeker—ordinary is no longer enough.

Unreasonable and *Extraordinary* is possible and can replace the ordinary...if you know how to access it.

We are at the changing of the guard for the invisible forces that create, maintain, and transform our lives. The amount of energy available for these forces determines the quality of our experience of reality. Through the ideas in this book, you can find more energy to access these forces and produce *Unreasonable* and *Extraordinary* change in your life and throughout the world.

While our personal development is vital, this book goes beyond what personal development offers; it delivers what many of the historical spiritual traditions have promised.

Just like a musical concert or poetry, and the writings of mystics and visionaries, this book transmits an awareness of and access to the gateway to a Next Tier of humanity.

The codes that organize our existence, what we manifest in our lives and interactions in the world, and the operating system (OS) that provides for what we interpret as reality are in the process of a massive and unprecedented upgrade.

I offer you, my fellow Seekers, access to what only recently became possible for more than a select few disciples of spiritual and transformational practice. What once took a lifetime of dedicated practice can now manifest in an instant!

Pursuing this possibility has been my life's journey. I was born experiencing that which I now know is the primary data stream before it manifests as emotions, thoughts, and what we consider to be important and real. This experience was terrifying to me as a child and has humbled me to my greatest gift.

Now, in my fourth decade of developing healing, consciousness, and transformational methods, and engaging in revolutionary academic research, I have assisted hundreds of thousands, and through those who have practiced these skills, countless others. I am offering you access to the codes of creation to upgrade your life and instantly influence your direct experience of reality.

To describe this unprecedented moment and the nature of the forces at work, the style of writing in *The Seeker's Code* must be unique. As you turn the pages you might find that a sentence calls to you. Some of these words might be speaking to you and require a moment or more to activate a new awareness or energetic. Some might illuminate truth and meaning that make you want to just stop and experience the significance in turning around your map of reality and giving greater understanding of your life.

Most books take a few unique ideas and spin them throughout the pages. Every page here is filled with novel spins on some of the most ancient spiritual promises linked to leading-edge science and the way of the *Unreasonable and Extraordinary*, and often appears to be magical. The Magic is Real™. We are poised for the Next Tier of humanity. What will be available to you requires a different type of communication and promises a new way of interacting in the mega-field of a higher-order participation and creation in life than you may be used to.

This book is written for Seekers, those individuals who are predisposed for this transition in how we, as information systems, individually and collectively are leading this evolution of what is possible for a new human experience and world.

You will know that there are profound intangible forces and data streams, and you will understand that a different energy is being ushered into our world as you continue to read. The words and the energies that perfuse this book will appear in the content, context, and beyond. You are invited on an adventure to new capacities, capabilities, and pragmatic linkage of the parts of life and teachings that you know are true and now available to you.

It's A Special Day!

You've just awakened knowing it is a special day. You hit the snooze alarm too many times so you could stay in your comfortable dream. Feeling excitement and agitation you remember that you are attending a formal celebration today and must be on time. You take a quick shower and prep yourself to leave your house. You hear the pendulum of a cosmic grandfather clock ticking as if overlying your reality. Tick Tick Tick. You think of the old friends who will be there, those who might show up, and the chaos that will likely accompany you. Tick Tick Tick.

You have your clothes laid out. You wanted to wear a particular outfit and someone—your spouse or partner, a friend, or the critic in your head—told you to trash what you had and wear something different, something radically different. And another voice said, "Screw it, just wear what is comfortable." It seems that this has been the theme in more lives than just yours these past few years. It is getting too familiar and tiring.

After you decide which voice to listen to, you attempt to put on your pants or dress, your shirt or blouse. You find your chosen outfit either is stained or missing a button, or you have contracted dunlaps disease—meaning your belly "done laps" over your belt.

Your friend calls you. "Are you awake, and ready?" Somehow, this hits you in a surreal way, perhaps linked to the Tick Tick Tick coming from some other place or dimension. Your friend continues, "We are picking you up in five minutes."

Something is wrong. What used to work doesn't work right now. You wanted so much to be comfortable. You keep working at it and finally the seam tears, or you can't get out that stain smack in the center.

And from that unreal and seemingly real place you sense yourself and perhaps billions of others asking the same thing:

"Are you ready?" Tick Tick Tick...

You sense it, you know it: these are not ordinary times. The old rules about school, work, relationships, business, the way we treat the environment, our money, what's important, what's correct or wrong no longer work. It no longer fits. It is permanently stained. Where, how, and when people gather, the rules of Democrats and Republicans, what is appropriate or not, and even what is important to you no longer fits. It's not only soiled—it's front and center for all to see. You don't know if you have something else to dress in that will hide that which you are or have become or what you want to be. Tick Tick Tick. No more time left. Here you are centerstage and the curtain is about to come up. You feel naked. No matter what you try on, it just doesn't fit.

You are not the only one. Tick Tick Tick.

"It was the best of times, it was the worst of times, it was the age of wisdom, it was the age of foolishness, it was the epoch of belief, it was the epoch of incredulity, it was the season of light, it was the season of darkness, it was the spring of hope, it was the winter of despair."

—CHARLES DICKENS, *A TALE OF TWO CITIES*

Waking Up

Your old or expected way to show up in life no longer works. You realize that you and most of the world slept too long as the greatest shift in human history had been occurring. How we live, think, interact, consume, share and, well just about everything, is either soiled or no longer fits. We have been busy consuming energy and information for our own benefit. We have been unconsciously going through life believing in the narratives shared and asking questions that can never bring us the liberation we must have for this Next Tier of humanity.

And if we did ask these questions, they were not even supported by a world that knew that there is soooo much **MORE** to reality than we have been shown.

More importantly, the way we dressed up for this party called life will no longer work. No matter how Humpty Dumpty tries to get back into his or her shell, it's a mess and will no longer work. There is a crack in the cosmic egg of the human experience of reality.

In the movie *The Matrix*, Morpheus offers Neo a choice between the blue pill of ordinary life and the red pill of something *extraordinary*.

The red pill leads to an uncertain and radically different reality that you know is calling you. It set Neo free from the computer program that was his reality. The blue pill represents a more comfortable prison. It would have allowed him to live in a world bound by the reality that the controlling culture wanted him to consume—as it consumed him.

For Neo, the red pill led to danger as well as adventure. For you and me, it leads to the *Unreasonable* and *Extraordinary*. This Next Tier is already hacking the codes that have allowed humanity to survive and also to destroy the Eden it was given. The sound of the clock ticking is the sound of the pendulum swinging back and forth between the best and worst of times. Tick Tick Tick...

The sense you feel that everything is falling apart is because the energetic that has been running the Matrix is collapsing. The game humanity has accepted as reality is run by a computer code that has been our companion, a code that attempts to control what we think, believe, and desire. The game is glitching. The code no longer works to achieve what is truly possible in this Next Tier of humanity.

Time to wake up. Tick Tick Tick...**TOCK!**

You Are a Seeker

You know there is **MORE**. You can feel it; you sense it; you know that something else unseen is waiting for us to show up—something raw, real, and so beautiful.

The light is cracking through the Matrix. You know that something very powerful and profound is rocking our world and that we are at the juncture of either the worst of times or the best of times. You are ready to take the leap and experience, truly experience, the radically different new energetics that are creating the apps that will play out as reality on your personal screen.

I will take you on a journey. It is a journey, Seeker, that you have been waiting most of your life to take. You have been waiting for someone to take your hand and show you the code that runs what you value most. I will guide you toward understanding and even changing the apps that frame your observations of the world, the narratives of your story, and everything you thought was real. By accessing these codes before they become emotions, thoughts, or reality in your world and life, you can manifest a new reality.

How?

Because if you are a Seeker—Tick Tick Tick—you know that this is our time.

You may ask, "Am I a Seeker?" If you have a hunger, a calling—you might be a Seeker. If you know there's **MORE** to life, and you want to have more, be more, and share more—you might be a Seeker. If you know that you want to constructively tap into **MORE** than the physical world influencing our lives and destinies—you might be a Seeker. It is this **MORE** that has been calling you. You have been on a trajectory to find and experience it. You've felt that calling for a while now and have been unable to answer it consistently. Until now. *That's* why you're reading this book.

Your hunger is for more than just personal satisfaction. You have a calling for a greater humanity, a greater human experience. You feel the pull to go beyond yourself and a hunger to illuminate and help evolve the human experience to a higher level.

This is what makes you a Seeker! In fact, you already embrace at least two of the seven tenets of *The Seeker's Code*, which you will learn about through these pages; you know there is so much more to life than what appears as physical reality or circumstance, and you are obsessed with going beyond who you have been.

Most people focus on trying to be somebody so that they don't feel like a nobody, and they experience life as if we are all separate people sharing a common world. Seekers know there is so much **MORE**. Seekers know that whatever connects us is real and sacred, and they want to take as many others with them as they can on this life adventure. As a Seeker, you know there is an *extraordinary*. You hear the calling, and you are ready for more!

You may have followed the rules of the culture to be who you wanted to be or thought you should be to be accepted or to be "enough." You may have achieved in some area of life, and beyond the short-term victory still felt empty—as your hunger was for something else that you could not articulate or find. Or perhaps you never made it as you hoped for or were promised and you have a calling to pull back the curtain and see what is truly real, powerful, and creative, and how to tap into it and make a difference.

Tick Tick Tick... This book will help you answer that calling for **MORE Unreasonable** and **Extraordinary** in at least one area of your life. It will help you understand the nature of reality and guide you through exercises to learn how to experience and engage with the energies of creation. The content, context, and transmission will help you be able to make the biggest jump of your life and be more of the change that you and humanity requires. Finally, you will know what's *really* behind the curtain, what's *really* running this show called life.

Through the discernments experienced here, you will discover just how you can effortlessly and instantaneously do that. *The Seeker's Code* will be your access to the *Unreasonable* and *Extraordinary*.

Through this book, you will learn the one (r)evolutionary distinction that will allow you access to *your Unreasonable* and *Extraordinary* anytime, anyplace, without having to change anything, let go of anything, develop complex new practices, or use effort. You will understand how you can rapidly turn pain and suffering, or a wound or trauma into a gift.

You will get to know why your life has been the way it has been, why your past or future is truly a source of pain or distraction from the magic of what is available in any moment, and how to transform this instantly. You'll discover you can transcend whatever challenges you may be facing in a relationship, in your business or finances, or in how you impact others and humanity, and make them instantly irrelevant by simply switching how you use your energy.

It's a Matter of Energy

"Energy is liberated matter, matter is energy waiting to happen."
—BILL BRYSON, *A SHORT HISTORY OF NEARLY EVERYTHING*

Focused attention always produces an effect. Prayer is an example of how directed thoughts or attention can make an impact. Thoughts, emotions, conversations, achievements, problems, opportunities, and manifestations are created, sustained, or transformed by one simple ingredient: your available energy. Too often, that energy is just not enough for who you are or who you are called to be. Your *Seeker's Code* adventure is about going beyond thought or mental chatter to experience and gain mastery of the rich energy that drives everything. This rich energy can be available for your personal use to create change and experience and manifest the *extraordinary*.

Ordinary experiencing leads to an ordinary life. Ordinary experiencing usually engages the thinking mind as the narrator of life. *Extraordinary* experiencing transcends that limited way of organizing and interpreting reality. You can either claim *extraordinary*, or your (or someone else's) ordinary will claim you.

For most people, ordinary is enough. They do whatever they can to stay in the ordinary lane of their ordinary lives. Occasionally, they may let themselves rise a little above or dip a little below, but on average, they're pretty much ordinary. Their lives, like a soap opera, after twists and turns, ultimately stay the same. They focus their thoughts primarily on themselves, what others think of them, or their circumstances. What most people call *extraordinary* is more of what makes them feel comfortable and successful or gives them relief from experiencing feelings that they are incomplete and just not enough.

I say, "Enough of that!"

When focused on yourself, the approval of others, or your circumstances, your reality will be limited because you are living within a matrix that offers just enough energy and information to keep you there. As you discover how to instantly have more available energy to download an app that guides you to play a bigger game, you'll radiate a different reality in the world.

Staying the same will never do for a Seeker. They must reach for *extraordinary* and create a larger scope of connection and participation. Seekers, like large enterprises with numerous employees and processes, need access to more energy to support them so they can make and distribute *extraordinary* products and fulfill *unreasonable* goals. Ordinary thinking cannot power the **Unreasonable** or **Extraordinary**.

By experiencing how to use unbound and directed energy, you'll discover your personal recipe for accessing the *extraordinary*. You can transcend the habit of trying over and over to *think* through your problems. With more available energy, a problem instantly dissolves and is replaced by an opportunity.

Tick Tock to the Next Tier

This book will help you learn how to access that energy. As a Seeker, you are hardwired to thrive in the next level of humanity, where energy is the currency for creating change.

Humanity is entering the Next Tier of the human experience where new energetics—allowing us to create change through energy—will shape how we live, consume, give, relate, and manifest. The actual source of energy for our bodies, relationships, business, and what we influence will change. What we're experiencing right now will change. We are at the transition point from the way humans have lived for centuries, the era of using force or violence to release the energy required to fuel our lives to make change. In the Next Tier, energy and resourcefulness are unbound and freely available.

In this Next Tier, no force or violence will be required. We might compete with ourselves to be **MORE** and collaborate with others to share **MORE**. And we'll still bind energy and value the physical world. The difference will be that we will choose to consume in a different way, in a way that consciously respects the source of energy that fuels our experience of reality. By employing the energetics of this Next Tier, we will be able to distribute more energy and opportunity for others.

Seeker, you can gracefully transition *now* into Next Tier dynamics by claiming the unbound energy and potential to access *Creation's Codes*.

Creation's Codes are the self-organizing principles that allow for the manifestation of everything in the universe. A simple way to see how *Creation's Codes* work is by looking at a spider building a web. What is propelling it to do that? What manual or book of directions is it following? What architectural plans? None! *Creation's Codes* program the spider, like all of life, to express this organizing intelligence and create its masterpiece.

Similarly, it's *Creation's Codes* that form the body, our emotions, the ability to think, our connection to the immaterial nature of life, and to the web of creation.

They are what creates the apps that allow a caterpillar to turn into a butterfly. In an embryo, they determine the precise moments when cells differentiate into lungs, into hearts, and into fingers. They underlie all cause-and-effect situations and help organize all aspects of our existence.

Creation's Codes are immutable. They create and manifest consistent with the amount of energy available. And while *Creation's Codes* are immutable, the amount of energy we have available *is* mutable.

We exist in something akin to an artificial intelligence program running *Creation's Codes.*

Through our focused attention, we can help *Creation's Codes* to manifest in ways that transcend what the AI program and cultural codes want us to believe is real. We can hack the cultural illusion and create something more profound.

We can learn to use energy that is consistent with our personal nature in such a way that *Creation's Codes* become available to us in their purest and highest order. Suddenly, we experience unbound energy that gives us new opportunities to download life and reality beyond the ordinary. We become greater expressions of the codes of creation.

In *The Seeker's Code,* you will learn the key to effortlessly accessing the unbound energy and manifesting more of your potential. You will also instantly participate in a higher-order of experience, where we are all connected as one Field—the cloud of data with access to every possible thought, feeling, and manifestation.

You have a choice—the red pill or the blue pill. You can choose to embrace your role as a Seeker. Seekers who become aware of, acknowledge, or accept the forces that *really* run our lives—the very forces that run the universe—will have a much easier time accessing *Creation's Codes*. It will seem effortless for them to initiate the changes they want to see in themselves and the world. Creation's apps will take over with absolute perfection. Your life will go beyond ordinary, awakening to the sacred and majestic nature of authentic energized conscious living.

I've seen people transform their lives in seconds when they have more available energy to access *Creation's Codes*. And here's the kicker: it doesn't take years of spiritual practices, and you don't have to let go of anything to do it. Although, after you experience these codes, your other practices will be enhanced. You can have greater health without having to work on it. You can often have a tremendous relationship and profound intimacy without having to get counseling, having to take a course, or having to do anything differently.

The key to it all is gaining greater mastery of your energetic nature and access to the invisible forces that direct your life and your experience of reality.

You don't have to change *any* of the circumstances in your life in order to have the *extraordinary* life you were meant to live. Why? Because it's all a matter of energy activating the codes that create everything in existence. And the time has come for you to learn how to use it.

Here's What's Coming

In the pages ahead, you will discover your personal recipe for using *your* energy to access the forces of creation. You will wake up from the limited life app that we all have believed was our container in life and realize it does not contain us—instead, it nurtures the ordinary that much of our conditioning and culture represents.

This book will explain to you why your life has been the way it has up to this point. It will explain what the heck is going on in the world these days as we are shifting from the energetic that is running the show to a radically different one. You will discover why you've been living the ordinary, or even sub-ordinary, and why things seemed to have dropped to a more painful place or to a less resourceful version of you. You will learn why your experience of life sometimes improves and becomes more resourceful and productive. You will understand how and why, at times, life required so much effort and at other times was filled with ease, and why you sometimes just managed to get by.

Most importantly, you will see why and how things can become *extraordinary*, and you will know that all that is needed for that to happen is the focused use of your energy.

Instead of being part of the breakdown of your health, relationship, or business, or assisting with the downsizing of humanity's potential, as a Seeker you can draw upon a higher-order set of codes that, with enough available energy, you will easily become part of the emerging renaissance.

This is a simple process. First, we will come to understand the basics about reality. Next, we'll look at how all available energy and all information and data available to us resides in the Field—that area that surrounds us all. The Field is an active information and energy cloud storage medium where all the potential information, data and the energy of the universe resides for our use. The amount of energy available to you (your E-State) determines the quantity and quality of information or consciousness that is manifested in your body and life.

With the basics covered, we'll discuss energy states—the state of available energy, or the "Real E-State" of energy, which is the aggregate wealth of energy available for yourself and your legacy. The richness of your energy is what allows you to organize your life to access the *Unreasonable* and *Extraordinary*.

This book will give you the tools to discover the one discernment that can profoundly increase your energy efficiency and information processing that impacts your interaction and attraction in the world. That is enough to take you from "I can't" to "I can." Or from "I don't know" to "Here's the answer." Or from "I don't like you" to "I love you."

This discernment can make the difference between just treating your condition or healing you, between leaving your relationship or transforming it, between being confused or instantly knowing, between experiencing post-traumatic stress or realizing (or *real-eyes-ing*) that it was really post-traumatic growth.

With enough energy to fuel your self-organizing wisdom, *Creation's Codes* can immediately transform the organization of your body, mind, thoughts, beliefs, roles, sense of self, and relationships to improve your intimacy levels, business, finances, and your collaboration with all of humanity.

This astounding metamorphosis happens without your need to do anything else.

How Do I Know This?

My life quest has been to find what I call a soul signature. What is the identifier that makes you *you*? What are the forces of attraction and manifestation that, like a magnetic field attracting iron filings, organizes your body in health and the people who impact your life, your relationships, your business and finances?

I studied for and received my doctorate degree in chiropractic because, as few know, it's based on a principle that there is an organizing intelligence in all of life that is transmitted through the nervous system. This was the beginning of my "professional" journey. This book is inspired by these principles—and so much more. When there is an alteration in the tension between the brain and body, like a violin string that is stretched, it alters the vibration and the music it plays. *Creation's Codes* communicate through the nervous system's vibrational sharing of information. With a distorted energy and information system, the orchestration of life is modified. Therefore, less of this intelligence can be personified and less energy is available to manifest the organizing wisdom. The nervous system links our body and Field to create our experience of reality.

Realizing information requires energy to manifest anything in the world, I was led down a path of discovery.

I had to find a way for new sources of energy to fuel the organizing wisdom and bring into existence the magical celebration of the *Unreasonable* and *Extraordinary*. My research focused on answering how could I and every person on Earth tap into the same intelligence that manifests all of creation? What are the codes, the apps needed for us to experience the illusion we call life in a way that is so much bigger than we are conditioned to believe?

As a healer, educator, systems developer, author, researcher, practitioner, and a soul-on-fire to help liberate and assist a new humanity to emerge, I have professionally taken care of at least a quarter-million people around the world. Close to 100,000 attendees have experienced my transformational events. I have taught many thousands of doctors. I have developed expanded models of healing the energetics of life and manifestation. Collectively "my" various methods have been practiced on all seven continents. Academians at various colleges and universities have studied the characteristics of new properties of the nervous system and of healing that occur with the spinal care I developed. Articles in various journals suggesting new maps of reality, healing, experiencing, and accessing an expanded reality have been published. Novel levels of coherence within individuals and between people have been demonstrated. We call that "entanglement," or as Einstein referred to it, "spooky action at a distance." We have discerned human identifiers and upgrades of the human OS.

The principles in this book and what led to them are lived by people of all walks, including world leaders, CEOs, thought leaders and celebrities. They're used by those creative geniuses and transformational and spiritual icons, athletes, coaches of all types and regular people seeking to be more, give more, and make a difference in some way, small or huge...and now by you.

It's Time

Imagine you are calling a phone number to reach an all-inclusive, adult, paradise vacation resort. You dial the number a few times and each time someone answers, to your surprise and repulsion, "City morgue." Regardless of which directory or online search you use to find the number, for some reason you continue to receive the same city morgue connection.

To get the fantasy vacation, you'll have to dial a different number. *That* is what this book is about. It is about helping you to hack the codes that lead you from city morgue to *Unreasonably Extraordinary* fantasy resort, and how to achieve this outcome each and every time.

Before continuing, be forewarned: instead of being given any answers, you will be given a new and exciting path of inquiry. This new set of questions will magically provide more unbound available energy for you to wake up from the matrix of ordinary and barely reasonable so you can experience the energy of what is true, real and profound. You will move from doubt or fear to trusting that you can tap into the energy that created the universe and use it to manifest change. And, you will know that what you do with your energy will impact your life and the lives of others. All of this will happen without the need to change anything in your life, do anything differently, or have to force or manage something. Just energize *Creation's Codes* and the organizing wisdom of life is now available!

BAM! TOCK!

It is time to admit and celebrate that you aren't like most people. You tried to be like others, and it just hasn't worked. You can act or pose like other more "normal" people who believe that this physical world is all that there is, and the one who dies with the most stuff wins.

They just don't get it. There is a whole universe outside and inside that is waiting for us, one that we can only access if we look beyond the life we are asked to live, beyond the commercially acceptable script inside a flat-screen TV.

You have a gift, knowing that there is so much more in the unseen and that "real" is like a curse sometimes.

What you are truly seeking is also seeking you...

Because you are a Seeker.

You Are Ready!

You are about to get an intimate look at the energetics that manifest and create all aspects of your life, and our collective lives. You will get to experience that which you sensed or hoped or prayed would be true. You are no longer alone or weird in recognizing that there are invisible energetics running the show in your life, our lives, and in the world. There is some perfect intelligence, perhaps a divine and sacred organizing wisdom that creates and moves mountains for us to manifest in life when we are coherent, filled with energy and more reverently connected to this source. It is finally our time—and time for us to demonstrate that circumstances are no longer the causes or limitations in our lives.

You've been waiting your entire life to expand into *MORE*—to live, radiate, attract, and manifest the *Unreasonable* and *Extraordinary*.

Now, it is time to dial up new apps transmitting the energized organizing intelligences of creation for more than validation or a momentary high. It is time for a new life for you and the people around you. It is time to be part of this tipping point for a new humanity.

You're finally able to get, be, and share what you were made for. There are seven statements that articulate those beliefs, knowings, and values that all Seekers have in common. They transcend our conditioning—often in spite of what we have been told is real and what we have been told to ignore or disregard.

Seekers, these *Seeker's Codes* are a spiritual knowing, a calling for you that many have forgotten, repressed or denied. The recitation of these seven declarations reunites you with a real and mystical force. It reminds Seekers through all of humanity—of what we might call *"Home"*...regardless of where we have been living.

We are in the midst of a great remembering for Seekers, which is occurring in the midst of a great forgetting of most of our connection with the same forces that create everything and everyone. This connection sustains, transforms, and awakens us to new energetics of life with a much more direct, graceful, effortless and profound access to the true organizing wisdoms of life, *Creation's Codes*.

Seekers, because you know several of the *Seeker's Codes* that prepare and initiate us for this new energetic, you will find that *Creation's Codes* will find YOU as you find them. The key is to experience and understand the instantaneous manifestation of these invisible forces made visible—as a new YOU, a new world, and a new reality. All of this manifests through the conscious and ecological use of energy and information for **WE**.

As you read or listen to the words through these pages and the transmission of this new energetic, remember that we were incarnated as stewards of this Next Tier for a more conscious humanity.

The Seeker's Code

I suggest you slowly repeat each of the *Seeker's Codes* sentences at least three times.

Three of these *Seeker's Codes* have two parts separated by a slash. The phrase after the slash imparts even more energy to the statement. With each code, state the entire code and sense the impact upon yourself, and for those who can, sense a resonance in the space around you. Next repeat the codes with a slash only up to the slash. Then repeat again with the entire statement. Take notice of any difference between the way two statements sound and feel to you. If there's no change, no worries. This distinction will become clearer as your journey continues.

1. WE KNOW THERE IS SO MUCH MORE TO LIFE THAN WHAT APPEARS AS PHYSICAL REALITY OR CIRCUMSTANCE.

2. WE HAVE AN OBSESSION TO GO BEYOND WHO WE HAVE BEEN.

3. WE SEEK A RICHER, MORE MAGICAL, AND EXTRAORDINARY EXPERIENCE FOR OURSELVES/AND FOR OTHERS.

4. WE WANT TO GIVE, GET, LEARN, AND LIVE WITH A BIGGER PURPOSE/INSPIRING PROFOUND IMPACT.

5. WE WISH TO ACCESS THE MULTIDIMENSIONAL ENERGETICS THAT MAGICALLY CREATE AND CONNECT US ALL.

6. WE RECOGNIZE THE POWER OF FOCUSED ATTENTION AND ENERGY/AND CONSCIOUS CHOICE.

7. WE HONOR AND CELEBRATE THE SACRED NATURE OF LIFE/AND WISH TO SPREAD ITS MAGIC.

Congratulations, Seekers! With this awareness alone, the apps in the game that have been playing, you have already begun to change. As you continue to gain access to the energy that will allow you to manifest and create in the Next Tier, I invite you to turn the page and allow yourselves to choose a new game, one that you can win and you can bring as many others as you'd like to come and win too. Choose a new game of life!

Acknowledge that you are a Seeker in at least one area of life. One area is more than enough to begin to access the *Unreasonable* and *Extraordinary*! You are a Seeker. You are ready.

It's time to read on. The rest of this book and this Next Tier of reality is calling you. Your journey has already begun!

Tick Tick Tick...frigging **TOCK!**

CHAPTER 2

———

THE JOURNEY BEGINS

THE FIELD OF POSSIBILITIES

"Energy is contagious, either you affect people or you infect them."

—T. HARV EKER

You are dramatically poised fifteen stories above ground, nervously seated on a classical wooden roller coaster. There is what is called potential energy bound up in the car and the tracks and within you. It is poised for major change, and in a moment this potential will be converted to other forms of energy to take you on an exciting ride.

The brake is slowly released as the force of gravity starts accelerating the car. Effortlessly, potential energy is converted into "work" energy and heat energy. It also creates fear and excitement and exhilaration energy for you as the car drops rapidly at dizzying speeds and then heads up again on the next hill.

This ride transforms bound energy, as expectation, or whatever you had been thinking or worried about, and is replaced by the sheer experience of the moment. The way that the energy is changed from one type to another within you, in that car, in other cars, in other riders, in the amusement park, and as the park relates to the larger system is called energetics.

Energetics is the science of how energy changes form within all systems: chemical, physical, social, the body, relationships, business, political, economic, environmental, and more.

I suggest that the conventional definition of energetics be expanded to how energy changes form in a system and *thus also changes the system.* Energetics influence the outcome of everything you think, imagine or do, and of anyone you interact with regardless of the apparent space between you and whomever else you can imagine.

In this way, the roller coaster can be a metaphor for your life, taking the energy that is bound and finding a way for it to be freed up to create change, taking your potential into potentiation—for your life and for everything in the world.

In this book, we will be exploring the energetics of the various aspects of your life, those that are working sub-ordinary, those that are just ordinary and staying there, and those that have the potential to be *extraordinary.*

The first step on that journey is answering one of the most basic, important questions: "What are you?"

What Are You?

According to the *Talmud*, a central part of Jewish scripture, "We do not see the world as it is. We see it as we are." This profound statement contains the secret and mechanism for developing your Seeker's "superpowers" and the answers that humanity requires. The questions it raises are simple and profound—none more so than "What are you?" This inquiry has been in my awareness since I was a child.

When I was seven years old, my teacher asked me, "What do you want to be when you grow up?" I told her that to answer that question I have to know *what I am now*.

Who am I? Why am I here? What am I made of? These are the questions that many spiritual texts have sought to answer or at least set into motion for life to inspire a response.

Always, the first question to answer, the asking of which is like tapping a series of perfectly arranged dominos is, "What am I?"

Over the decades, I have danced with the various answers to this question, and I have helped others do more than answer this: actually live it. The answer has rocked and continues to rock my world and the world of others. And I assume you are reading this to have your world rocked. An added bonus to this gig is that the world we live in will be similarly rocked—transformed or even awakened.

Before you can be rocked, I must ask you one question: what is your tolerance for *extraordinary*? And I mean, "Oh My God, is this *extraordinary* even possible?" In some of the chapters ahead, the light might shine so brightly you may want to put on shades—that is, your custom personally designed shades! These shades were designed by the voice in your head that sees *extraordinary* and says, "It is bullsh*t." This voice is part of the same shaping energy of the culture that, at best, wants ordinary.

To know what you are and to ride the roller coaster to *extraordinary*, you must recognize that we're made of **MORE**! You know it, and I know it. Maybe it's time you get on board, Seeker, with the forces that made you from your mother's and father's seeds and pushed you, and nudged you, and directed you, and held you through some times where you would not, could not, and did not want to see or be with the *extraordinary* magic of creation.

Aunt Sadie's Journey

Let me show you the true potential of *extraordinary* in your life. A few years ago, a company in California, let's call it Aunt Sadie's Organics, was losing business and disappointing customers. They shared that their problem was they relied on one supplier for the food source necessary for their creation and distribution of their main product which was their primary source of revenue. They had a critically timed big launch planned that was essential to the growth of the company. They gambled "everything" on this expansion, and nothing further could happen unless it was a success.

Everything began to go wrong when their one major supplier couldn't provide enough for their launch. Unable to get supplies, they couldn't create their products. Customers were disappointed. This is a common reality in today's world with the distribution of international suppliers' products being bound and there not being enough energy to change this.

The owners, employees and managers were understandably distressed. At this point, their hopes for growth disappeared, and they were struggling to just stay afloat. They searched to find alternatives and found themselves thwarted at every turn. In fact, they seemed to attract even more troubles along the way, including a large lawsuit that was looming. Eventually, the team realized they were trapped in a downward spiral: the more they focused on what was wrong, the more time, money and hope was lost. For the company to survive, something had to change. A different approach was needed.

A consultant familiar with my teachings about the influence of energetics on the creation and organization in life and business was engaged. She spoke with a respected company executive to consider the different levels of energy that ignited or extinguished the bound potential energy available for change and transformation.

Since the term "corporation" comes from the Latin word *corpus*, meaning "body" or, in a collective sense, "body of people," she recognized that change was needed in the team to ignite the energy for manifestation. The energetics, conversations, actions, and vision of the employees needed a more coherent focus.

It became obvious that the simple truth playing out was a lack of constructive available energy pervading the office culture, collective mind and finances. The focus on a seemingly unsolvable problem, ordinary thinking and the ceiling of thought being "poor me, poor helpless us" had to change.

The CEO and management had been in similar situations in which their companies lost resources and had failed. They were leading and unconsciously broadcasting a Field of bound (unavailable) energy and information linked to those painful points in their lives. This further supported the manifestation of a dark cloud that became pervasive throughout the company. The conversation and focus was on what was not happening and how to avoid this from happening again on their watch. What was being experienced was a dramatic example of the expression, "Where the attention goes, the energy flows."

Since it is always the darkest before the dawn, how could they ignite and harness or direct the light in the darkness? Might a different source and level of energy somehow create a tipping point in the signal the company was broadcasting to the larger system and initiate a different outcome for the company?

After all, where the energy flows, attention and manifestation goes!

With the help of the consultant, those working in the company realized that they were utilizing energetic strategies counterproductive to the desired outcomes instead of ways that would ignite greater available energy to attract and create new perspectives.

One of the executives and a manager seemingly at the same time recognized this. After experiencing it, it was like they were hit by the light of truth. They realized **MORE** was needed.

MORE is the path for the Seeker. Less is the path of loss. When this was recognized, something happened. Since the company was being coached about different levels of energy and how this played out for them, they recognized some fundamental principles that influenced and regulated the way things and people show up in all areas of life. Pure awareness of where they were at, without attempting to change anything, opened something up.

As awareness took hold that the energetics are what really pulls the strings on our experience of reality, it ignited the light of dawn upon the darkness. That light spread. To those at Aunt Sadie's, it seemed magical as the impenetrable mist of doubt, fear and lack dissolved into the light.

In just moments, employees, management and executives began sitting straighter, held their heads more erect, took deeper breaths and irradiated a sparkle in their eyes and a palpable sense of momentum fueled by some knowing of the future. This was spread amongst the team as a collective energy.

What had seemed impossible, *unreasonable* or unexpected was now in process. Some other force was back in action. It was that same force that inspired the vision of the founder and the employees' commitment to the company's purpose.

"Welcome to the *extraordinary*," the consultant said.

For the first time in weeks, the individuals and collective company could step back from their issues with the supplier. Suddenly, they could look at the bigger picture. They asked: What is the purpose of the company? What are we producing for people, and why? Are we sure we're doing something in alignment with our highest purpose and adding value to our clients' lives?

With more energy available, they were able to ask bigger questions, and these bigger questions further switched the energy they were using to power their thoughts, giving them a bigger perspective on the system that they were part of. Their energy led them to different answers and led them to a new perspective, one in alignment with their highest purpose and focused on more than just their struggle for commerce. The energy available opened whole new dimensions for many of them, and activated a world that they had forgotten or perhaps had never before experienced.

Magically, two days later, the supplies were released from quarantine, and soon after that the lawsuit against them disappeared. More innovation and new clients flourished.

You Are Data

This story could be your story. It could have been about your health and the real way that you turned things around, or about your relationships, your finances, or how you shared the gifts you were made for and followed a calling that personally invited your larger participation in life.

To capture the same instantaneous and almost magical manifestation in your life, you must first understand the nature of energy and your relationship to it. To that end, I ask that you now take the time to answer this question: what are you?

Seeker, you are interpreted data. And, therefore, everyone and everything in the world you observe is also data manifested.

The thing that turns data, or information, into a usable form—into the apps we choose to shape or influence our reality—is one thing. Or maybe it is a non-thing...**it is energy**!

The amount of energy you have available helps that data to become code. Code is data that is prepared to be used by an information processing system, like a computer, our body or a corporation like Aunt Sadie's. The quality and quantity of our interpretation, the meaning, and how we respond to this code depends upon how much *energy* is available to turn potential into reality.

We see and experience the world with the same amount and type of energy that we are. The more light (energy) we are in the moment, the brighter life gets and the easier it is to experience the magic that is here and within you. The less light we are, the more difficult it is to see what is really going on and our attempt to achieve, love, heal or manifest requires more effort.

Energy is the currency of change. Energy is neither created nor destroyed. Instead, it is changed from one form to another, making energy available to do "work" to fuel the actual codes that create, sustain, and transform your life instantly—in a way that is consistent with your true nature and the nature of all systems. That is what this book is about.

With enough energy, the qualities of our bodies, emotions, thoughts, and manifestations are upgraded with a larger bandwidth of potentiated potential.

You will discover strategies to transform your consumption and radiation energy which will transform the quality and quantity of the data you manifest.

As the Talmud verse mentioned earlier suggests, everything in the seen or apparently real world is created, sustained, "redeemed" or transformed by invisible forces. These invisible forces are the primary reality. I call these forces *Creation's Codes*. Our ability to access *Creation's Codes* determines everything and even the no-things that become everything.

When I speak about *Creation's Codes*, I am referring to a vibrational light and data transmission that manifests creation's potential impact on all aspects of our reality, our capacities, and our existence. *Creation's Codes* express the apps of the various self-organizing energetic intelligences that many of the spiritual traditions refer to. This is that which creates the thinker that can think, the lover than can love, and the physical attributes that provide for these. With the activation of unbound energy, their traits and capacities are created.

Before there is an achievement, a plan, a goal, a desire, a hope or a dream, there is an intangible force or impulse, a data stream that comes from another dimension or time.

Our ability to grasp this, interpret this and act upon its guidance with enough energy to manifest its outcome determines how we perceive, act upon, and create during our life and the legacy that follows us.

This is an example of EpiEnergetics.

What Is EpiEnergetics?

EpiEnergetics is the conscious and ecological use of energy and information to manifest the *extraordinary*. *Consciousness* means that you are aware of your own existence and the environment around you. It means that you recognize that it is you interpreting and interacting in the world. *Ecological* like in the story of Goldilocks and the Three Bears means that you don't want to use too much or too little of the chairs or the bed or the porridge, and in our case, the energy. You want the least amount of energy and information to get the greatest "cluck for the buck."

Epi means "beyond, between or around an object or person." Electricity does not pass through a wire; it jumps in the "Epi-space" around the wire. A nerve impulse does not pass through a nerve; it travels in the Epi-space around the nerve, just as thoughts do not exist in your head or brain. They are the nervous system's vibration or oscillation that links your brain to the Epi-space around you to create meaning.

"Epi," in this context, is the space between the physical world and the space around it. The *epi*dermis is the outer layer of the skin. It is the point of union of the physical bound body and the multidimensional reality and information beyond it.

Therefore, EpiEnergetics is the term I developed to describe a novel and revolutionary way of experiencing, understanding, and influencing the world. It is the way of the Next Tier of human existence and the ambrosia of Seekers.

It recognizes, honors, and advances the union of the material and non-material, between the seen and unseen, between potential and manifestation, between energy and consciousness. It is the means of transformation, awakening, bringing the mystery into reality and helping reality to awaken to **MORE**.

This will become more apparent as you experience the ideas and practices in *The Seeker's Code*.

EpiEnergetics helps you to know and live more of your personal way of moving from the sub-ordinary to the ordinary to the *extraordinary*. In the chapters to come, you will discover your personal recipe for what you experience as reality.

"Everything is energy, and that is all there is to it. Match the frequency of the reality you want, and you cannot help but get that reality. It can be no other way. This is not philosophy. It is physics."

—ATTRIBUTED TO ALBERT EINSTEIN

To impact the world we see—our tangible reality—we must dial up the invisible forces, the energy that we use to experience, interpret, and radiate that which we are. And my fellow Seekers, the energy that fuels the codes that create our reality, is what we can effortlessly get acquainted with, harness and change.

Through EpiEnergetics, nothing else needs to happen. You can have an impact on your environment, your work, your play, your love or the space you live in. It is hard to believe, and this is because it is *unreasonable*.

This transformation and manifestation is possible because not only do we see the world as we are, it sees us the same and meets us there. The EpiEnergetics of our realities collide, caressing, seducing, influencing and constructively or destructively interfering with the energetics we express and radiate in the moment.

What's even better is you can help transform the lives of those you focus your attention upon without attempting to change them. Instead, you wish to inspire more available energy for them. Through our connectedness, you *can* become the change you wish to see in the world.

And the most wonderful part is that change can effortlessly happen in just a moment! You will discover how you can experience the oh-so-sacred moment that "everything" changes. You'll see areas of your life where things may be a little messed up, due to a power (and therefore accessible energy and information) shortage. I am sure that you or those you care most about have patterns in health, relationships, business or perhaps with intimacy that have been full of drama, finding a cause for blame in the past. Or you may be practicing an energetic that promotes potential calamity in the future.

This is possible for you and for everything through EpiEnergetics, and also through the connections that bring us together in the Field.

The Field

"The field is the sole governing agency of the particle."

—ALSO ATTRIBUTED TO ALBERT EINSTEIN

The Field is the force of attraction or repulsion of everything and everyone. It connects everything to everything else and to *no-thing*. The Field contains energy and the information of all of creation. It is the information cloud that we must tap into to give meaning to life and to prod for creation and manifestation.

This informational Field (or data storage "cloud") is within and around you. It has enough energy to manifest itself as physical reality. The way the ripples of your informational Field interact with other informational Fields, from a subatomic quantum level, to the molecular level and finally, to the visible body level, creates the dance of life.

Every atom in existence generates a Field. The difference between a proton and electron generates a charge. The spins of electrons create a charge and the spins on electrons also create a quantum reality sharing of information across time and space. Each of these tiny Fields influences larger ones, just as larger Fields influence smaller ones.

All communication begins and ends in the Field.

You, me, the sun, the moon, the stars and everything you perceive as solid reality is at its basic core an energetic and information Field. The Field exists in all the spaces that are around and between all the matter. And it's more than just empty space. It is made of energy and information that influences our lives. It exists around the atoms that make up your body, your cells, organs and you. The Field communicates and vibrates, and its vibration is a communication between parts and between you and others. This vibration or oscillation is the language of life.

These vibrations are expressions of data and are intrinsic to all communication. They exist in all dimensions and communicate between them.

The Field is truly vast and includes nearly infinite smaller Fields. Some are truly immense. There is a cultural Field that influences how we think, what we want, what we like and don't like, how we behave and what we should and should not say or do. We meet the Field before we meet the person, and each Field is influencing our possible experience and manifestation in life. As we have more unbound energy available, we can begin to influence these Fields, and we can choose to be ruled by them, choose our degree of participation or choose how we actually can transcend them.

There is a Field at a sporting event and different Fields for the home and visiting team. There are Fields between political parties and religions. When driving, for example, between Italy and Switzerland, there is a palpable Field shift. Even though Italian is spoken on both sides of the border, the Field is different. It's the same as if you were to travel between France and Germany, or in the USA, between the far northern and southern states. There is a different Field in New York City than across the river in New Jersey. There is a different Field between art, chemistry or business students. There is a different Field for Seekers and non-Seekers. Once we recognize that we are all playing and being played by Fields within Fields, we can further answer what we are—and also where we need to go.

Your Field is a small subset of this larger Field. The human biofield or auric field is an electromagnetic field that is also the information cloud our nervous system connects with to play out the apps we consider to be reality. It is associated with states of consciousness. How it influences gene expression, membrane function and our lives is the subject of the highest level of academic inquiry.

I am fortunate to know, care for and collaborate with some of these people. I have spoken at conferences and am involved in studying and finding new ways to understand and experience the connection of this Field with the human nervous system. I have developed methods in healing and living that influence and actually evolve new properties in the part of our personal Field that we can directly influence. I call this the EpiField. It is here that you can adjust the sails on the winds of creation toward the *extraordinary*.

Our Senses Are Field Sensors

Ultimately, the subtle changes in the energy of your Field influence all your senses, emotions, thoughts, actions and meanings.

Our senses relay subtle energy changes in our immediate Field to the central nervous system. The central nervous system, which coordinates all body parts and functions, interprets the vibrational and electromagnetic signals it gets depending on the amount of energy available. This also determines the meaning we give it. Is it a threat? Is it a gift? Is it interesting? Is it fascinating? Is it something to be avoided? The emotions, thoughts and meaning also reflect this interface between the nervous system and our Field.

Vision is a consequence of the change in photons in your Field that hits your retina. That information is carried to the brain, lighting it up and is interpreted as what you see. Hearing the roar of the lion two kilometers away on the African Serengeti is created by subtle energy changes in the molecules of the atmosphere in your Field that hits your eardrum. This data is carried by the energy of the vibration to your brain for your interpretation. Similarly, smell is your experience of the disturbance of your nose and brain receptors triggered by a chemical change of information and energy in your Field. The Field is also at work in our preferences. Have you ever walked into a room, seen somebody and instantly thought "I have to talk to that person"? That thought came to you because somehow your Fields resonated in a way that said "pay attention here" as data between the two of you was activating something in the space between you, asking for more to manifest.

Have you ever walked into a room where the tension was so strong, you could "cut it with a knife"? You just *knew* an argument had just happened. You can feel the energy of the argument still there in the room. We tend to like or move toward those people or experiences that add more energy and give us more resourcefulness. These are the people and experiences we are drawn towards. We tend be repelled by people or experiences that drop our energy. These are the people and experiences we dislike.

Imagine these senses amplified thousands or millions of times to redirect your life in a constructive way.

You are always influencing and being influenced by energetic Fields. Any change you make to transform, grow, achieve or love is, more or less, first associated with a change in how your Field is unconsciously—or as you will learn here, consciously—engaged. Your behaviors and even the organization of your body and life change.

Spiritual Traditions Work in Fields and Codes

Most spiritual traditions—including Judaism, Christianity, Buddhism, Hinduism and Islam—give their own names to these Fields that organize the capacity to have a body that can feel, think, manifest, and experience the true nature of our spirit. These Fields are considered fields of consciousness that transmit information about our existence and help us manifest. I consider the information in these Fields as apps for specific use of data transmitted in code—*Creation's Codes*. Everything in existence and all potential is information. To access information, it needs to be broken into bits of data. In order to be utilized by an information processing system, such as a living cell or organism or a computer, it must be converted into code. This is how biological systems work. The organizing wisdom of life (*Creation's Codes*) makes us the architect of all that we experience as reality by giving us access to its larger codes. When we think as a spouse, business owner or student—or in any role or emotional state—we then take that code and convert it into an app to play it out in our lives.

The quality of what is created with these codes is dependent upon how much energy is available to manifest the information that is your body, emotions, thoughts, relationships, business, finances and impact upon the Field of humanity.

When people take hallucinogens or some other mind-altering drug, they experience more of the unbound information of the Field that is activated in spiritual states. Yes, even these spiritual states exist because of the magnitude of information activated beyond the bound roles and identity of the mind. When losing oneself in lovemaking, spiritual rapture, or an experience of true healing, everything drops away and there is no-thing to think about. Without even a thinker, you are experiencing more from the Field and its unbound potential.

These consciousness states, cherished and described in the writings of so many religious mystics, are accessible through the Field. Each of these states is available with its corresponding level of energy to manifest information. In the coming chapters, you will learn about the different energetics that potentiate your life through your Field.

Often, when some *Thing* is bothering you, or you can't achieve some *Thing*, it is because the thing is bound energy, bound information, and unavailable for transformation; there is no available energetic to transform the bound energy into change. In **The Seeker's Code**, we call for the needed unbound and the no-thing to light up the codes of creation—the organizing wisdoms of life. The organizing intelligences of life do not have to liberate anything. There is no breakthrough to be made. As soon as the light is on there is more energy for the forces of creation to just create something better. You witness it and smile knowing there is something bigger in charge.

The Universe Is Created through Fields

The Field is the force of attraction or repulsion of everything and everyone. It connects everything to everything and to no-thing. The whole universe is created by and inside everything in the Field.

Within and around a seed is a Field. This Field is organized by the particular **Seeker's Code** that creates what I call "the Weaver." The Weaver lines everything and everyone up at the right place and time for the optimum unfolding.

The Field attracts the sun and calls the worms and insects to it to create nitrogen for fertilizer. As a tree emerges in the fertile soil, it provides shelter to house a seemingly infinite number of organisms. The overlapping Fields attracted by the seed's Field communicate in alignment with *Creation's Codes*.

The Field attracts the right insects to the tree to pollinate the flowers and to protect against predators. It produces fruit, some of which falls and rots at the base of the tree returning nutrients to the soil and attracting other insects and animals. Some stay on the branches until they are ripe. The ripened fruits attract animals that consume it and defecate the seed-laden waste, burying it with their claws or carrying the seeds in their fur to later fall elsewhere. Or perhaps the Field calls the animal to store the seeds for winter or to bury them for later growth.

If one of these seeds was planted in an indoor pot, or perhaps in a less supportive environment, it would still be a tree. *Creation's Codes* would still be at work modifying the tree in relation to how much energy was available and the tree's direct connection with other trees. Its life would be modified to still represent the best tree-ness possible with the degree of connection and energy available.

When a tree is cut down, through chemical signaling manifested by *Creation's Codes*, the "parent" tree will call others through the root system to provide further nutrition to the existing stump.

The influence of one tree can be immense not only for the creatures around it and within it, but for all of us. We now claim that too much carbon dioxide is creating climate change at a rapid rate and that this is bad. Well, please remember that carbon dioxide is what plants call food. That tree living out its ideal tree-ness grows larger and absorbs far more carbon dioxide.

Plants transmute or deactivate many of the toxins that humans have brought into this world, and some say that they also clean up many of the destructive thought forms that humans create which are consequences of bound energy.

The larger system is always at work through the Fields or the earth, wind, water, metal, etc. The seed that became a vast, life-giving tree within a forest was coded in the Field around the tree, using forces of attraction to bring everything that would support the tree's survival and growth. Just as the tree shares the fruit of its presence in the web of life, *You* too have a Field around you that helps create you in the forest of humanity. With enough energy, this Field transmits a beacon consistent with your designed nature and has a force of attraction and manifestation for higher-order life. It manifests across space and even time to organize you and code your Field with the most fertile and juiciest "fruit" that your existence has promised for humanity and the web of life. The tree can nurture vast amounts of life and purify the world. So can *You*!

EpiEnergetics is how this is potentiated. You will discover that the one distinction helping these connections is a greater bandwidth of information between you and the forces that drive the cosmology of your life. The tree grows larger when connected to the large forest. The same is true for *You*.

What happens when we take a moment to appreciate the organizing intelligence of life and instead of taking it for granted we experience *awe* for its presence? When we observe and experience the tree using the sun's energy to move toward syntropy and growth as it shares its Field with the forest, we can access the data codes to magically transform the energy that is all around us—like the tree's energetics of taking one form of energy (sunlight) and transforming it into work energy. This is methodically and perfectly guided by a higher dimension, and it is usually invisible to us. It does not have to be.

I invite you to become aware of the phenomena of life sharing its gifts through awareness of the energetics of creation, the system that you are really in, what you truly participate with, and your personal recipe for activating the various states or levels of energy.

Creation's Codes are embedded in our Fields. And what is it that's needed to access them to organize your life from the cellular level to its larger destiny? Yes, you've got it...available energy.

With your conception, the Field of the seed that would become you also sets into motion and will create throughout your life the Field of attraction for the highest version of *You*. This highest version will attract the largest constructive and ecological influence upon the fabric of creation.

And this, too, will be revealed, my fellow Seekers, through these pages...

Being "Outstanding" in Your Field

SEEKER'S CODE #5
WE WISH TO ACCESS THE MULTIDIMENSIONAL ENERGETICS
THAT MAGICALLY CREATE AND CONNECT US ALL.

Throughout this chapter, I have made a point of showing how energy is at the center of all change, both for breakdown with a loss or growth and transformation with gain. We have discussed how energy transfers in the "epi space" between things, how our existence as data connects to the energy to transfer information, and how valuable energy is to *Creation's Codes* working through the Field.

Gaining access to more unbound, instantly available energy is what this book is about: how you, Seeker, can have and share (through your energized Field) more available information that becomes your body, mind, spirit, and your calling in life.

In other words, your available energy is what you will use to perceive the world and respond to the Field's changes. When you don't have enough energy, you process and express less bandwidth with less information, and therefore, your world is smaller. More energy and your whole universe is larger, with more information, more connection and more access to the abundance of the forces of creation.

Whether you want to quit your job or relationship because it's too stressful, or you love and are seeking to grow and commit even more to it, has little to do with your circumstances. It has everything to do with how much energy is available to you when you're focused upon your job or relationship and the way you interpret and experience life. Remember, less energy available, more pain, breakdown, loss, and downsizing of your life. You want to run away or escape. The more energy available, the more excited, enthusiastic and engaged you feel,. Your Field does the "work" in manifesting richer, deeper, further out, and constructively **MORE**.

You could have the darkest memories, with the darkest emotions, stemming from the darkest trauma, and the way you interpret it—whether it is a blessing in disguise or a curse—will be based on your available energy. Less energy will lead you to determine it was the worst thing ever and life-defeating; more energy means you will see it as a gift. The circumstances do not need to change. Claiming and practicing your higher-order energetic in your authentic nature will sponsor a different version of *You* with a different experience of reality.

An analogy I frequently use to explain the impact of receiving more energy when you think on a global scale is one of the interplay of magnetism with iron filings. You can think of the individual pieces of iron as parts of your life, each one representing a person or thing that's important to you: your relationships, your health, business, finances, family, etc. You can use your mind to attempt to put these filings where they belong in your life. Perhaps, as you fall asleep or when you awaken, you take inventory of each of these iron filings and look to align them and keep them organized. You might reposition the relationship filing closer to you or move the business filing further away—only to realize that, oops, you forgot to pick up your kids after soccer practice.

No matter how much effort and focus you put into it, life has a tendency to fall into disorder.

What if, at this point, you remembered that you had an electrically powered magnet? All you would have to do is turn it on. Suddenly, all of those iron filings that represent aspects of your life could line up perfectly and bring thousands of others from "wherever" to magically engage in the place that the Field calls them.

You see where we are going. The Field contains information and energy for everything that is meant to be attracted and repelled from your authentic integral signal of creation. Instead of trying to line up your life where parts fall away and break down and attempting to fix what does not work, you can choose a much more elegant and magical option. You can know the nature of the larger system that runs every aspect of your life and potential life paths and experience and allow it to organize and manifest.

Creation's Codes will be powered by your energized Field to attract those areas of your life that were not sustainable and consistent with your higher nature and to create a current to bring other people and events in synergy with your Field. The energized Field, like the magnetic field (which is one of the tools of *Creation's Codes*), instantly aligns parts of your life without you having to use effort or force.

Similarly, finding *your personal recipe* for your use of energy to manifest *Creation's Codes* is like putting a powerful magnetic field in action to line up each aspect of your life. This more energized and higher-order Field enables you to broadcast your authentic beacon—influencing others and attracting what is needed to serve your higher destiny.

A Ripple on a Pond

Now picture yourself or someone throwing a rock into a pond. The rock sends a ripple throughout the whole pond. Each of us with our incarnations are like stones dropped into the pond and the energetics of our Field and life intersect with the ripples of other stones that we will sometimes knowingly but usually unknowingly influence and be influenced by.

Ripples are carrier waves in the pond (field)
of information potential for our
individual and collective lives.

With enough energy, the ripples meet,
constructively influencing one another and reality.
Coherence of information and abundant energy
are more impactful than distance.

We all are connected
in the multidimensional field of potential.

Figure 1

The ripples, powered by energy, are ripples of data about our individual and collective gifts. The more available energy you have, the stronger your ripple. It joins with others' waves in synergy, collaboration and creates a force for change, curiosity, victory, tenacity, breakthroughs, awakenings and a pathway to take as many with us as we can, carried by the winds of creation and constructive manifestation.

In every moment, we are either cursing or blessing whatever we're thinking about. In other words, you are affecting or infecting with your thoughts. When we blame ourselves or others for why we are the way we are, or why we were hurt, then every time we think of one of the people we blame, we create competing waves with them. These "interfering waves" diminish the available energy and bind their waves, helping hold them—and us—right there, unable to liberate our story about why we can't be *extraordinary*.

When you develop a relationship with your Field and have more available energy, your ripples and others collide, increasing your impact's signal. Synergy and syntropy (negative entropy) happens! Magic happens! When you think about somebody else, they will think about you—that's synergy and **MORE**—it's quantum entanglement!

SEEKER'S CODE #6
WE RECOGNIZE THE POWER OF FOCUSED ATTENTION
AND ENERGY/AND CONSCIOUS CHOICE.

Time to explore the energetics that determine the quality of your focused attention, conscious choice, force of attraction, manifestation, and impact—Your Energetic Legacy.

CHAPTER 3

===

YOUR ENERGETIC LEGACY

THE E-STATE

"If you want to find the secrets of the universe, think in terms of energy, frequency, and vibration."

—NIKOLA TESLA

Manifesting the *Unreasonable* and *Extraordinary* for **MORE** requires us to have access to *more* energy. Through these next three chapters, I will guide you on a journey to understand and experience the various levels of available energy. We will discover what they are, what they look and feel like, and how they influence your life. You will learn why this is important for you and all of us, especially now in this rapidly changing world.

Having access to an instantly available renewable source of energy for your life creates new opportunities and transforms existing ones. The energy you require and desire to organize and advance your life is in many ways like a financial investment strategy.

Using the unit of exchange we call money as a metaphor for the energy we expend, we gain, lose, transfer and use it to create. Energy is what runs the economy of our bodies.

Keith Cunningham, considered one of the top experts on business mastery, publicly trashes the commonly heard phrase "It's just the cost of doing business." At his presentations, he speaks of this as a misguided and risky concept. Instead, he shares that it is important to consider every expense, check, money transfer, and credit card payment as an **investment**. With every investment, your balance sheet **loses, gains, or stays the same**. The same is true of your level or state of available energy.

Throughout your day-to-day or long-term vision, you invest your thoughts in family, friends, home, healing, relationships and so on. With each investment, you may ask: "Was there a net constructive wealth created for yourself and (or) for others? Was there more light and more possibility manifested within view on the horizon? What was the result when you invested your time, love, attention and wisdom into someone? Did it set her into motion to re-invest the energy, direction, guidance and love that you shared into a new vision, perspective or action that put her—or someone she knows—in a position for *MORE*?

We use energy in ways that manifest more or less in our lives. You and whatever or whomever you invest in either loses value, gains value or stays the same. This is true of everything in your life.

The Game of Energy Is the Game of Life

Most of us have some experience with estates—either planning our own or inheriting part of someone else's. An estate covers the entirety of your financial worth—including your liquid assets, investments and debts plus the cumulative value of houses, furnishings, cars and jewelry. Some of this is unbound and easily used immediately; some is bound in debts or long-term investments and hard to use immediately.

The values can be hard to measure or understand on our own. Because of this complexity, for major financial matters, many of us hire some-one to assist us. We are able to ask our advisor to determine what is left over for us to either survive, be more comfortable, or grow and share with others.

These three choices reflect the standing of our estate and the three levels of our E-State, or the state of our energy. This is the energy available to us while on this earthly plane. It is also the energy we can leave for others to add opportunities and value to their lives. I call this our **Energetic Legacy**.

As with estate planning, it's the wisdom of our energetic investments that determines the quality of our energetic legacy. For instance, real estate traditionally has been considered one of the most valuable long-term investments—unless the value is bound up in a mortgage and the overall property value has gone down. When the value bound in the mortgage exceeds the value for which you can exchange it, the property is considered to be underwater.

When you are "underwater" energetically, you are in an *Energy Poor* state. This is when the bound energy exceeds the available energy. It's a losing investment. You may have felt this way as you were taken by ambulance to the emergency room or rehab center, or in a difficult relationship that seemed like it couldn't be saved, but you wanted to just survive just long enough to leave before it killed you.

Your energetic real estate might not be "underwater." If after years of repair and putting lots of work into it, your real estate sells for roughly what you bought the property for, it isn't a loss or a gain. Everything comes out even. It maintains the status quo. In the meantime, you may have lost out on more profitable investments or opportunities, or the profit may have been consumed by rising inflation. When you experience this in your finances or life, you are *Energy Neutral*. It's when your relationship is just okay. Lacking in passion or intimacy, life with this lover is a "partnership." There is effort. Most of the time life is too busy, or just satisfactory, with no energy left over for more. Or it's when you are just healthy enough to avoid the hospital and are managing your condition and circumstances.

These are two possible states of your energy and your real estate. A third exists. You might find this when you place your property on the market and have an open house. To your delight, so many people are interested in the house that a bidding war ensues. At the end of the day, you're in contract for 20 percent over your asking price!

This abundance of energy/opportunities is called *Energy Rich*. It's when everything seems possible, and the world is full of new options. That state is passionate, enriching and exciting. You're so energized that you can run a marathon *and* go out dancing that night!

Revisiting the real estate metaphor, what if you could change your real E-State in an instant so that your energetic assets could go from underwater to that bidding war? What if I told you that you can increase your energy, the net value of your life and what you bring to the world?

You can! It all starts with understanding energy and knowing your current E-State.

The Nature of Energy

Energy is a unit of change. It is required to fuel *Creation's Codes*—the forces that organize information into reality. The amount of energy available to you determines how much of the information or data stream is interpreted as emotions, thoughts, meanings and manifestations. This data is what the computer screens of our minds interpret as reality.

Most of the time in life, **no matter how real it seems, you don't experience reality. Your personalized experience of what reality is—or is not—is determined by your energy state.**

The amount of energy to access *Creation's Codes* of organizing wisdom determines the light you shine and the beacon of attraction between your body-mind and the world. This is reflected as the quantity and quality of your manifestation and impact in all areas of life.

In an *Energy Poor* state, you have just enough to survive.

In *Energy Neutral*, your goal is to have relief or be comfortable. Progress takes effort. There is little energy left over and valuable opportunities are missed.

In contrast, when we are *Energy Rich*, our greater forces of attraction and tremendous bandwidth of information illuminate the blossoming of opportunities. This blossoming is like the Midas touch where everything turns to gold—or perhaps to NFTs or crypto—for you and everyone you connect with.

Your whole range of experiences between hell and heaven are triggered by a simple change in the amount of your available energy. The question, then, is how to get more energy.

Energy has most commonly been made available through extreme life changes, trauma or loss. This liberates bound energy in a rather "rude" way like how a robber or the IRS might forcibly "unbind" non-liquid assets. This is not the only way to attain more energy. Other ways are also available. Through the teachings in this book, you can have access to energy in a manner as simple as bathing in the sun's energy on a warm spring day.

With one simple switch, one energetic alteration, you will have your own moment when everything changes for you without any pain or upheaval. You'll discover how to tap into your once unconscious competency and make it conscious—that's when things work magically! You'll move from "we don't know how or why" something is the way it is to "this is how it magically is." You'll start waking up in the morning and instead of saying, "Oh God, it's morning," you will naturally call with gratitude "Good morning, God!" Instead of asking,

"How can I get through today—or have a more comfortable day?" you may find yourself wondering, "How can I accomplish more and love more than ever before?"

For those with a superabundance of available energy, rather than, "How can I have an *extraordinary* day today?"—you will just naturally ask, "How do I make a much more constructive impact?" Because, Seeker, that's what you are called to do—to be the constructive change that changes your life—and the world. It's the ultimate win!

SEEKER'S CODE #3
WE SEEK A RICHER, MORE MAGICAL, AND EXTRAORDINARY
EXPERIENCE FOR OURSELVES AND FOR OTHERS.

All of these statements have one common predictive factor—your Energy State.

Your Energy State (or E-State for short) is your *real E-State*. It is your energetic currency for change. Your real E-State is the amount of energy you have available to create impact.

When we change our E-State, we change how we experience, interpret and respond to our circumstances. The E-State determines the quality and quantity of *Creation's Codes'* downloads and uploads for a different reality.

Remember, everything is ultimately information potentiated by energy. The amount of your available energy, when focused, determines how you experience, interact with, transform or transcend your circumstance. Therefore, the ability to know and select your optimal E-State is vital for attaining the *Unreasonable* and *Extraordinary*.

Now please be aware that reasonable and ordinary are often just fine. You and most of humanity got that down! This book is for you Seekers who want access to what is way beyond this baseline. I will keep contrasting the difference between the ordinary and effort and the effortless *extraordinary*. Most important is knowing your strategy for when you want to and must be the change that you wish for yourself, for others, and for humanity's legacy.

In this and the next two chapters, I will reveal the nature of each E-State, so you know where you are with this most important asset. Once you have this understanding, you will be able to have access to and consciously allocate the perfect amount of energy for the greatest result.

Transforming Your Understanding

> Someone asks you, "How are you today?" What do you say? Do you respond about you, or do you refer to what is happening in your life? Do you talk about your circumstance, your situation or what you cannot solve as if all of this is *YOU*?

The assumption we too often make is that our circumstance, problem or opportunity is our reality. We assume that we must change our circumstance or situation to be better or happier.

To move forward, this assumption must change. When enough energy assumptions that do not support you effortlessly change, a different data stream is accessed.

Most of us think in terms of effort instead of energy. We believe that if we work hard enough, study hard enough and put in long hours of struggle, we will then be in the position to enjoy our lives. I propose that there is no trophy for effort. Instead, it's the result that matters.

We believe that if we change our circumstance, work harder, get a promotion, make more money or have a different relationship, we will then feel like we are enough and will have a better life.

To some degree this is true—for a few moments. The same *YOU* will be using the same apps to observe your life and world. When you use high, low or neutral energy for uploading and downloading information within the Field, you'll get the equivalent high, low or neutral reality.

What fuels true transformation into action is something other than effort. Instead, it is the moments of inspiration and the energetics that push you to be more, share more and shine more light upon whatever reality you consider sacred.

When you go beyond the belief that your circumstance determines what is possible, you play a different game in life. Instead, you recognize that your E-State determines how you experience your circumstance, and how capable you are to create change. The following simple analogy will further reinforce the powerful influence of your level of available energy in your life.

Your Energetics Standard Is Like H_2O

Think of your circumstance as H_2O. Take the energy away from the two parts hydrogen and one part oxygen, and the structure and Field of the water—its properties and nature—change. Water without energy becomes ice. With even more energy it becomes steam. Each phase of water has different physical properties. This applies to our bodies and lives as we vary the amount of energy available.

Frozen

When life is like ice, all possibilities are frozen. There is an absence of energy. Nothing can move when encased in ice. Overwhelmed by the all-pervasive ice, you feel helpless that there is no way out. With your options gone, you cannot see beyond the seemingly solid obstructions before you.

You are incapacitated, paralyzed and incapable of moving in any direction—like a deer frozen in the headlights. You feel an all-pervasive feeling of helplessness looming on the horizon. When frozen like this, you have just enough energy to survive and not more. To protect against further breakdown and potential death you conserve energy and downsize the information stream that makes up your experience of reality. Therefore, without an aware thinking mind on line, there can be no judgment, blame or even the ability to identify a problem. It is as if no one is home. All is locked out! You are immobilized, frozen and have a sense of impending doom or death. Perhaps this is about your life itself, a relationship or your business is about to go bust. Energy is needed to move in any direction and remove you from the suffering.

This is Energy Poor.

The Big Thaw

You survived the ice age.

With the increase in energy, the ice began to melt. The molecules were vibrating more, and what was solid, or appeared that way, was changing. Some cosmic switch had flipped. POWER ON! The game of being aware of life had just begun.

With this energy, *Creation's Codes* can activate your capacity to engage your brain and Field to have basic thinking about this or that. Now that you have survived freezing, you can focus upon the blocks of ice remaining in your life as problems or obstructions.

Water is pooling around the ice. There is not yet enough motion in the water to take you anyplace. It does eventually start to carry you away from the ice, and then the trickle stops. It brings you back to face the ice or problem. While still mostly solid, with more energy, you are thawing out and discerning your options. There is not enough energy available for you to solve the problem. Shivering, you see a remaining slab of ice and remember the feeling of helplessness when bound in the ice. Rather than simply hoping to survive, you now crave safety and comfort. Nothing can significantly change. Although it is cold, the water nonetheless carries a little bit more information.

You will use effort to try to make the problem go away. And try you do! But nothing really changes. More energy is needed than you have. You really want everything to stay as it is so you don't freeze to death or get carried away to where the water is too deep. The higher part of your brain cannot yet access enough data from the Field to truly wake you up from the freeze. You are not really aware that you have decided on the status quo. You hold on to whatever offers comfort.

This is Energy Neutral.

River Rapids, the Adventure

As more energy enters the system, the same formerly frozen H_2O molecules vibrate faster and bump one another with massively more energy. Most of the ice has melted, and a potential river rapid that you were concerned would neutralize you now offers an exciting adventure. This river meets other tributaries bringing you new opportunities and attracting more information and possibilities. These are consistent with your now energized executive higher brain choices. The switch has flipped again. The whole POWER STATION IS ON.

Small blocks of ice are still in the river. With far more energy in the system, you are offered a wider range of realized information—too much even to consider *anything* as a problem.

With more energy and the synergy happening with a greater bandwidth of information, you now experience the ice as stepping stones to **MORE.**

Situations that were immutable are now mutable because the ice that bound the information and opportunities has melted away. Circumstances you had formerly considered to be obstacles blocking progress, preventing healing, destroying a relationship or causing a business to fail are suddenly hit with energy and light. Significantly more data is organized by *Creation's Codes* for greater manifestations and opportunities. You step up and claim **MORE**. The river of water is the momentum in your life propelling vitalizing energy through your body and attracting more of the same from your Field.

BAM! A new idea, a new relationship, a new perspective or a new opportunity comes out of "nowhere," and your standards, expectations and hopes of possibilities magically change. Synergy emerges. A change in your E-State has happened. **YOU ARE ENERGY RICH.**

Row, row, row your boat gently down the stream. Excitedly, courageously and more resourcefully you access a greater bandwidth of information potential and attract constructive manifestations. You share data and opportunities with other streams among you and neighboring canoes.

You recognize that wherever you go on this journey, something bigger is guiding you. By using this river as an opportunity to deepen and share your energetics with others, something is changing. It is so *unreasonable* and *extraordinary* that you sense an acceleration into the biggest **MORE** of your life. It almost feels like you are about to take flight and soar above this river of energy!

This is where you, Seeker, can awaken to a higher range of what is possible on the way to the *Unreasonable* and *Extraordinary*!

SEEKER'S CODE #2
WE HAVE AN OBSESSION TO GO BEYOND WHO WE HAVE BEEN.

The "Mist-ic" Experience

You Seekers always want to know what might be next and you fantasize about the world beyond or within physical form. Although this book is geared to you having more easy access to the Energy Rich state,

I will share a tiny taste about what is beyond Energy Rich. **MORE** will come later...

After a massive infusion of unbound energy, the same chemical H_2O now has continued its transformation from solid to liquid and on to steam or mist. It is no longer really visible as it disperses throughout the space. This also happens with you. You can experience the energetics beyond the bound body and sense the connections to everything and everyone.

You have transcended your experience of the physical world as your primary reality. You have access to new dimensions and an initiation into quantum reality. As the mist passes through spaces and diffuses everywhere, so does your awareness. It touches everything and everyone—adding value, love, and we-ness to the world.

The cosmic switch through the wormhole has flipped. The Sun's Power is ON!

With even more energy, the coherence in your body-mind and Field is so abundant that now your focus is beyond yourself. It becomes a collaborative **WE**—for people you know and even those you do not yet know. The game is full-on!

The Energetic Payout

In this book you will discover how to flip that switch. You will learn your energetic recipe to change your E-State. When you seek comfort and relief from your problems, or when you claim opportunities, you will discover what E-State propels you to get to the other side—and ka-ching ka-ching, you will then get the payout. Furthermore— ka-ching ka-ching—there is enough abundant energetic payout that others will benefit from your Energetic Capital also. A separate you is replaced by experiencing the connection to all. As both quantum physics and most spiritual traditions suggest, the Energetic Capital appreciates funding a new evolving humanity.

Who must you be for this to happen? You must be someone who is at least Energy Rich. When Energy Rich, you can instantly claim or further invest that payout. You've got it, it's got you, and you know it's a done deal. Get used to this idea. It's our target—both individually and collectively.

Seekers, you know this. You sense this, and this is your new baseline for **MORE**. To claim anything, energy is required, and the bigger the claim, the more energy is needed to harness the information and create and organize a new reality.

When Energy Rich, you have more bandwidth. Your energetic Field and awareness expand to benefit more people in even bigger ways. You create, exude and shine because this is what you are made for; it is what we are made for. In fact, you can have so much more energy that the *water* turns to *steam*. You transcend the experience of the bound light of a single body that many spiritual texts speak of, and you wake up beyond all cultural conditioning to experience *Creation's Codes* directly beyond the boundness of desire or thought. This is called **Super Energy Rich**.

In this E-State, accessible are data streams from the higher possibilities of super or meta-human existence impacting the flow of time and reality in multiple dimensions. What you thought was real is revealed to be an individual experiencing the world and its problems, solutions, and opportunities in a projection from an app that is missing the most important bits of information. You awaken to experience the energetic threads that connect us all through the apps that were once available only to a few mystics.

You knew on some level this was possible. That's why you agreed with the first principle of *The Seeker's Code*.

SEEKER'S CODE #1
WE KNOW THERE IS SO MUCH MORE TO LIFE THAN WHAT
APPEARS AS PHYSICAL REALITY OR CIRCUMSTANCE.

Now it is possible to live it.

Most people have the energy available to be content with the status quo, keeping things on an even keel and living their ordinary lives by rote. Especially for Seekers like you, people who want to transform the world into *extraordinary*, more energy must be made available.

How do you get more energy? You find a new way, supported by the Next Tier of humanity's energetics. And that starts with becoming aware of the difference between the various states of energy and what they mean for your life.

Pure awareness influences your energetic nature; how you experience, interpret, observe and live in the world. Pure awareness of how you create, manifest, attract and impact through energy is a game unto itself. Instead of requiring trauma to liberate the energy needed to more fully live and manifest in your life, pure awareness of your energetic nature and your relationship to your Field provides the energy to transform these relationships.

As we've seen, there are four levels or states of energy that can instantly change: Energy Poor, Energy Neutral, Energy Rich and Super Energy Rich. They each support different states of awareness, change, influence, synergy and Oneness. Each supports your degree of effort or effortlessness, the way you interact in the world, and whether your life is subordinary, ordinary or *extraordinary*. In these next pages, you will meet each one of them and get to know the standard they establish for what is possible and what is not.

The focus of the teachings in **The Seeker's Code** is to find your *one* discernment that can flip you between states and in an instant transform the life apps you use and what you experience and broadcast to others. The immense value of this one discernment depends upon your awareness of the gifts and limitations of your E-States.

Breakdown, Stasis, or Buildup

A.K.A. Your degree of sizzle and fizzle depends upon...*Your E-State.*

Ashes to ashes, dust to dust. Increase your E-State, or your life goes bust!

When a domain of life—such as health, relationships, business or impact upon the Field of humanity—fizzles out, it is analogous to once solid wooden logs turning to ashes spread across a cooling fireplace. It is a fact of nature that opposing forces of life and death affect every system. The systems in our lives are no exception. There are forces that break things down and forces that build things up. The difference between breakdown or buildup is based on the amount of available energy. In living systems, however, the difference is more complex. We have *Creation's Codes* to keep us from fizzling out into nothingness. Once again, and many more times to come in this book—and if I see you in person—I will repeat: you will experience that the degree of sizzle or fizzle depends upon *Your E-State.*

Everything is information plus energy. The amount of energy available in a system determines how *Creation's Codes* organize information/data into everything you consider to be reality.

You will find that I repeat this often. It is important that it be front and center in your thinking. *Creation's Codes* are the organizing wisdoms that orchestrate what we experience and manifest in life. This includes our bodies, our relationships and everything we see or experience in the world. Because you are a Seeker, you are predisposed to the energetic superpowers of the new energetics for humanity.

Or as one of the *Seeker's Codes* states:

SEEKER'S CODE #5
WE WISH TO ACCESS THE MULTIDIMENSIONAL ENERGETICS
THAT MAGICALLY CREATE AND CONNECT US ALL.

To further understand this idea, let's look at the wood in the fireplace you had imagined. That wood is a thing. *Creation's Codes* organized the tree from a seed by creating a microenvironment around that sprouting seed, with insects and animals perfectly organized for its unique needs. When there was no longer sufficient energy for that tree's root system to connect to the other trees in the forest—to keep breathing the carbon dioxide in the air and to power itself with the sun's light—it could no longer continue to exist as a living tree.

What was left was its corpse. This is called death.

Somehow remnants of that tree called wood wound up in that fireplace you enjoyed while sitting by the fire.

When a match was lit near that wood and a small spark of energy touched it, the piece of wood could no longer self-regulate and maintain its form. The energy came OUT of the wood as fire. The energetics of the system changed the latent or potential energy in the wood to heat and light energy. The information we interpreted as wood ceased to exist. Instead, we had ash. **Entropy**, the scientific term for the dissolution into nothingness, had taken over.

Information (Data) + Energy = Manifestation

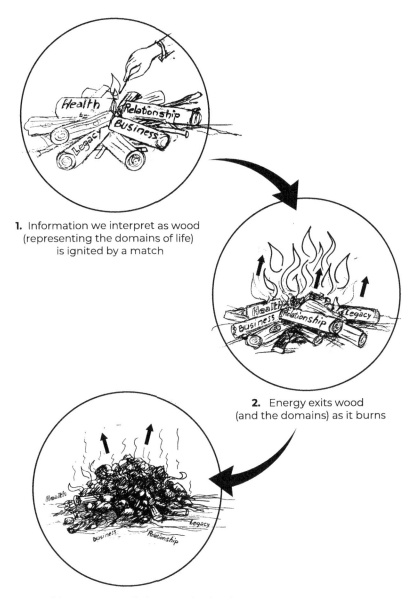

1. Information we interpret as wood (representing the domains of life) is ignited by a match

2. Energy exits wood (and the domains) as it burns

3. Without energy, all that remains is ash

Figure 2

Creation's Codes organize the information to create the architecture of our bodies and lives. And what is it that's needed for us to stay alive and resist the calling to dissolve into nothingness? Yes, you've got it. The answer is *Energy.*

Energy is needed to facilitate creation. It is your E-State that ultimately determines the quality of your experience and manifestations in life.

We perceive information from our Field, and it is given meaning through our nervous system. With our focused attention, we provide unbound energy to fuel *Creation's Codes.* These divine forces of self-organization transform us to become and inspire needed change.

SEEKER'S CODE #6
WE RECOGNIZE THE POWER OF FOCUSED ATTENTION
AND ENERGY/AND CONSCIOUS CHOICE.

To be alive is to have the superpowers to reverse the call of entropy— the Darth Vader of our life, the angel of death to whom we eventually surrender. Our lifespan is how long we can defend against our eventual dissolution and "meeting our Maker." The process of breakdown, breakup or dissolution is where there is no longer enough energy to fuel the codes that make living tissue and prevent breakdown.

This breakdown or growth is more than about our bodies—it influences whatever, whomever or wherever focused attention is directed.

Non-living systems break down because there is no energy to activate and adapt the matter to the changing environment. As the energy leaves, the information we identified as wood ceases to exist. All that is left is ash. When you repeatedly use the same hammer to drive nails into walls, in time the tool will wear down. This is entropy in action with non-living forms. In contrast, as a living self-organizing being, with repeated use your hand will build up calluses, your muscles strengthen, and your bones and cardiovascular system will grow stronger.

More or Less

When fed with a stream of unbound energy, *Creation's Codes* create the capacity to adapt and change as needed. With an abundance of energy running through you, these codes can then constructively influence others.

The capacity of living things to grow and get stronger while non-living things break down is called **Syntropy**. This "negative" or reverse entropy is positive for us! Instead of only survival or comfort, there is sheer magic. There is thriving, growing, evolving, being **MORE** and bringing **MORE** to the Field of all of humanity. The degree and quality of syntropy in your life is dependent upon, you guessed it—*Your E-State.*

SEEKER'S CODE #3

WE SEEK A RICHER, MORE MAGICAL, AND EXTRAORDINARY EXPERIENCE FOR OURSELVES/AND FOR OTHERS.

Energy adequate to fuel *Creation's Codes* reverses the tendency of everything to break down and disperse. The binding and directing energy and information into physical form through syntropy affects the many people and interactions in your life.

Through knowing your E-State and other discernments I am sharing in *The Seeker's Code*, you will gain the capacity to help reverse the tendency toward dissolution. With more available energy and the novel skills you'll learn, your life and energetic interactions with others can effortlessly sponsor the building, growing and evolving to something way beyond what they had been. **YOU** will help the Next Tier of energetics to create a more magical and profound **MORE**!

Although finding answers may lead one to greater certainty, it rarely changes a life. Instead, it fortifies who you already are. In contrast, asking new questions fueled by humility and curiosity opens a door to novelty and creativity. Questions that expand our awareness of the size and nature of the system we participate in, and how we can serve the intelligence that creates life, invites more information and Energy Richness.

Who am I? What am I made of? Why am I here? How does life organize? In what ways can we be more individually and collectively aligned with our unique energetic signatures? How can we create a life consistent with the forces that create us? How can each of us be part of the tipping point toward a Next Tier of humanity? How can we invite change consistent with this Next Tier?

These are questions I've often asked myself for close to half a century. They've guided my theories, my practices, my innovations and university research, and they have placed me on a passion-filled quest like few have ever known. It led me to what is now called EpiEnergetics and to the (r)evolutionary content in this book. They've led me to you, and through the Field, led you to me.

Ahead are ways I've discovered to access the forces life uses to create and manifest **MORE**. To access these forces, you must come to recognize the illusion of separation that leaves us feeling disconnected from others. This pervasive illusion is as crazy as a tree being separate in the forest, a separate ant within a colony or a bird being alone in a flock. Remember, the fish that does not swim in the community is called dinner. *Creation's Codes* organize all of life and orchestrate the symphony of our interdependence in the community of life.

When you first register a new company, it is simply you plus a name. Then when you hire staff, it is you and the staff. Problems, conflicting needs, and opportunities develop. In order to continue to grow the company, more information consistent with the company's uniqueness and the vision of the creator must be accessed.

As we move up the ladder of E-States, the energy organizes a larger circle of communication between parts. It is like going from a single-cell organism to a multicellular organism like a worm, and on to one with more systems like a fish, and then a more complex self-regulating system like that of a human. With greater complexity, more information about one's existence and how to adapt and self-regulate is essential. As we expand our system to larger gatherings of our species and others, cooperation, collaboration, and more available energy are required.

The illusion that we are separate dissolves as we achieve higher E-States. The experience of lower E-States is one of separation, and life seemingly happening *to* us. With higher E-States, life happens *for* us. With the Super Energy Rich state, we *give back to* life, adding more Energetic Capital as *we* happen *for* life.

In this book—through its words, stories, the spaces between the words and the transmission of information—you will learn to know these E-States and how to access the more syntropic, synergistic and connected state of energy richness.

And it all starts with getting to know and experience the E-States—how to recognize them, and later, how to instantly shift from one level to the next.

Energy States

Energy Poor E-

Breakdown, Survival, Collapse,
Leaking Energy, and
Downsized Existence

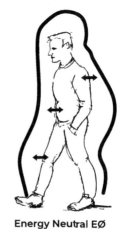

Energy Neutral EØ

Effort, Status Quo, Fit In,
Be Accepted, and
Nothing Actually Changes

Energy Rich E+

Abundance of Energy and Perspectives,
Optimization, Field Synergy, Achievement,
Status Quo Transcended,
Constructive Influence

Super Energy Rich E++

Beingness, Awakens to Invisible
Forces of Creation that Connect Us,
Superabundance of Energy,
Information in Multidimensional
Existence, Quantum Entanglement,
Spiritual Existence in the Midst of Real Living,
Others Awaken

Figure 3

Next, we will further explore the first two E-States.

CHAPTER 4

YOUR DOWNSIZED LIFE

ENERGY POOR OR ENERGY NEUTRAL

In this chapter, we will begin the in-depth exploration of the E-States. Here, we will focus on Energy Poor and Energy Neutral. These are the states that prevent change. In these states we either break down or maintain the status quo.

Let's get started.

Energy Poor

She was frozen in terror, separate, and alone in the midst of others' celebrations. She had no thoughts. There was a primal sense that the end was close. Perhaps this is death. It had that stench. She had no way of avoiding it and not enough energy to try. A darkness pervaded everything. It was not that she did not care. There was no one there anymore to care. She did not even remember why she was like this. It just didn't matter. Nothing did.

This is the experience of Energy Poor.

Energy Poor systems are dying systems. They are breaking down. They are becoming less and less. They are fading. They are becoming dust.

Entropy is tearing away at whatever domain of life is involved. Energy is lost past a threshold of existence.

It sucks energy, and yes, it also sucks.

Energy Poor feels like death. Whatever we experience in an Energy Poor state, we want to run away from because if it continues, we sense we won't survive.

Think about a relationship you've been in where no matter what you did, it deteriorated. Or maybe you have a business that you pour so much time, attention and money into, yet in spite of the massive infusion of unbound energy, it is heading toward bankruptcy. Those are examples of moving into Energy Poor. When you are Energy Poor, your basic existence and survival are in jeopardy. That which in the past, present and future you create, interact with, or focus your attention on tends to lose energy and downsize with difficulty or pain. You experience helplessness, loss and a profound separateness that you are sure no one else can understand.

When Energy Poor, there is hardly enough energy available to power your thinking mind. You function in a primitive, infantile state, overwhelmed by the sense of reality as darkness, powerlessness, and futility. You are immobilized. You are not really "here." Your entire life and awareness are downsized, and the information stream you use to interpret reality becomes sparse like a dry desert of meaningless data.

When you are Energy Poor, there is no judgment or blame. There is not enough energy to fuel the *Creation's Codes* that allow the mind to think. In the place of thought, there is a state of pure resignation that all that was, is, or will be is to be taken away, lost. What remains is absolute suffering.

You, like a deer frozen in the headlights, are paralyzed and helpless. There is no conversation. Your posture is collapsed, your breath is shallow and your eyes have no light. Since you require more energy to survive the way you are, you will unconsciously draw it from the Fields of others. It takes great effort to interact with others as this requires more information processing than you have available to you. And your hunger for energy drains others who also feel it.

When you are Energy Poor, there is not enough energy or data available to make any decision or contemplate any action. Someone must make decisions for them and get them emergency care. The sufferers may be taken to drug rehab centers because they are so far down a path of destruction, someone else must intervene to save them from themselves.

If someone has been struggling to fight a disease, he will reach a point where he is on the verge of collapse. There's no "me" left in the person, just a sense of urgency and an inability to take action.

Fortunately, it is rare that a person is truly Energy Poor in all areas of life. It is far more common to be Energy Poor in some areas while others are Energy Neutral or even occasionally Energy Rich. That one poor area, however, is almost nonexistent. You don't seek to improve or even consider this area. You may be an entrepreneur who is Energy Rich in the business world and Energy Poor in relationships, leading to the death of intimacy with your spouse. Since you are only one person, eventually the Energy Poor rot will infect other domains.

Since you are reading this book or listening to the audio, you, the person engaged with these pages, are definitely more than Energy Poor. It is the only way to be able to even read and have enough energy to fuel the thinking part of you. With that said, there still may be aspects of your life that are approximating Energy Poor. Those areas are drawing their energy from the parts that have more available energy, leaving your overall state more Energy Neutral.

The other E-States will each have a checklist to discover whether you are in that energy state. There is no Energy Poor checklist. Since you can't think clearly, a checklist would do no good, nor would you even have the motivation to read it.

Energy Neutral

"If you took one-tenth the energy you put into complaining and applied it to solving the problem, you'd be surprised by how well things can work out. Complaining does not work as a strategy. We all have finite time and energy. Any time we spend whining is unlikely to help us achieve our goals. And it won't make us happier."

—RANDY PAUSCH

Congratulations. In Energy Neutral, you have survived. You have the comfort of being stabilized and have avoided collapsing into Energy Poor. You, or at least a particular part of your life, no longer has the terror or stench of impending doom.

I consider Energy Neutral to be the most prevalent addiction in the world and a contributor to all other addictions. The primal need to survive has evolved. With a notch more energy available to organize more data into a better reality, you have upgraded and expanded your interactions and capacities in life. Now there is enough energy to create and organize a "you" that thinks in ways that brings you into compliance and alignment with the cultural matrix, or group-think. Being liked and accepted is essential to support the status quo and survive as a society. That cultural matrix draws powerfully upon your energy. In my early days of my healing practice, I provided care for Susan, a lady in her thirties who was in a wheelchair. Being in a wheelchair was common with her diagnosed condition. During the first few months in my care, the energy and information flow between her brain, body and life increased. Her health, beingness and ability to function progressed significantly. She started walking on the beach and began a relationship with a wonderful lover. She built a very successful multi-level marketing business, and she was flourishing. A few more months had elapsed and she was running over a mile a day on the beach.

Susan was an officer in the local disease support group and asked me to address the members to shake up their addiction to a given prognosis and help them "take back" their power to heal and thrive.

I accepted the challenge. I spoke about the power of healing and the idea that the power that created the body heals it—as long as there is enough energy to fuel this power. I also mentioned that getting better involves more than managing the condition or slowing its progress. Healing is beyond the disease; it's about the person.

I continued by sharing that regardless of the name of the debilitating condition, ultimately the disease is a consequence of not having enough energy for *Creation's Codes* to be expressed. And that the audience—as individuals and as a collective—had a power shortage and might want to consider a trained professional to help them switch the power on!

This was too much for them. The members of the audience were focused on survival and managing their conditions. I was speaking about the *Unreasonable* and *Extraordinary* possibilities of what healing meant—possibilities beyond their diagnoses and prognoses. This was way beyond the cultural Field supported by the medical care establishment and beyond their capacity to raise their ceilings by considering **MORE**. They were considering only what they wanted less of in their approach to disease care.

My talk was interpreted as if I were a villain—not respecting or accepting the seriousness of their condition. I was asked to leave, and my patient who organized my visit was scolded for inviting me to give people false hope.

Despite listening to her sharing of her personal transformation and victories, which they also might have noticed during the prior months, the members could not hear her. The evidence of this truth was competing with their Energy Neutral belief that their condition was the reason that they were ill. Instead of aiming for a reduction in the symptoms or just hoping for remission, Susan suggested that managing and healing were different objectives.

They were too trapped in Energy Neutral thinking to see her point.

The job of the practice of medicine traditionally is to avoid Energy Poor so that the person does not die. The traditional goal for medical therapeutic interventions as seen by insurance policies is to "restore a person to their prior minimal state" before they drop to a subordinate state. It is considered a success therefore to assist patients in providing relief from Energy Poor breakdown and to help them stay alive. This means arresting the possibility of Energy Poor and upgrading the patients to a solid Energy Neutral state. Physicians want to bring their patients to the next level beyond surviving—to where things are manageable. The aim is to bring them back to ordinary. This can save a life. The challenge occurs when they expect or want more than what Energy Neutral can deliver to them.

The doctor is socialized to be Energy Neutral, as their profession is based upon finding a problem and then helping people move away from the pain and other effects of the illness caused by the problem. In fact, this reminds me of a joke that reflects the social expectations of the culture that conditioned my mind and Field.

The first Jewish president calls his mother to invite her to the Passover Seder at the White House. His mother says she can't go because of what I call "blah blah blah." She gives reason after reason. The president gives solutions to each of these reasons, and finally she runs out of excuses not to go to the White House. "OK son, I guess (sigh) I will go to the White House to join you for the Seder." Two minutes later, she speaks with her friend Sarah who asks, "What are you doing for Passover?" The mother responds, "I am going to my son's place for the Seder." The friend asks, "Which son, the medical doctor?" The mother sighs again and says, "No, Sarah...the other one!"

Note the way someone, in this case a son, is rewarded by his mother and others for achieving that which the mother's culture values most. When someone is neutral only one perspective at a time is accessible. One is right and the alternating perspective is wrong. One is supported and the other is rejected or attacked. The alternative perspective to one's cultural Field matrix is often punished. Please remember that both our words and our thoughts give testimony to our E-State and affect the E-States of others.

The post-World War II Jewish culture elevated being a medical doctor so much so that it was the epitome of acceptance and the cultural proof of success. It is as if a child of that generation was first valued when he got his MD degree.

So, in this story, even being president of the United States of America was not enough for his mother. Another example of the Energy Neutral cultural Field "matrix" of social conditioning, or the neutral reaction to it, is represented by the saying on popular tee-shirts worn by female chiropractic students when my wife Jackie went to chiropractic college in the 1980s. It touted, "Be the doctor your mother always wanted you to marry!"

When we are Energy Neutral, we seek acceptance of our stories through our cultural conditioning by our peer groups and by society at large. The expectation from the societal perspective, and its mandate, is to support the existing cultural Field of Energy Neutrality. Through cultural, political and governmental regulatory agencies those below and significantly above Energy Neutrality are deemed either confused, or dangerous. They must be made to be compliant with the status quo or punished. This supports the survival of the tribe or culture as it is. Characteristics of neutral are living within the matrix of group thought—ours, those we like, and those we don't. We are in a world of judgment, both fitting in and reacting to it. We experience temporary highs and lows, balancing toward the middle. We have lots of conversation and lots of trying...yet nothing, no-thing changes. Our thoughts give us stability and provide more energy than being frozen in the headlights. Still, the car doesn't go anywhere.

In this state, we think at the level of thoughts that will allow us to judge, blame, create boundaries, establish rules, and maintain stability. We believe our thoughts are real and that they run our reality. We aim to avoid experiences that could destabilize the system, and thus we create the risk of dropping into Energy Poor.

The purpose of Energy Neutral is to make sure that nothing will sustainably change. We may measure or be proud of how far we have come or become distressed that it was not far enough, but we are still on the same circular treadmill.

Here is a statement that someone shared with me in preparation for an event she was attending. Her words: "I was considering the possibility of beginning a relationship soon, and I realized that since my past relationships were so traumatic, I would first have to open my heart and heal more."

Can you sense how bound she is by her thoughts? Her bound information and energy are causing her to have one foot on the accelerator while the other is on the brake.

When Energy Neutral, there is an immense amount of energy turning and churning and going no place. One current opposes the other and nothing changes. The energy is bound. It's ten points up and then ten points back down—always ending up at zero. Remember that all thoughts are reflections of the individual's E-State, and the thoughts that arise perfectly match the energy and data available at that moment.

With neutrality, there are always reasons why you don't have, didn't have, or won't have more in life. Happiness is when life meets your expectations and you achieve comfort, relief, safety and the status quo. There are rules for everything—about what is good, bad, right or wrong. There are rules about people, relationships, roles and circumstances.

We stay Energy Neutral to fit into our tribe, our cultural Field. It helps to assure us that we are accepted or liked. Because humans are social creatures, the next level of survival is following the way of the tribe or culture to protect us from harm.

In most of the world, if you don't follow the rules of the culture, if you question the status quo in health, relationships, business, finances or your masculine or feminine nature—or perhaps if you are not liked—you will be excommunicated, punished, rejected, shamed or possibly even killed.

We are seeing this more often in the USA and other countries with the rise of more politicization and corporate alliances between governmental agencies and media outlets. The level of mind that is fueled by neutrality is primarily about social compliance, judgment, rules of engagement and stories about why life is not better. This level of the mind, below the level of executive function, can only see one perspective at a time—and that one is right while all others are wrong.

In this state, you'll do whatever is possible to avoid what is real or true as it might significantly change your life. You are living in the AI program of your conditioning. The matrix's codes and your cultural conditioning, which seem real and immutable, are running the show.

> If someone asks you, "How are you today? Good?" you might respond, "How can I be? I just had an IRS audit." Or, "How can I be? My daughter is ill." Or, "How can I be? I have arthritis." Since there is not enough energy to create a real you beyond the matrix, you are your experience of your circumstance.

There is no you.

There is not enough energy for you to truly experience yourself or anyone else. Instead, you are a list of your goals in business, relationships, and health. This list is what you were programmed by the Field to want. It is total AI. You will find a person, a husband, a girlfriend or an employer to fill the space on your list. Life is its administration with effort, and you avoid asking, "Is this working?" or "How can this be more effective?" You will try, you will hope, you will look to fuel yourself from the places where there is only unavailable (bound) energy.

It is an energetic purgatory.

Your life equals your excuses as to why things are working this way. And if you do say you want more, you go about it in a way that will not work.

"Pay no attention to the man behind the curtain."

—THE WIZARD OF OZ

In a key scene in the movie *The Wizard of Oz*, Dorothy (played by Judy Garland) and her entourage are seeking to come out of their wounded scarcity and unfulfilling existence. Each believes if they get some resource that they're lacking, their lives will be wonderful.

After a long journey and tremendous effort, they are granted an audience with the great and powerful Wizard in the land of Oz. They are greeted by a frightening, giant floating head with a booming voice and spectacular presence. At a moment of being scolded by the Wizard, Dorothy's little dog Toto pulls open the drapes with his teeth. This shocking opening allows them to see what is really behind the illusion they were believing to be real.

The opened curtain reveals a timid little man in front of a microphone, manipulating the projected floating head and trampling their hopes. Attempting to sustain the illusion and maintain his power, he fumbles with the curtain and cables while calling out, "Pay no attention to the man behind the curtain."

For almost a century this statement has been a metaphor for resisting peeling back the image believed to be true and maintaining the status quo. This is the central core of Energy Neutral and the cultural matrix. Under no condition is one to question the illusion. Energy neutrality perpetuates. People can continue their day-to-day lives relatively unconscious with limited access to the larger data stream and insufficient energy to pull back the curtain. "Pay no attention" refers to what is behind the curtain of our thoughts, the media, our family and our peers—and ultimately restricts the manifestation of our energetics.

You see this in the world today. Like Toto, anyone who attempts to pull back the illusion that the cultural matrix creates to maintain a low level of reactive energy is censored, excommunicated, shamed, ridiculed and in many places may lose social rights or privileges. The Energy Neutral system cannot sustain more energy, more bandwidth— or even the questioning of the cultural narrative.

Questioning the cultural narrative takes a higher level of energy and information. To those invested in the Energy Neutral baseline and the stories of the matrix, this is confusing and painful. Whatever one believes is reality will be defended. Each level of consciousness thinks that the one below is regressive and the one above is misguided, confused or dangerous.

When you are Energy Neutral, you are sending conflicting signals into your mind, body and Field. This is essential to avoid momentum. This way, you might not truly succeed or truly fail. You are in the middle land of sludge and effort. Having competing smaller waves of information increases your stress response. This compounds as the limited energy and data availability organizes your experience, and your impact in life is chipped into small manageable bits about yourself, others and your environment.

Much more energy and more simultaneous perspectives from which to choose are needed for your stress response to become a growth response. In Energy Rich, this can happen in an instant—and that is for the next chapter!

Your body is responding to the safety of Energy Neutral. When you are seeking this comfort, any thought or action that might go higher or lower than Neutral is often seen as an enemy and to be avoided. Thoughts *prevent* any *actual experience* of reality beyond the AI matrix, which you accept as reality. To you, the *unreason-*

able is unthinkable, and *extraordinary* is just a tee-shirt or a dumb bumper sticker.

Higher than Energy Neutral often disturbs those living in the lower Energy Neutral matrix as they are encouraged to live as they are, or to fight with their reality. As Pope Frances stated in his book *Encountering Truth*:

> And we are like Peter at the Transfiguration: "Ah, how wonderful it is to be here like this, all together!"... But don't bother us. We want the Holy Spirit to doze off...we want to domesticate the Holy Spirit. And that's no good. Because he is God, he is that wind which comes and goes, and you don't know where...he is the one who gives us consolation and strength to move forward. But: to move forward! And this bothers us. It's so much nicer to be comfortable.

When people rise above or fall below Energy Neutral, there is systemic, cultural and political pressure to stop them—or get them to comply with the status quo. Otherwise, they can become a disruptive force in the family, school, company or community. Traditionally, regulatory agencies in the world are focused on preserving the current political, economic and social system as it is. Regardless of which political party you belong to, the party's job is to ensure you follow their belief system if you are to be accepted by its members. Energy neutrality is an evolutionary mechanism to support the tribe and has been a necessary stage in development for humanity. It is also regressive and limiting when overused, overvalued or when our information processing and energy availability outgrows its ceiling.

While there is comfort or safety in being Energy Neutral, the downside is you never really change. You don't get to experience a high (or very low) for long. To protect you from an energy surge (up or down), you avoid experiencing true passion, joy, victory, love or celebration. Instead, everything is a concept. There is nothing authentic that you can acknowledge or truly experience when Energy Neutral. You are owned by the groupthink and the cultural matrix. There is an avoidance of true experience. Life is about drama or about fighting against drama. Data for data's sake or information without wisdom replaces the raw and real.

Your apparent difficulty or massive pain or pleasure with your spouse, children, employer, government or friends has little to do with them. It is the nature of the neutral E-State.

How does our Energy Neutral mind convince us that this is for our betterment? Why don't most see neutrality as just one way, amongst others, to choose to experience reality? It isn't only about our need for survival. In a word, it's about happiness.

Happiness is a goal that obscures the *extraordinary*. Happiness is when life equals what you think it should be, based on your alignment with how you've been conditioned by the expectations of your cultural Field. When you are aligned, you are happy.

In a car, neutral is a place to just glide, without using more energy to shift gears to move ahead, or in the case of reverse, behind. Life is often necessarily between gears. It is like the energy saving capacity that hybrid cars have when idling. The **Unreasonable** and **Extraordinary** is not meant to be the basic idling of your life. Energy Neutral is a fine strategy for being happy or content, not challenging the system, changing direction or looking to influence anyone or anything.

Happiness, relief, fitting in and being liked are good things. After a productive, creative or impactful day, it is great to veg out, perhaps with a loved one and dig into your favorite decadent ice cream, chips or other "comfort" food—without a care about nutritional value. While watching mindless, predictable movies on Netflix, you fall asleep in the middle of one, with the empty food container on the floor. The next day neither of you remembers how the flick ended—or even going off to bed. Ahhhh, just some of the mindless wonders of Energy Neutrality and the seeming comfort of being asleep at the wheel of life.

In contrast, *The Seeker's Code* is about those times you wish to make a greater impact and transform yourself, your relationships, or your world. To do this, you must access the **Unreasonable** and **Extraordinary**. This requires using a greater bandwidth of data converted by **Creation's Codes** into apps that effortlessly provide for a higher-order participation with life. Energy Neutral will annihilate those choices, desires and hungers—and the very outcomes you seek for yourself and for others.

If your Energy Neutral state is one where your cultural norm is to live in the middle, even an experience of great fortune will somehow balance out. Should you receive a windfall of a couple million dollars, something will happen to balance out that windfall. If you go to a transformational retreat, have a personal coach, have medical treatments and make significant progress, life will throw you something seemingly outside of your control to crash or drop you lower again. The same is true with your relationships and business. Great success will be followed by great failures or vice versa. At the core of neutrality is effort, more effort, and even more effort again. You may even go many miles from where you were and—**BAM!**—like a predictable scene from the classic movie starring Bill Murray, *Groundhog Day*, you wake up each day in the same scene. You have been there before: you make changes, and the next morning you wake up again to find that you are back where you started. In Energy Neutral, be it low or high, you have substituted effort for progress, and if you "effort" enough, then you are absolved of the lack of progress.

> Have you been there? Do you know others who stay on this hamster wheel and do not know they are on a wheel and can step off? Or do they go from one hamster wheel to the next? Their reality is about which wheel they are on.

Picture a flea that jumps in and out of a jar repeatedly. A glass lid is placed on the jar while the flea is in it. When the flea senses the lid, it quickly learns to limit its jumps to just before it hits the barrier. On the internet, I read that the next generation of fleas have had this conditioned response passed on to them, and these young fleas don't attempt to jump beyond the barrier recognized by their parents.

If it is on the internet, or your favorite blog, it must be true, right? Or perhaps if it is on the liberal left or the conservative right media, it must be correct? Or perhaps, it is right only if it is in the middle "more balanced" mainstream media.

Being trendy, buying trendy, eating trendy, being in the trendy "right" places, advertising the logo of the trendy brands you purchased, being seen with trendy people, listening to trendy music or purchasing trendy art is the epitome of Energy Neutral.

The same is true with social and political causes and language. Perhaps you know nothing about classical music, and someone asks you if you like Bach. You pause and with a prolonged look of seduction say, "Ahhh, Bach..." Or you know nothing about jazz and say "Coltrane," nodding with a look of knowing. Or, perhaps you reject that culture to be accepted in the not-trendy trend!

A hipster, whose identity is being "hip," has also been defined as a bohemian counterculture advocate. By definition, a bohemian is a person with artistic or literary interests who disregards conventional standards of behavior. This can be a Low Energy Neutral opposition to the norms expected of the culture.

Or it can also simply be an arrogant snob. Isn't that a Low Energy Neutral perspective? Busted! Will you still like me? You will? Oh, what a relief—that makes me happy! (Smiley face.) Now I can go back to responding to the trolls on the internet...just kidding!

Did you hear about the hipster who drowned?

He was thrown into the mainstream!

When you are Energy Neutral, you'll get a specific college degree because that's what's expected of you. You marry a certain way or kind of person, so that you continue in the life patterns you are familiar with.

All your roles as parent, child, husband, wife, business owner, man or woman are meant to help you feel like you are enough if you follow the rules of the culture. Neutral follows the cultural expectation and vision for who you have to be in order to no longer have the hunger that you are not enough.

My wife Jackie reminded me that the word culture begins with the word cult. A group that is very different from the main culture is called a cult. Hmmm...when you really think about it, all cultures started out as cults. After all, how different is "cult-ure" from your cult?

A person might be considered a hero or patriot if his team "won." If they lost the battle, then they may be considered a dangerous revolutionary or a terrorist. Is this Energy Neutral "game" familiar? Too familiar? Have you had enough of this?

Not Like My Father!

We can see all these elements in this next example with Josh.

Josh is Energy Neutral and really works hard to feel like he is enough. He does whatever he can to NOT be like his father. Instead of being indifferent, he seeks to be engaged. Instead of being judgmental, he attempts to be accepting. Instead of forcing his children to eat meat at every meal, he raises them on a mainly plant-based diet. Instead of being a traditional medical doctor like his father, he is an alternative health care practitioner.

While successful at appearing to people in the way he wishes to be seen, he is miserable. He is still experiencing his role as a father from a place of not wanting to be like his dad. Naturally, his father has a similar energetic pattern, and they play the same father and son energetic games. Unconsciously, since both are Energy Neutral, this father/son energetic dance continues and all stories and emotions stay the same. Ups and downs happen, as you may expect, but ultimately nothing changes.

No matter how well he does as a father, his children will still experience many of the feelings that he did because his Field is pushing against what he does not want. He is opposing the culture of his younger years, and his children experience his effort. Owned by the matrix of his conditioning, he lives in a concept world. All roles are designed for acceptance, social compliance, and support of the prevailing cultural Fields.

When you are neutral like Josh, no matter how diligent you are, nothing changes with any lasting sustainability. This is what neutrality is about. No matter how hard he tries, because of his E-State, Josh is unable to really change the father-son relationship. The E-State speaks before he does and shows up before he does! As living beings, our Fields communicate louder than we do.

In neutrality, there is no change. And often, people are unable to see the part they play in their own struggles.

The Two Levels of Nothing Really Changing

We've looked at Energy Neutral in general terms. Now, Seeker, we will take a closer look at the two levels of Energy Neutral: Low and High. Each shows up differently, and both ultimately will defend against the possibility of real change because of their associated energetic addictions to effort and neutrality.

Low Energy Neutral

In this state, you have thoughts, judgments, and rules. You also have new goals: comfort, relief and the desire to fit in. This focus on survival is no longer only for yourself—as it was in Energy Poor—it is unconsciously for acceptance within the culture that conditions you.

Here's an example of Low Energy Neutral that you are likely familiar with. You call a friend who has been going through—or rather is IN—a tough time. Let's call her Hope. You tell her that you bought concert tickets for her favorite pop band that just happens to be in town that night and she is invited to come as your guest. You offer to pick her up and suggest that afterwards you can both go out to her favorite club for BFF (best friend forever) time.

She should welcome such an evening but is hesitant. If she goes with you, she might no longer have the certainty and safety provided by keeping her energy level in conservation mode. Right now, joy, community, celebration, and doing things that she likes require a level of energy beyond her current energy ceiling. If it gets too good or too vibrant, it will require a different pattern than the rut she is in currently.

None of this is in her awareness. For Hope, there is only one perspective at a time. She alternates between different ones as she settles on reasons why things are stalled or just too much in her life.

Because she is in a Low Energy Neutral state, she focuses on a belief, thought or story that downsizes her experience of life. She is "supposed" to be home minding her burdens. Even the scent of actually having fun is viscerally disturbing as it will no longer allow the thoughts that give her the certainty to keep her E-State above Energy Poor and maintain control. If the E-State changes in Low Energy Neutral—then stability is lost, and there might be more problems to contend with later.

Unconsciously, even the promise of celebration is beyond Hope's current energetic identity. She will do whatever she can to focus her attention on whatever mess she can to use as an excuse for her Low Energy Neutral mentality.

After a couple dozen text messages, Hope resigns herself to going to the concert. She says that she will meet you there. You know, somehow, she won't make it and will come up with a reason—other than the real reason that she did not really want to challenge the energetics that have been sabotaging her life by going to the concert.

Eventually, she gets into the car—at a time that would, even without traffic, have made her late. However, either the car runs out of gas because she forgot to fill the tank or her credit card does not work, or some other seemingly unrelated event happens. Life conspires to support her neutrality.

When you tell her you expected this, she gets angry that you are mis-understanding her or her situation. For her, they are one and the same. In Low Energy Neutral—and this is huge—**circumstance or situation equals reality**. People in Low Energy Neutral do not experience people; they experience roles, scripts, and personalities, and they react to their experience of the mismatch between what is happening and what should be happening. They want to change their circumstances to avoid that feeling of not-enoughness.

The concert is not happening for her. Hope goes home to do the laundry, pay the bills or find some other administration of life that seems so important it obscures that she is not fully here or alive or in charge of her LIFE. Her life is owned by her conditioning, her stories and her circumstances of the moment. She sends you a text: "Sorry, my car ran out of gas. I really tried and wanted to go. Thank you for taking care of me. I guess it wasn't meant to be. —Your BFF"

> Do you know someone like this? Has this happened to you in some area of life? Has this ever been you? What do you sense about your energy, thoughts and emotions with this story? As you think about that time, where in your body do you feel constriction or heaviness? Are you thinking of this situation with lots of breath, or are you barely breathing now?

One thing you certainly know from such moments is that unlike in Energy Poor, where there is no judgment, in Low Energy Neutral, there is plenty! The focus is on questions like: Am I good? Am I right or wrong? Is someone else good or bad or right or wrong? Working, putting in effort and struggling all mean you're on the right track. Therefore, you're good, and if something should go wrong, well, it's not your fault. As you have experienced and witnessed, there's always plenty of blame available to go around and around.

Let's reflect on the curtain scene I mentioned earlier from *The Wizard of Oz*. When in Low Neutral E-States, we will not even consider that there could be a curtain in front of our eyes. Everything we think is to maintain an illusion so that we can live relatively unconsciously, as an actor playing a part in a virtual script of life. In general, the strongest need of the psyche is the obsession for life to equal our expectations. This is called happiness. Relief and happiness go hand in hand. When Low Neutral there is no higher mind present to question your values, roles or effectiveness. I saw an awesome bumper sticker in Boulder, Colorado. It read, "Judgmental People Suck." In Low Energy Neutral, we have lists of what we want and don't want; what we like and don't like. The list—whether on paper, a device, or in our mind as a definitive concept—is for all our roles and relationships. Good/Bad, Right/Wrong, etc. We are offended if something happens to impact the "wrong side" of our lists.

These lists created by our response to our role models—like our parents, caretakers, or our culture rewarding or punishing us—are unconsciously playing the apps for our roles. They set into motion our attraction and repulsion strategies in life.

We choose our partners, jobs and identities from this neutral matrix without recognizing that we are indeed character actors in a play. Once the characters we play are established, we automatically cast others into the roles that best fit our pre-written scripts. We do this without seeing what is behind the curtain.

We only want to do what we are "supposed" to do, and our lives "should" look like they are "supposed" to look. We may be missing excitement, intimacy or our secret dreams coming true, but that's okay—we fit in with our society. We are offended easily if someone appears to question our reasons for why we don't actually want more. Drama is the domain of Low Energy Neutral, and it serves as a distraction from experiencing reality. It is all about how things should or should not be, and it keeps us in a world of concepts, a matrix of neutral thought.

After finishing a week-long event, I remember being awakened at 6 a.m. by a friend shouting about the stress, fear and anger she was experiencing in regard to what someone did to her and what that person was supposed to have done instead. I calmly suggested that my wife and I start our day with constructive energetics, experience positive outcomes for as many concerns as we can think of, and that we just do not do drama. I told her that I knew she was upset, and I would love to speak with her when she reached a more resourceful state. Then she could share what constructive and inspired solutions her transformed version would create.

This was an Energy Rich response. Before we actually go there, we still must visit with High Energy Neutral.

Opening the Door to High Energy Neutral

Knock, knock… Open sesame!

Stress hormones, inflammation and the sympathetic fight or flight nervous system inhibit the pathway to your higher brain through what is called the prefrontal cortex. This area behind the forehead is the doorway to the higher and more sophisticated processing of the cerebrum. This is the seat of greater bandwidth of information, executive function, optimization and synergy.

When in Low Energy Neutral, your stress hormones and flight-or-fight response reduce the blood supply to the prefrontal cortex, your gateway to higher brain function. You don't have the access needed there to support an Energy Rich E-State. You also unconsciously consider that energetic state as a threat to your Low Neutral experience of reality. You have no desire to knock at its door. Higher brain access is beyond your security clearance. Your energetics instead hang out in relationship with the more automatic and lower part of the brain.

You must be at least High Energy Neutral to be knocking at that door. High Energy Neutral allows you to get one foot and one eye into the higher brain, giving you a spark of energy and a bit more information flow to manifest as reality. You now know there is a Sunday brunch buffet of possibilities already prepared for your enjoyment. With this additional resource, you now know there is more and have a hunger to eat at the brunch buffet. Nevertheless, security clearance will say, "Everyone out—especially you!"

You went past the long line by telling the cashier that you had to go to the bathroom and had the opportunity to view the mouthwatering abundance of foods awaiting you. Covertly, you reached out to taste a small tiramisu at the dessert section. After being caught nibbling, security escorted you back to the end of the line.

While getting a taste of what was to come, the line for the buffet got longer. You saw and had a taste of what is possible for those rich enough in energy to be hungry for **MORE**.

Although now separate from the buffet, you are High Energy Neutral and know what is possible. You will work to remove or get past any obstacles to getting there. The desserts and opulent opportunities await you. While in line, you plan your strategy.

Visiting the wizard's words again, "Pay no attention to the man behind the curtain," it takes a different turn for Dorothy, and for you, Seeker. In a High Energy Neutral state, you know that something is obscuring and keeping you distant from your goals or destiny. You will take a path to improve yourself and be able to peel back the illusion. You are "working on it." You are no longer terrorized by the projection, and you acknowledge the curtain. With this said, the curtain—and the intimidating projection above it—is no longer real. Your focus is on what is behind the curtain, the unseen energetics running the show. For you reading this book, they are the codes that we interpret as reality. The projection is the illusion of the cultural matrix and what has kept you busy with effort.

Now, breaking out of its spell, you know there is more than you had accepted. The *unreasonable* awaits. You have tasted what is beyond your prior security clearance. Squeezing ahead of the line, you really start working at getting beyond the illusion of separation. With a taste and view of so much more awaiting you—*Seeker's Codes* one and two are bubbling over like freshly poured champagne!

SEEKER'S CODE #1
WE KNOW THERE IS SO MUCH MORE TO LIFE THAN WHAT APPEARS AS PHYSICAL REALITY OR CIRCUMSTANCE.

SEEKER'S CODE #2
WE HAVE AN OBSESSION TO GO BEYOND WHO WE HAVE BEEN.

High Energy Neutral

"I know what to do, and I am working on it!"
—PERSONAL DEVELOPMENT AND TRANSFORMATIONAL PATH DEVOTEE

As your peek at the luscious brunch buffet suggested, this next level of neutrality is seductive. It is when you have enough energy to begin to engage your executive brain functions enough to know what is not working, and when you seek to be more.

In this state, you actually work on improving your health, your finances or your intimacy. You embrace the personal development teachers, speak their jargon, and live their culture. You know what you must do to establish a plan. It still requires effort, although now there is enough energy to move toward change. You know what the problem is, and you sense that there is an opportunity on the horizon. You truly get that this is about you and you becoming more resourceful. **You are looking for the resources to make you resourceful.**

Getting back to the fleas in the jar, in the following two paragraphs, you will experience two levels of energy neutrality and the game of going between them until we claim Energy Rich. Notice how I change my "voice" between that of the low and the high neutral states while keeping Energy Rich at bay:

I have not read academic studies to see if the flea experiment is real or only occurs under certain conditions. My Energy Neutral strategy does not care if it is true or not; it just proves the point that I am sharing. So, screw Energy Rich. It just confuses people.

My High Energy Neutral state wants to know if I should include this in the book or not, as there might be other explanations for what was reported. After a while of going back and forth, I have decided that I will continue to search for the truth, and because it's so tiresome looking for validity, I have just decided to edit this out of the book until I can be one hundred percent sure.

True or not, the Low Energy Neutral Donny says, "Screw it...keep it in the book." High Energy Neutral Donny asks which metaphor is the best and really keeps looking for the right one; that is, until fatigued when I finally choose one that may not actually be the best—in spite of seeking the best outcome. While neutral momentum continues in a circle with some short detours toward great places, it never actually arrives at any of them.

To give me the illusion of certainty (so I don't have to question reality), I decide the story about the fleas is true. There is nothing to have to consider, as it must be true; after all, it fits into how things should be. I feel better and much more relieved and comfortable.

Let us visit with Austin. He told me that he desired to feel the energy of love for himself and for others. He declared that he had a HUGE wall over his heart.

He believed the obstruction was blocking his progress and decided what he would have to replace it with. This level of thinking is characteristic of High Energy Neutral.

Austin said that he would like to replace the wall with something more life-giving. He had a hunger to feel love and gratitude for his own life, which had been missing. And he was sure that if he felt this love for his life, he would then love others. He claimed with assurance that he knew the problem, and he had to find a solution.

Knowing Austin, I was excited that he had recently moved from blaming his situation and considering himself a victim to focusing on what was still blocking him from becoming more accountable and responsive to *MORE*. He affirmed that he knew what obstruction had to be resolved or how **he had to be *MORE*** to get to success or victory. The solution he had chosen was focused, clear and declarative.

This is not necessary or optimal when Energy Rich, yet it is perfect for High Energy Neutral. This claiming of a solution for more is necessary at high neutral, and because it is still neutral, nothing will change other than the setting of new things in motion to create change. Energy Rich and its much-expanded data stream is needed to manifest a new effortless reality, as the Field simply reorganizes your life.

When Energy Rich, like river rapids, life flows without obstruction. Austin was part of the way there, though he was not yet playing with a full deck of cards. The High Energy Neutral cloud obscured Austin's vision and experience of the forces of creation that were already reorganizing his life.

Seeking to remove the blockage over his heart or to find love and gratitude first for his own life would keep him neutral and busy for years. How would you know this? If he was High Energy Neutral, he would seek to improve his lack of resources, and any choice made would miss the mark in reaching the objective. He wanted to feel more love within himself to bring to others, and this had not yet happened.

As Austin spoke, I saw the neutral flag waving in my face. There was only enough energy to consider changes—not enough to fuel *Creation's Codes* with the bigger bandwidth required to make choices. Like an Energy Rich rapidly flowing river, if instead of trying to remove the wall around his heart, he just acted as he would if there were no longer a blockage, a different reality would reveal itself. In Energy Rich, you attract opportunities and collaborations just like individual streams and tributaries that meet in an energized river of possibilities.

If Austin helped others to love more, he would discover he was already there. The Energy Rich actions and synergy with others would melt more of the ice—as it would the wall he experienced around his heart—making his neutral desires irrelevant.

For a few moments, he would sense that he was enough. Knowing this is possible, he would be driven to continue to love and serve others. For Austin, the key to experiencing his love and fulfillment was in helping help others experience their own. With enough available energy, this would shift his lack of resourcefulness to instant resourcefulness. Like ice melting, his wound would become a gift.

We will revisit this later in the context of how to know your strategy and make that jump from working and striving to experiencing instantaneous transformation through the gift of energy richness.

> In what areas of life have you moved from low neutral to high neutral? After months or years on the "path" or "doing the work," does victory still seem out of reach? Or have you for a moment touched or tasted it before the tide took it out again? At least you know it is possible. The energized current will bring it to you as you align with your authentic energetic nature.

When people are in High Energy Neutral, they have the energy and perspective to work on things, use the latest technology, engage in personal or spiritual development, and study the situation or problem. These things are vital stages of development.

How many times have you or someone you know bragged about how they've been on a spiritual or personal development path for decades? This is so seductive and addictive because it provides the promise that we can end a circumstance and gain more resourcefulness. So, we work on it, over and over. This repetition is a function of neutrality. We are still removed from the synergy, the Epiphenomena, the actual *Creation's Codes* that effortlessly align the "iron filings" to exactly where they must be—propelled by the Energy Rich Field.

You may do daily exercise to make sure you look good and stay healthy. How much time each week is devoted to these routines to help you feel better about yourself and your body—or to help you get through your day more successfully? You commit to more of these routines and to doing them harder and harder. You can imagine the victory; you still place an image of your future dream home or your ultimate lover on your mirror. You recite your daily mantras, and review your new goals. These are all wonderful things to do as you become more aware of the gap between where you are and where you are being called to be while you seek more resourcefulness to become that person. Still, you are living a conceptual existence. What if there was no more effort, trying or searching needed? What if you could have results by adding an energetic so that the invisible forces could help you be more of the change you must attract?

When you are in High Energy Neutral, you think it takes time to work through change, process the information to assimilate change, or to get the right people on the team. You have your spiritual practice to get ready for the day. You have your line-up of daily supplements, potions and lotions to optimize your day. You follow a diet that is sugar free, dairy free, gluten free and hopefully not taste free! These are all good things to do. Consider if you are truly doing it to be

MORE, or are you moving away from the neutral fear of loss of health, vitality, etc.? Either you are looking to add a missing resource to your health, relationships or business, or you are seeking to instantly be more resourceful. In neutral, even when High Energy Neutral, you are focused on your lack of a resource and working to remove a blockage in your life. You believe that if you only added this one more thing to your routine and were committed to working at it, etc.—you would then arrive.

What is missing here is *Creation's Codes*, the organizing wisdom that acts instantly as the electromagnetic Field to effortlessly align you with a much more substantial and impactful life. With the knowledge that this is the central force of creation and manifestation in your life, you do not have to change anything. Remember the forces that made the earth, moon and stars, and the egg and sperm that became you, the same forces that made you miss the bus or turn down a different street just in time to avoid a tragic loss or gain an opportunity of a lifetime, are on call for you 24/7.

These forces guide our lives. The degree to which we get to experience, become aware of, and participate with these codes and the apps they create for us is dependent upon what? Yes, you are getting it...YOUR energy state.

Do you need to know what your liver is doing right now or how you are making blood cells? You just know something has your back! And this is what you must always remember. In High Energy Neutral, we get glimpses of it, but we still put forward effort. We think we are separate and distant from the outcome and if we only did more, did things differently or gained another resource—we would get there.

When Energy Rich, you no longer believe. You know, radiate, live that you are actually there. And there is always *MORE*! I will hold your hand along the way to this greater *MORE*. Ultimately you will have enough energy and bandwidth or information to hold the hands of others, adding more energetic capital to their lives.

I asked a respected spiritual avatar in India why he had promised the highest-level supporters of his vision that their greatest wishes would come true. I mentioned to him that one of these supporters shared with me that his wish was to be a billionaire. The guru nodded and said, "It will be done." I asked him how.

He said that these people made a decade-long commitment to the foundation for the awakening of humanity. He explained that the person who wished to be a billionaire would in a few years desire other things, and what he once thought to be important would no longer matter to him. He and other supporters would realize that the true richness of the world is already theirs.

The Language of Neutrality

When I asked a guest at our restaurant dinner table if she would like dessert, the guest replied, "I'm good." "Good" is not *extraordinary*; it is neutral.

The rules of *extraordinary* are of a different universe, and so is the upgrading of life beyond ordinary. I did not ask her if **she** was "good." I wanted to know if she had the desire, the passion, the hunger or the fascination to consider dessert.

Was she simply neutral and preferring to avoid the experience of being offered something **MORE**? What if she had given a more energized response like, "Thank you, the tiramisu at this restaurant is said to be wonderful. I will pass for now. Let's do this another time, and I will remember to save more room in my tummy!"

Do you sense the difference? You might say, "Well, 'I'm good' is just the way people speak these days. It is a common way of responding"— to which I answer, "Yes, it is common, and 'common' is another word for neutral. It is a way of saying, 'I am part of this group. Look at me. I am part of the status quo.'"

This is not a state in which you can expect *Unreasonable* results and *Extraordinary* outcomes.

When neutral, even High Energy Neutral, there is still additional coherent energy needed for your Field to instantly turn on the apps for greater manifestation. As you move into High Energy Neutral, you know what has to improve, and sense what is needed for **MORE**. *You* can almost taste this **MORE**. The gap between where and who you have been and who you must be seems to shrink. As you get closer to that **MORE**, your entire world has the possibility to change.

Suddenly, something happens that you did not have to work at previously. Someone just brings you what you were searching for. You witness some connection between yourself and others that creates a sort of synergy. There is nothing you have to do to get there. This is an 'oh my goodness' moment, as somehow you become aware that there is an observer observing your life—and that the observer is *YOU*. You see the world from more than just one perspective and find value in each of them.

Energy Rich has just launched, and it is wonderful. You are ready to peel (or melt) away the illusions. You are so ready...yes, ready for a new *unreasonable*, raw, real and profoundly *extraordinary* life!

"I'm good" is only one example of Energy Neutral entering our vocabulary. The words which we select always reflect our existing E-State. All thoughts, all words and all communications are characteristic of the amount of available energy that our central nervous system has as it collaborates with our Field to experience what we call reality.

There are words or phrases that demonstrate how and exactly when we rise or fall between E-States. I invite you to a brief course in Energetics Vocabulary 101.

Observe how people use language reflecting an Energy Rich state and can in a moment drop to a habitual state of neutrality when they go a bit higher than their identities will allow.

Some words work well if you wish to maintain or drop to neutrality. They reflect the energetic drop of the person using them and bring along the one to whom the communication is intended. "But" is such a word.

Think of the lyrics of great love songs. Very often, they are filled with words that are Energy Rich about seduction and powerful declarations of love. Often, they also will drop the energy into neutral with a word like "but."

A But-ectomy: just what the doctor ordered.

An example of this drop in energy is seen in Carole King's popular song "Will You Love Me Tomorrow?" After an Energy Rich statement that the lover is entirely hers and a full declarative statement about receiving love, King asks if she will still be loved tomorrow.

WOW, what a radical drop to Low Energy Neutral. This happens in life more often than the sustaining of an Energy Rich E-State or merging into Super Rich during an experience of "out of your mind" lovemaking.

A "but-ectomy" is required in those lyrics. What is apparent is that the person describing this night had just moved up a few degrees in energy and therefore found a way to drop the energy in a flash to maintain her Energy Neutral state.

Another example of this is the use of the word "however." "We have expanded our business by 200 percent and have an abundance of funds conservatively invested. Our employees are thrilled to work with us. However, we don't know if the supply chain problem will wipe out much of our progress as we may not be able to maintain our deliverables."

This began with declarative statements about his business and finances and then sank the ship by launching the phrases that followed with the word "however."

The beginning of this business narrative is Energy Rich, and immediately after the statement about employees, the energy significantly dropped with the word "however." Now, we are Low Energy Neutral with "...we don't know...problem...wipe out progress...may not be able to..."

Let's now consider Sarah's response to Michael's marriage proposal: "I love you and want nothing less than to spend my life with you, but you do remember the pain I had in my prior two abusive relationships. However, I am willing to consider your proposal as I will do anything for you."

What do you notice about how you experienced Sarah's statement? Were you uplifted at points? Did your energy level drop at other points? Were you inspired? Can you sense her conflicting information or data streams canceling one another out? This is characteristic of Energy Neutral. Do you relate to this?

Sarah started out great, with a declaration of her love that was high up on the Energy Rich meter. When it comes to relationships, intimacy and trust, Sarah experiences these at a Low Energy Neutral. Oops, her neutral identity in relationships has to immediately balance out the Energy Rich claim with the statement, "want nothing less," using two negatives in a row to cancel out the richness and take the taste of love right out of your mouth.

And while the energy was low, her further journey into the sludge was reflected in her stacking past pain to the present opportunity to be in a relationship she truly wanted. This reflects the E-State Sarah was in when making that statement.

Her then adding the word "However" was just in case there might be any signal in the Field or her partner's mind about her affirming any commitment. Sarah is "willing to consider"—a Low Energy Neutral statement—to make sure nothing changes, and she finally winds it up with a contradiction to her willingness to "consider" with an affirmation that she will do anything for him.

Whew!

How do you feel or think about this? Is any of this familiar to you or someone you know? What's pulling the strings on what she is verbally manifesting is not about past wounds. It's about the amount of energy available.

This is the kiss of death to even the idea of a relationship. This is at the edge of Low Energy Neutral and never makes it to even claim Energy Neutral.

You can see how the E-State dictates what is or is not possible. Please remember that the thoughts we think, the words we use, and the actions we take are perfect expressions and actual testimony to the amount of energy available to us to organize our lives.

Changing a word is far from the solution. Since energy attracts information and determines our level of consciousness, attentiveness to our E-States is a primary factor. Pay attention to the man behind the curtain of the illusions of what is real and important in your life.

The use of "never" and "always" are also clues that we are currently Low Energy Neutral.

"You never cared about me." "You are always angry." Sense the energy from those statements as compared to "I love the way you care about me." Or "I apologize for triggering your anger. I promise to show my love and caring in a way that works better for us."

Language works the other way, too. Going from Energy Neutral to

Energy Rich means going from confusion to knowing. **The only time you will think or say something like, "I don't know," "I'm not sure," or "I'm confused" is when you're Energy Neutral.** Confused means that the amount of energy and bandwidth you have, and the way you are experiencing the world is insufficient for *MORE*. It is a call for more available energy and a more effective observer or lens to interpret your experiences.

Energy Neutral Checklist

Some telltale signs of Energy Neutral:

You...

- find a reason why your life or things are not better and link it to a "because."
- consider your circumstance to be your reality.
- rarely ask, "Is this really working?"
- substitute the real for the familiar.
- substitute roles or scripts and rules for people.
- seek to manage your experience or circumstance rather than get beyond it.
- drop your expectations so as not to feel like you've failed or you're not enough. Or, you raise them so high that if you fail, you'll have a reason why that feels better.
- have a down that exactly manages your up, and vice versa.
- react against the status quo by joining a similar subculture where you want to be liked.
- are effortful.
- are moving away from rather than toward.
- are avoiding blame.
- are offended.
- have "issues."
- seek to be trendy for acceptance or approval.
- define progress in terms of relief or the comfort it brings.

- live in a concept world that is more about the ideas of things and people than your experience of them.
- place people and events in distinct categories so as not to have to question the story you are telling.
- believe your thoughts are reality.
- are confused.
- get stuck in the "how to" without considering the "why."
- find reasons why not.
- articulate or think in negatives: what you don't want, what you won't do, what is wrong, and what you don't like.
- see polarities, judging that one side as good, the other bad: one right, one wrong.
- believe in one objective reality.
- narrow the size of your system.
- seek causation or blame.
- manage conditions, circumstances, relationships and money instead of claiming *MORE*.
- drop your standards in life and somehow—deliberately or unconsciously—downsize or sabotage your opportunities or those of others.
- mute extremes to be reasonable or more palatable to yourself or others.
- share that you have been on a spiritual or healing path for years instead of arriving at that spiritual destination.
- want to do only the things that you like.
- dislike something, so you think it is wrong.
- may know what must happen to get there and there is still a distance.
- seek more resources to be resourceful.

YOUR ENERGY NEUTRAL INQUIRY

In which of these domains in your life do you use effort, experience ups and downs, and feel nothing changes: health, relationships/intimacy, business/finances, or your impact on the Field of humanity?

Place your hands on your chest, wait about ten seconds, and give voice to what does not change. Why do you think this is? What do you have to say about this element of life?

Take note of what you said, your posture saying it, and your level of energy. What did you sense or feel?

Now, instead, reach up with both arms extended out and palms facing away from your body. Give voice to the same thing. What changes? What does not change? Why do you think this is? What do you have to say about this element of life now?

Most people find a difference between these two experiences. What did you notice?

Did you find the experience to be different with your hands on your body as compared to up in the air? Did you find you were stating different things? Was one of the two more about what is okay or will be okay and the other about what is messed up?

If you answered yes during the exercise, your E -State changed between the two, just by doing this—without having to change anything else. This helps you to know that instant change in your experience of life can happen without having to first change your life.

The second your E-State changes, your experience of a problem or circumstance in life that is scary, terrifying, worrisome, upsetting or depressing—such as a relationship, a loss, a job, a financial problem or a health concern—suddenly is different. For many people, they can't remember what they were concerned about a few seconds earlier. That upset was only an upset at a Low Energy Neutral level. When in High Energy Neutral, the upset is transcended by the situation or circumstance. Instead, it is about the gap between where you or someone else is now and where they must be to access greater resourcefulness.

The awareness and acknowledgment of an energy differential, its rapid influence through a different range of emotions, thoughts, behaviors, beingness, and direct and indirect outcomes is a key to mastering the gifts of this Next Tier. This creates an opening for you to jump through to the Next Tier Energetics in your life. This subtle and profound shift is a function of your consciousness and ecological use of energy and information. You have just been put on the Junior Olympic team holding the torch of the big-time games for this Next Tier of humanity.

"It Seems the Same"

As you practice this exercise, if you're not sure if you are truly sensing differences or imagining them, know that there is nothing wrong with you. If you are saying and experiencing the same things with both hand positions, you are likely Low Energy Neutral and are repeating what your conditioning asks of you—at least for that domain of life. If your energy neutrality has become such a drug to protect you from Energy Poor and anything beyond neutral, know that the drug effect can wear off with more available energy to provide for a greater information flow with which to experience and upgrade your life.

The great news is that when you recognize that your current experience of what is important seems real and your options at any moment are simply an app you are playing, then a new source of energy and light starts becoming available to jump-start your stalled Seeker's engine.

As you read more in this book, you will come to recognize that two distinct information and energy flows are available for each of us. One locks you into energy richness, and the other makes sure you are in neutral land and cannot get out of the swamp of confusion or effort. After one chapter on Energy Rich and Super Rich and one on the nature of the Next Tier, we will dive further into these two methods, and you will have more resourcefulness, and gain even more from what I am sharing.

Beyond your thinking mind, you likely already intuit that experiencing, observing, interpreting and living opposite your natural, authentic, and optimized energetics will consistently drop you to Energy Neutral. These warmup exercises will give you greater insight and help you to find your authentic way—so that you too can gain the power to transform and be a beacon of energy richness.

The juncture where High Energy Neutral meets Energy Rich is an exciting place.

Bridging the Gap

High Energy Neutral is the target for most of your daily life. This is the state in which you are willing to look with curiosity at various options and alternative ways of manifesting what must happen next. There is still a binding of information and energy. For one reason or another, nothing truly changes. Since it is Neutral, there will be no real change between your thoughts and your Field—nor between your Field and the force of attraction for a new reality. You are climbing the ladder to the diving board. Jumping is actually still ahead.

While the gap between High Energy Neutral and Energy Rich is very small, their differences are HUGE. A small spark can create a wildfire of change. This gap is between thinking, planning or working on something you want to happen—moving toward something or someone for greater optimization or greater impact—and the superpower of Energy Rich. It is a totally different experience of life with a tangible influence on more than just your Field.

Your EpiField and those of others connect—resulting in a very real and noticeable increase in resourcefulness. Next Tier Energetics do not have the need for loss or trauma to liberate energy and access the information to create a new level of engagement, synergy and the seemingly magical force of constructive attraction. It's analogous to the difference between rowing a boat against the current or being carried along by it.

The current is the direct experience of *Creation's Codes* organizing the *YOU* who is observing and narrating your life and reality. In Energy Rich, as opposed to the jump from poor to Low Neutral or low to High Neutral, you are energetically exchanging into a different, more affirmative, more capable, more empowered and more actualized *YOU*.

This difference is truly incredible. Let me illustrate it through the story of Nancy. She told me about the relationship she'd experienced between the amount of energy available to her and the impact it had on her adult son. After ten years of sobriety, her son had relapsed into severe drug addiction. He was in a deeply psychotic state and wanted to kill himself.

Nancy knew that more was needed of her. Attentive to her son's Energy Poor state, she focused her E-State from low to High Energy Neutral and expanded her perspective to also include others who could support him.

She did this while she was miles away from them. She knew that in an Energy Rich state someone who is Energy Poor can flip to neutral, and someone neutral can momentarily experience Energy Rich. As she thought about her son and those who were near that might help him, she instantly and magically transformed the connection between herself, her son and others.

In his prior experience with hospitals, her son had been told that he could not be admitted with addiction until he was discharged from a rehab therapy center. The rehab center said he could not be helped there until he received hospitalization to first medically control his psychosis. The bureaucratic Energy Neutral field of medicine/disease seemed to seek efficiency for the masses while missing the personalized and effective attention needed by individuals.

During her participation in my one-year AlchemE course, her energy level shifted, and she consciously moved from Energy Neutral—with no capacity to bust out of the matrix that limited her and influenced her son—to so much *MORE*. A burst of resourcefulness flowed through her body-mind-spirit and Field as she remembered Energy Rich.

Instantly, she observed herself watching a rerun of a lousy old movie. She felt that she and the system her son was locked into was like a hamster on a wheel, furiously trying to get almost anywhere else. She knew that there was *MORE*, much *MORE*.

Through becoming aware of the energetic strategy that was running her life, and by choosing her authentic way, she had more than enough energy for the organizing forces of life to abundantly ignite the Field of others. Nancy accepted that to achieve greater Field synergy and quantum entanglement (oneness) with her son, she must represent the energetics of the change that she and her son needed. She chose to become more of that change.

With enough energy, one person, like one lit candle, through sympathetic resonance, can ignite or activate another. The EpiSpace between each of us is real. This is the place of mystics, philosophers, creatives, lovers, artists, Seekers and *MORE*. This happens constructively and more consistently once we are launched beyond the grasp of the matrix and move from High Energy Neutral to Energy Rich.

SEEKER'S CODE #3
WE SEEK A RICHER, MORE MAGICAL, AND EXTRAORDINARY EXPERIENCE FOR OURSELVES AND FOR OTHERS.

Nancy temporarily had an energetic exchange into a different version of herself with a more coherent Field and much more expressed information. This version, more consistent with her true energetic nature, sent a different signal through her Field, which was broadcast to her son's Field influencing him and those who cared for him. For the rest of the weekend, she had a future vision for her son with the full flavor of victory.

Knowing that the change already happened in the future, she called the hospital and asked for the help of the head administrator. This time she had full positive expectancy supported by her Energy Rich state. Her Energy Rich interaction with the administrator triggered the future reality.

Magically, the system and those entrusted with her son's care became more mutable. His care plan was transformed. The hospital agreed to treat her son, and within a few days her son's psychosis was stabilized. He was sent to the drug rehab treatment center. This is very different from the immobilizing conflicting conditions that existed previously.

SEEKER'S CODE #5
WE WISH TO ACCESS THE MULTIDIMENSIONAL ENERGETICS
THAT MAGICALLY CREATE AND CONNECT US ALL.

This is what true Energy Rich does. It creates synergy between an individual's Field and that of others for coherent engagement. Super Rich creates even more. The same *Creation's Codes* that, when energized, make the stars, planets and life on Earth are now so much **MORE** available.

"Commit your affairs to the Lord, and your plans will be manifested."
—PROVERBS 16:3

When Moses came down from the mountain, the tablets he shared were not ibuprofen or whatever you think is missing; they were tablets of faith—faith in whatever is the source and the way of creation in all areas of life. We are frozen light. And we are here to share that light as easily and naturally as we breathe, move our fingers, and walk on this Earth or dream of a new world for us all.

Sense the difference in you—your posture, the movement of energy within yourself, your facial expressions, your breath and your emotions—as I relate the impact of Energy Rich and **MORE** for more than just Nancy and for more than just yourself. Think of people who might jump up one E-State as you become Energy Rich. Consider the possibilities of spontaneous reorganization to a higher order without even attempting to fix, heal, transform or change them. How? The answer is too simple and profound for most of us to imagine. With more light and bandwidth available to you, might this spark a remembering in them of the **MORE** that is possible?

I know that this Seeker's Code #5 has just been activated for you as it was for Nancy, her son and others. Now, my fellow Seeker, like the "charge" assigned to students at a graduation ceremony, here is the mission being passed on to you:

SEEKER'S CODE #7
WE HONOR AND CELEBRATE THE SACRED NATURE
OF LIFE/AND WISH TO SPREAD ITS MAGIC.

Now, read the sentence up to the slash, after the word "life." What are you thinking and feeling? What is your energy level like? Add the second part of Seeker's Code #7. What is different as the system grows to take action to inspire others? Now, let's take this from a High Energy Neutral statement of wishing to spread this magic to something so much more Energy Rich and engaging with the Field...

We honor and celebrate the sacred nature of life and are consciously and with full tenacity spreading its magic...

With whatever it frigging takes!

This is the energetic Nancy used, and you can too.

Whew. I trust that you are beginning to recognize the difference between energy states and how "the real stuff" starts beyond neutrality. Claim *extraordinary* or the ordinary will claim you. While circumstances or situations differ, Nancy and her son's story is also your story. It is humanity's story in these raw and fragile times.

Most of you will find something in this that you really know is true and possible. You don't know exactly how to do this—but you do know there is **MORE**. The divine forces that fill the interspaces of the universe await our conscious focused attention and the unbound energy that will activate *Creation's Codes* for the higher-order reality that is awaiting us all.

In High Energy Neutral, you've got the transformation and personal development language. You are sensing momentum toward achieving your desired reasonable goal. You work in a way to make it happen effectively and often efficiently. And now, effectiveness for more than yourself is calling. You are changing. Once Energy Rich, synergy, syntropy and direct access to *Creation's Codes* are available. High Energy Neutral is a good place to rest—just don't expect things to fundamentally change. For this we must engage in Energy Rich as it engages us with even more than we can reasonably expect.

With High Energy Neutral poised and ready for *MORE*, the countdown begins.

Tick Tick Tick, the pressure and excitement for massive momentum builds.

10, 9, 8, **Tick Tick,** check systems again and prepare for takeoff.

7, 6, 5, **Tick Tick,** do your exercises and state your goals.

4, 3, 2, 1 **Tick Tick,** have positive expectancy and rehearse for blastoff.

It is as if we can hear the mission control of the National Aeronautics and Space Administration (NASA) in Florida announcing to the NASA team in Texas (responsible for the rocket launch after the rocket clears the tower)...

"Houston, we have ignition."

TOCK!

You have launched with a power thrust igniting *Creation's Codes* for more than just *Your MORE*! The communication from High Neutral has been passed on to Energy Rich to take you on your next Seeker's adventure!

We're off to live the promise of the *Unreasonable and Extraordinary* with Energy Rich and Super Rich.

CHAPTER 5

GAME ON!

ENERGY RICH OR SUPER ENERGY RICH

"Set a new standard. Step up. Step Up. Step UP!"

—TONY ROBBINS

Set the standard for your E-State—it is from there that all possibilities and realities emerge.

Energy Rich is truly where our transformational journey begins. This state is what allows us to set a higher standard and serve as an example that inspires others. It exists beyond the world of defense and stress responses.

Entering this state may be inspired by massive pain or loss, ripping you and humbling you to claim a bigger **MORE**. Even without significant loss, in a High Energy Neutral moment, you may have recognized that you have been playing too small of a game in some area of your life. This awareness alone, with acceptance of the energetics leading to it, can add the spark to fuel your choice to jump through the gateway between High Energy Neutral and Energy Rich. Until you go beyond planning it—until you make that choice to jump—nothing changes.

Claim *extraordinary* over and over, or ordinary claims you!

Perhaps you chose to act on a whisper of remembering what you were made for in the past, or a shout reminding you to step up now for your future legacy to happen.

From Lost Resources to Gained Resourcefulness

I shared the story of Aunt Sadie's Organics in Chapter 1. We "met" them in a Low Energy Neutral state. The circumstance at the heart of this story was that their main product was stuck in quarantine. Because of their shared Energy Neutral state, they believed and energetically broadcast that the circumstance was becoming a solid and immutable block of ice, keeping them from surviving. As they drifted toward Energy Poor, they felt it was quickly becoming a fatal reality. You now know that seeing a "problem" as reality is a quality exclusive to energy neutrality.

However, at that point, there was enough energy to search for a way to resolve the problem (to melt the ice).

With yet another massive jump in available energy and a significant rise in the ability to organize new possibilities, Sadie's Organics was able to make a vital shift. This was the shift from "working on it" while still in the neutral experience of being "separate from" to the characteristic transformation of "being there" in Energy Rich. **With this profound shift from lost resources to gained resourcefulness even the concept of a problem no longer existed.**

Instead, with more energy, the ice was no longer just a trickling stream, but became a flowing river—fluid and mutable, with its current transformed into a constructive force of attraction. Syntropy replaced impending entropy, breakdown and loss was replaced by growth and gain. Employees were involved with and celebrated this transformation. Epiphenomena were occurring as even some along the manufacturing and supply chain, as well as the end users and their families were enriched.

In Energy Rich, with more available energy, the problem became increasingly irrelevant. What remained was an opportunity for cooperation and elevation to at least a transient state of energy richness.

A Challenge to Step or Leap Up?

A challenge is a constructive way to see a problem. As a noun, "challenge" is still about an obstruction, like the ice in your way on your path to **MORE**. Though a slightly more energized problem, it is still about the lack of a resource to let you move ahead. There is a circumstance or situation that is still beyond your control.

As the current gets stronger with more energy, the word "challenge" goes through a metamorphosis; it becomes a verb. It's about what you can do to be more resourceful. With enough bound energy transformed into "work" energy, you can change the way you are experiencing the situation. Instead of the challenge being a noun requiring a missing resource, and goods being withheld, it is about what *YOU* can do about it. With Aunt Sadie's, it was about the individual and collective resourcefulness of the team representing the corpus or body of the **corp**oration. Step up, step up—or perhaps *leap* up—to **MORE**.

In this context, challenge is an invitation offered to you to take part in a contest or perform a feat. Energy Rich requires that you both welcome and choose to accept the challenge. Now, with the additional data stream, new apps are created that provide collateral streams or currents to help fulfill your personal **MORE**.

This is the launch of Energy Rich. Power on!

Bobby, a dear friend of mine, said that fame and fortune are often confused. Too many want the illusion of fame, and this by itself usually leads to a path of destruction for them and others. This is because it is about taking and binding energy mostly for oneself.

Bobby said to screw the fame, and that he will take the fortune! Fortune is associated with an abundance of accumulated Energetic Capital that offers you—and those inspired by you—expanded opportunities that add value to life.

This next story is about a boy who had neither fame nor fortune. He chose to see his problem as a challenge. Ultimately, he manifested both.

Ralph Lifshitz was a shy boy constantly ridiculed because of his last name. As it is natural for a child—and important to survival in a culture—he yearned to be liked and accepted. This need being threatened can be traumatic. Energy Neutral states are predisposed to stress responses.

For little Ralphie, this was very stressful. Ralph's experience of rejection was even more strongly felt as a teen. Living a Low Energy Neutral existence, Ralph was the last to be chosen for most teams. While his name did serve as a lightning rod for attacks, his energy state furthered this. His Field was likely conditioned to both his experience and his broadcast of his Energetic of rejection. Eventually, he decided he'd had enough. At about thirty years of age, he chose a new standard. Ralph decided to redirect the sails of the ship of his destiny. He chose to view the problem as a challenge to overcome, and his quest began. He decided to perform a ritual to affirm his personal transformation and energetic exchange into a new Ralph, a Ralph playing new apps.

Welcome, Ralph. Welcome, you. Welcome, Seekers, to Energy Rich. Do you sense the transmission of energy and information also calling YOU to **MORE**? Goodbye to trying or hoping. Goodbye to "peeing in the wind."

Ralph officially changed his name. He began studying fashion design. No longer bearing the anchors to the social stigma associated with his past name, he was energized by his new future. Energy richness helped bring on the codes that provided for choosing a new identity and creating the synergy that manifested opportunities. His energy richness was further fueled by courage, tenacity, and a spirit of "whatever-it-takes-ness."

Now one of the richest men in America, **Ralph Lauren** stepped up to his personal challenge and developed a multibillion-dollar global presence in the fashion industry.

The Nature of Energy Rich

Dusty Springfield's hit song "Wishin' and Hopin'" illuminates the difference between energy neutrality and richness. She sang about what I consider the Energy Neutral busy-ness of wishing and hoping, thinking and even praying to be with someone. Using this as a metaphor can serve as a teaching for manifestation. You've got to show the person, the larger Field, that you care by making their needs your needs. This is Energy Rich—with bandwidth greater than just for your wants. You must create enough Energetic Capital through congruent and conscious purposeful action. Take them, or the outcomes, for more than yourself, into your arms and heart. Your uncommon-common Field will be a force of manifestation.

When you're in Energy Rich, the polarity, the blame and the dogmatic beliefs and doctrines that people use to define themselves simply disappear. The rules for interpreting our experiences and measuring success and failure with an Energy Neutral lens are no longer relevant. The stain in the center of your garment of life that you were ashamed of—your wound, story, or perhaps the team you oppose—is simply no longer you.

Energy richness activates the precise *Creation's Codes* to create and grow the higher brain and link it to the larger Field. This activates your capacity to make more decisive and effective choices. Conscious and deliberate actions add momentum and a palpable depth and elevation to your life. Access to your higher brain's connection to the Field allows you to see multiple perspectives and optimize your choices to live, create, and attract more of your **MORE**. Experiencing the powerhouse of choice, you chose to be the one who chooses where you focus your attention and E-State for the outcomes that best serve an expanded you.

"Always remember that your focus determines your reality."

—JEDI YODA, STAR WARS

Focus is an expression of your E-State. In Energy Rich, your focus is more coherent. It's like a laser—directed and aimed at the higher outcome, with enough energy to seduce it into existence.

True energy richness requires development of the upper or executive mind that begins in teenage life and continues until about age thirty. In the absence of significant levels of stress and associated biochemistry supporting a neutral state, new pathways are available. Through *unreasonable*, novel or *extraordinary* experiencing, higher levels of brain information, coordination, a bigger reality and greater human performance are possible.

Creation's Codes organize brain structure and its connection to the Field, sustaining the use of both sides of the higher brain. With sufficient energy, it sends signals down the spine and out into the Field to optimize one's experiences and opportunities in life.

For communications to get to the higher brain (cerebral cortex), much more energy is required to organize a more complex and integrated reality. Amazingly, that energetic change sparks a transformation that, once begun, self-perpetuates. The process creates new more efficient pathways between the brain and the Field. Your net available energy to create and manifest is far greater than the spark that first ignited your energy richness.

Transcending the uncertainties and the neutral loops of what, where, when and how liberates us to the greater energy of WHY. This has the energy to foster coherence in answering the rest.

How many of your challenges or pains in life are about: How is this going to happen? How will I (or someone else) do it? What should I do? Which step goes first? When should I start? Where must I be? When, where, what, and how are identifiers of Energy Neutral.

When your *WHY* is big enough, your how, what, where and when will find you. "What" finds you and creates synergy in your Energy Rich Field. It does it through the ripples in the pond of humanity's information Field intersecting between your Field and the Fields of others. This enhances synergy, cooperation and the emergence of new properties. In Energy Rich, what you seek seems to be also seeking you.

Trans Is the Solution

The prefix "trans-" means "beyond, across boundaries, or to cross over." Personal "trans"-formation indicates that we have crossed over to the other side from the previous form of our bodies, thoughts, actions, or creations. This also refers to a system—be it political, economic, environmental, or social—moving from where it was to where it ends up. "Trans," in this context, means that we have crossed boundaries to create a new emerging "something."

Something emerging that goes beyond, creating something **MORE**, in a higher order than existed before, is the secret in all trans-formations, healings, and awakenings. This is what is sparked by love, passion, courage, curiosity and many other expressions of unbound energy and emotions. Each of these states can light up your body-mind-spirit—and Field—to take a higher-order action consistent with your higher potential.

Whenever the ripples of information in your Field collide with another's there is an emergent property that is less or more than the two of you. If any one of your Fields is at least Energy Rich, then **BAM** a novel property, potential, creation or influence occurs between the two of you and the larger Field of humanity.

I mentioned the term "emergent property." This is a property of a system that cannot be anticipated from the parts or elements alone. Something that was not visible or formerly available is added to the mix to suddenly allow a new version to appear. A higher-order reality fueled by unbound energy with newly available information is required to create what appears as *Unreasonable* and *Extraordinary*. When we become Energy Rich, our Field creates emergent properties, qualities and forms. The larger we experience our system, the more ripples of others we can constructively engage with as part of this collaborative *MORE*.

A + B = C

Many movies (and books) involve a main character who endures a crisis, tragedy or loss that drops the person from a high level of energy to neutrality. Predictably, someone or something comes into his or her life who adds novelty and activates some of the more energized emotions leading the main character to a more alive being-ness. Together you see there is a potential for the two characters to be brought to an *extraordinary* level. As you take the ride with them, you hope that they don't screw it up by ignoring the potential of their union by instead hiding in what might initially seem like safety and comfort.

Person A sends ripples out in the pond of humanity as does person B. When their ripples meet, a novel interaction happens and a new property, C, occurs in this A+B union. C is the result of the dance between each other and their information and energy Fields and can be more or less than the information Field of either person A or person B.

It is as if C is a new being formed from their union. From this point on there is really no longer an A or B. This is important to know in all relationships. It is also the power of energy richness to create the functional dynamic for *MORE*.

The new "system" C is an evolution of the individual A and individual B that we started with. This higher-order "C" makes it difficult to return to the pre-union state when either A or B drops into Energy Neutral. It is as if the separate A and B personae no longer exist. Remember that evolution and transformation transcend the lower order and include the novel beneficial elements of each. What you, as the person watching or reading, finds exciting, frustrating, confusing, inspiring, compelling and annoying is this neutral dance between A and B. They are attempting to maintain their separate A-ness and B-ness while you await the characters getting to an Energy Rich C-ness!

C, a new property of the system, is what we are observing in the range from—oh no, he is messing it up—to great, this will be the best love affair ever. This is all dependent upon their new combined E-State, and how we view it. Our participation with them determines whether we want to end the story now or switch to another one. When neutral there is a power struggle within A and within B and also between A and B.

The main character grows, evolves, awakens—and then something happens. Forgotten, hidden, denied or withheld information comes to the surfaces from A. The Energy Rich system of C requires that A and B upgrade. Until Energy Rich happens there is not enough energy to move the story or the actors along. They are bound to split back to just A and just B once you've finally caught a glimpse of what C can be! Life creates it that they go along their ways as the same Energy Neutral A and B people. There is not enough energy to create anything. Everyone must get out of the pool until they can feel the ripples of each of them constructively intersecting to bring C back into the swim.

One of the two characters drops to Energy Neutral, and the wonder, magic and transformation is forgotten. Somehow a spark of Energy Rich hits one of them. A massive electromagnet pulls them together so that they can add value to one another and become something more than they could ever be separately—Person C. There is synergy that happens. They see the magic, the effortlessness and want this more often or maybe forever.

This spark of richness reminds you of Seeker's Code #6.

SEEKER'S CODE #6

WE RECOGNIZE THE POWER OF FOCUSED ATTENTION
AND ENERGY/AND CONSCIOUS CHOICE.

It just takes one of them to remember Energy Rich and focus their attention on the *Unreasonable* and *Extraordinary* of their union and how they are one. With this remembering, the Energy Neutral alienated, isolated, rejected part of the data stream is lit up. They either are merged into the higher-order C, or they are not because it is just no longer relevant.

Most challenges associated with energy neutrality are **trans-formed** by conscious choice when fueled by bigger whys, reasons, and visions. This is only possible with an upgraded E-State and data stream potentiating a larger experience of the real system in which you participate.

The bigger you see the system that you participate in, the bigger your why can be. The more alphabet letters and the larger the information Field you participate with, the more energy is required to organize your world and the growing access you have to the infinite consciousness, allowing you to make an impact.

This consciousness expands your perceptions and interactions in the world. Remember how Energy Neutral led to only one perspective? In Energy Rich, two perspectives can happen simultaneously. You don't think one thing is right and the other is wrong. Instead, you use a higher part of your cerebral cortex and discover how you can optimize everything. In Super Energy Rich, we go beyond what we personally want as there is no separate me or you. Something else exists—and we are part of this something.

This has an impact on those around you. If you are Energy Rich and those around you are confused, upset, doubtful, or attached to their reasons of why or why not, they will become more coherent, upgraded by your coherence and energized E-State.

Energy Rich excludes categorization and separation—the very polarity of society that we experience in Energy Neutral. I was recently asked, "Are you a Democrat or Republican?" This is a common Low Energy Neutral question, negating the other infinite possibilities for political parties and organization.

To consider anything more than the two main parties requires that you have more bandwidth and energy richness to determine which of these seems to support or best reflect your personal values.

In an Energy Rich state, you "trans-cend" considering yourself a Republican or Democrat—or a Libertarian, Socialist, or any other confining category. Instead, you are a person choosing to support the policies of a current party. Or you might view today's world and choose to support some conservative and some liberal policies. Therefore, after considering multiple perspectives, you'd vote for a particular candidate or support a party that best represents your vision for the nation or world. This is called trans-partisan politics.

The key here is that *YOU* choose! You choose your why and you focus on the outcome with positive expectancy and an abundance of energy coded with information.

Lost in Trauma, Found in Faith

Personally witnessing countless individuals over the years—reading more than a hundred thousand "forms" before, after and between events and speaking with people, clients, and friends—it seems that a switch always flips as people reach that higher E-State. They seem energetically and pragmatically "exchanged" into different people.

As an event begins, I often ask individuals if there is anything about their health, wellness, personal development or evolution that they wish to share with me. I remember Ellen, a woman participating at her very first event. Let's call her "Ellen A." She answered like this:

I am a sexual abuse survivor sober for fifteen years. My neck still hurts from a car accident where a drunk driver side-swiped me four years ago. I am in psychotherapy for my PTSD. It is generally under control, yet I do have night terrors. My ex-husband stole from my accounts, pretty much taking everything from me.

> What do you think her energy state was? Why do you think so?
>
> Do you know folks who offer a similar narrative when you ask how they are doing? If you ask how their healing is going, do they respond by talking about their trauma, circumstance, or problem?

Ellen was obviously in a Low Energy Neutral state when she responded. She stacked reason after reason why she could not be better, and after a while, the reasons became her identity. The thoughts that habitually cycled through her awareness were perfect manifestations of the amount of energy she had available. Her identity was in her circumstances and the painful events that defined her.

She was using an Energetic that was focused upon loss and being a victim. She thereby amplified this in the Field and attracted more of the same. When I asked an Energy Rich question about her health—not her illness, symptoms, traumas, or circumstances—she could not even consider or comment on it as the amount of energy and information that would be needed was not available.

After Ellen had been to a couple more events with me, "Ellen B" answered these questions with a truly Energy Rich response like this:

I am finding my way in life. Opportunities for new friendships and maybe even a new lover are developing.

I switched from a talking therapist to a body-centered (somatic) therapist so that I can be more connected to my body, which is no longer a trap for me. I am taking courses to prepare for a leadership position in the human resources department at work. Oh, at times, my neck hurts and sometimes I feel anxious. I am riding it to wherever it takes me, and Donny, please know that I am well.

How does this narrative impact you? Are you flat in your response to it? Are you annoyed? Are you inspired? What is your energy level like when reading this? What would it be worth to you to be able to switch yourself from Ellen A to Ellen B?

This example demonstrates the difference between Ellen's amount of available energy determining which data stream is converted into the codes that play out in her Ellen app.

Her second answer had much more energy. She was focused upon optimizing life and her relationships. Life was now more than just about herself. This required more energy and more bandwidth of information to reorganize her prior downsized life, emotions, thoughts and focus. With a more Energy Rich baseline standard, her Field attracted **MORE** instead of less. Synergy happened, new opportunities flourished, and she decided in faith to help others. Full on with greater resourcefulness, the presence or absence of resources was no longer relevant to her state.

She was exhibiting all the features of Seeker's Code #4.

SEEKER'S CODE #4
WE WANT TO GIVE, GET, LEARN, AND LIVE WITH A
BIGGER PURPOSE, INSPIRING PROFOUND IMPACT.

This is what happens within seconds of experiencing Energy Rich. Immediately, *Creation's Codes* enhance your information access, flipping your experience of your Field and impact upon it.

By becoming Energy Rich, you're instantly more resourceful through your greater availability of energy to potentiate the codes for the apps of life. There is nothing to work on and no circumstance that has to change. Change your E-State, and it seems like you are a different person—or the same person, now with access to so much **MORE**.

Help Others to Move Up One E-State

Most of this book is about how to instantly move from Energy Neutral to Energy Rich, from ordinary to *extraordinary*—in a way that doesn't require having your stuffing ripped out or having to first change anything in your life. Your energy abundant and radiant coherent Field—with *Creation's Codes*—creates thoughts, emotion, physiology, focus, language, posture and rapid manifestation.

Your radiant Energy Rich Field, with greater bandwidth of information engages the apps of raw, real and at times beautiful transformation. Once in this potentiated Field, observe how things really happen in life. Synergy is created aligning you and others.

People transform lives when they are Energy Rich—their own energy sparks more available energy for others in the cooperative Field. Being Energy Rich creates a magnetic momentum that brings more energy with it. This is the force of attraction.

We've all experienced this kind of attraction from momentum. Ever get very interested in something? Let's say you become super-excited about yoga. You're practicing it every day. You're thinking about yoga, talking to your friends about it, and suddenly...everywhere you go, you notice something yoga related. There are yoga studios all over the place, yoga clothing ads popping up in front of you, and other people into yoga become part of your experience. When you are Energy Rich, what you truly value becomes more visible and accessible in your life. This is the ka-ching, ka-ching Energetic Capital you are sharing with the Field.

You can help others reach this state without having to do anything. Just as you see the world as you are, similarly, you impact the world as you are. Your elevated E-State upgrades the E-States of others.

"Co-here-ence." When parts of a system function as one, greater coherence is created wherever or with whomever it meets. It is about experiencing and acting upon the **MORE** that others might not see. Your Energy Rich Field inspires those who are Energy Poor to move to neutral in an instant. Those who are neutral often become rich. An Energy Rich state is coherent with available unbound energy that is ready to do its job. In physics, it is "work energy," which creates change.

When you are Energy Rich, your coherent and effective focus is to constructively create. You are a momentum and manifestation machine. You shift from focusing on getting rid of pain or disease to improving well-being, or from escaping poverty to finding abundance, or running away from an unfulfilling relationship to discovering novelty and passion. What you choose to focus your attention on is what becomes your reality. Things just click in Energy Rich. They form in alignment with the organizing intelligences of life through the codes that create all of reality.

SEEKER'S CODE #7

WE HONOR AND CELEBRATE THE SACRED NATURE
OF LIFE AND WISH TO SPREAD ITS MAGIC.

Energy Rich Checklist

When Energy Rich, you choose:

- knowing over believing.
- courage over fear.
- power over force.
- fascination over dogma.
- effectiveness over effort.
- creativity over lack.
- flexibility over rigidity.
- purpose over personalities.
- synergy over competing efforts.

- decisiveness over uncertainty.
- opportunities over problems.
- progress over working at it.
- curiosity over confusion or judgment.
- declarative statements over maybes.
- novelty over certainty or comfort.
- pragmatic enthusiasm over complacency.
- multiple perspectives over a single way.
- discussions and actions over arguments.
- measurable results over we'll see what happens.
- momentum and transformation over sameness and stagnation.

Conscious choice with full determination is a natural and necessary tool of energy richness. When you are Energy Rich, you:

- remember your why before your what, where, when or how.
- experience manifestation through cooperation and synergy as you optimize with positive expectancy.
- know your larger outcomes with confidence.
- speak through your Field, both before you enter the room and after you leave it.
- transform perceived obstacles into opportunities.
- confirm that your systems—business, finances, health and relationships—are adaptable so that you're truly prepared to thrive.
- seek other opinions, options and challenges so that you can improve your relationships with the forces that create and attract.
- are beyond even considering if you are liked or accepted because you know outcome and success are higher orders.
- stand, walk and speak with confidence and a coherent, natural determination.
- create synergy with others and inspire them to find a way to step up to what really matters—with attitudes like "whatever it takes," "of course," or "yes, I will."
- uplift those who are Energy Poor to rapidly become neutral—and those who are neutral to experience Energy Rich.

In Energy Rich, your attention is upon optimizing your life—knowing that through the Field you also help others to be their very best. This represents success to you. It happens without coaching them. It happens beyond you. There is a palpable energy and an abundance of opportunities.

Success is often about reaching your goal. This goal is often about fulfilling what you believe the cultural Field (the matrix) considers the marker of finally being enough. Being accepted in the culture and avoiding not-enoughness is a hallmark of energy neutrality. Even in a High Neutral state, the feeling of enoughness or success generally lasts from only hours to days.

Having more success—beyond being liked or accepted—because you are **MORE** and want to achieve more is the beginning of Energy Rich. As you get to the height of Energy Rich, victory calls, invites, and beckons you with a bandwidth seducing your entire being. More than just about your personal transformation, your Field now uplifts others.

Activating an upgrade of your larger system impacts your relationships, your business, a larger outcome of healing and a new dynamic of personal interactions or intimacy. The metamorphosis is about you and your Field—about a new standard of how you cooperate, interact and create greater synergy $(A + B = C)$ with others. It is more than you or others being better or more. The entire room you are in or thinking about pulsates with a synergy that it is here. Ready or not, it is happening. The path is open, and you are holding the torch for victory.

You know, experience and expect the outcome of a higher order that begins to manifest through energy richness, putting Creation's Codes into action. You may want to be in the upper percentage of people with the healthiest immune systems—where infection, cancer and other concerns are no longer possible—and if they do occur, they are self-regulating. There you can experience a higher sense of success or victory.

You no longer have as your goal the specific lowering of your blood pressure or protecting against a heart attack or stroke. Instead, you optimize the cardiovascular system's synergy and enjoy testing this new system. Instead of minimizing stress or conflict in your relationship, you choose for your relationship to be a model that others seek to emulate.

When you are in Low Energy Neutral, you want to talk to Dad about the issues that kept you and him at odds. In Energy Rich, you phone him letting him know you are getting tickets to a ball game with his favorite team. Or perhaps you go fishing with him or take him to his favorite restaurant. You forget he is your "father" since he is more than this role. You show him you care about him more than you would a friend. Now his B joins your A, and the Energy Rich gets you both lost in a higher-order C. You cannot even remember why you withheld your love from him in the past.

Do you sense the difference? Is reading this inspiring you? Do you feel a quickening, a coherence or a sympathetic resonance with this? This is the calling of Energy Rich. It builds and builds. When can you recall even a moment of Energy Rich in your life—or someone you know taking the higher path that Energy Rich requires? In what area of life do you claim Energy Rich? And what is your reason why?

Energy Rich is where we wake up beyond the Energy Neutral compliance with the cultural Field. Liberated, you begin to create a greater influence in the Field of humanity than the conditioned Energy Neutral and AI Fields of the culture had on you. You awaken to a new reality, and often you influence others without even trying.

This is not the end of the E-State spectrum. At the upper end of Energy Rich, you can transition to Super Energy Rich. At this point, instead of feeling more accomplished, successful, meaningful or proud, you feel like you are not enough for what you are here for. Somehow this is now a welcome feeling as you sense something that is more than enough calling you.

The next level is beyond even wanting to achieve for achievement's sake or feeling that you have arrived and are enough. Somehow you experience that there is so much more than your mind can create or build. There is a calling from another dimension where *Creation's Codes* take you from the cocoon of the mind and this four-dimensional world into a new species—to a space beyond your own separate self and thoughts and anything you know. It is something that you somehow remember: from where or when is yet to be determined.

As you move to super richness, you realize that so much of what you considered to be adverse events, traumas and losses in life were perceived through your low energy state. Now with abundant energy, your prior believed obstructions to reality are dissolving. You are already realizing (or real-eyes-ing) that your entire sense of who you were or wanted to be was fraudulent. This mist of awareness shines brighter than anything you've experienced before. What is truly behind the curtain of mental illusion is illuminated—and it is sooo much more than the mind can comprehend.

A higher order calls, cracking you open to more light, spirit, love and intimacy through a direct connection with *Creation's Codes*. This widescreen view humbles you to the reality of the forces of creation. By yourself, you are not enough and never will be. You are created and shaped by a larger intelligence and must first have enough energy and the massive bandwidth needed to experience it. You sense this, and you welcome this new awareness. It is as if you still love an old childhood friend, and you are about to move on to something beyond your experienced reality. It is exciting!

You realize that all you own owns you. The funeral car has no luggage rack. With the innocence of a child, you wake up to the non-material, non-bound world—one that meets us with gratitude and whose currency is love, the soul's truth and grace. It is a calling to magically serve.

And speaking of magic, what lies ahead when the curtain between the bound and physical world is pulled back? More than synergy and cooperation between you and others, there is collaboration and quantum entanglement. You wake up to an experience beyond the mind—described and promised by many of the spiritual traditions—only accessed by a few. Now, Seekers, with the light of Super Energy Richness, it is available to *YOU*.

To go beyond your desires, your roles, the limits of this physical world, this time dimension and the rules of physics for engagement and reality, we must claim the energy to organize the potentiation of our soul's journey. This is the Seeker's greatest calling.

This juncture from Rich to Super Rich is experienced as if you are in a packed stadium in the championship game and the less-rated team is on the verge of a miracle. A player, who was injured earlier in the game, sets up to kick the ball. You are compelled to stand up and witness. Thousands in the stadium and around the world are inhaling the fragrance of impending *extraordinary*.

Something else had just manifested in the stadium. It is called Super Energy Rich. You and thousands are doubting this can happen while the seduction of victory and the Super Rich Field is building through this player. He kicks the ball a distance never seen before. It flies past several players who sense they are already witnessing a miracle. SCORE!!! This unlikely player accessed the Super Energy Rich Field as it accessed him.

There is no longer a player making an impossible play, or a team at the bottom of the ratings list creating the impossible. It is the city, the state, the country and even the world celebrating the rise of spirit beyond anything the mind could conceive of happening. Yes, goal, score! The stadium goes wild. More than the celebration of a player, a team, or a sporting victory—a rebirth of human spirit awakens. The light becomes even more visible.

The energetic differential is even more apparent. It is broadcast around the world by more than just television. Technology and humanity now transmit a larger signal as everyone and everything constructed are vehicles to be taken over by human spirit, soul, one-ness and the higher order of *Seeker's Codes*. Hundreds, thousands and even millions around the world are hugging each other. Radical political and social class distinctions no longer matter. At timeless moments we are embraced by **MORE**. We have witnessed the **Unrea-sonable** and **Extraordinary**—the answer we all need at this delicate and dangerous time between tiers of consciousness.

These are the energetics of moving from Energy Rich to Super Energy Rich that I have helped many thousands to experience. It is part of what I describe in my book *The 12 Stages of Healing*.

This part of how *Creation's Codes* work is super available in the Next Tier. Now you, too, are being asked to step up—or leap up to con-sciously and ecologically adjust the sails for a new future—a future borne of a changed past.

SEEKER'S CODE #5
WE WISH TO ACCESS THE MULTIDIMENSIONAL ENERGETICS
THAT MAGICALLY CREATE AND CONNECT US ALL.

Super Energy Rich: MIND BLOWING!!! Absolutely OUT OF THIS WORLD!!!

"Oh, my God, I never knew how beautiful it could be."

This declaration exemplifies the moment when a Super Energy Rich state awakens us.

Imagine looking out a two-story window—mesmerized by the majestic mountains and a shimmering waterfall cascading over sun-drenched rocks. You notice a purple light permeating the emerald-green haze rising from the falling water. A divine palette of crimson and yellow leaves spiral in heart-shaped vortices, seemingly summoning your heart to join in the symphony. A kaleidoscope of colors sparkles like a diamond under the brilliant lights of a high-end jewelry store.

Somehow the scene turns into computer code, and strings of light rise from all of nature. These strings dance with joy, and you witness *and* participate with all of creation. The mountains, clouds, waterfall, trees and birds oscillate in and out of existence—between "reality" and pure code.

The scene is intoxicating. You reach out through the glass to touch what seems so real, so strange and so familiar. The window looks so clean and the light so bright, you almost forget that there is a glass pane between you and the outdoors. You lean your entire weight toward the vision, and to your astonishment, you feel yourself falling. You fall out of the window of your mind, *out of yourself.* Something is happening. You welcome it as it welcomes you. It is sacred, pure and transmitting something to you. Perhaps now for the first time in your life, you have open access to it.

Pure love fills your heart and permeates the interspaces of your mind. You now know something. You do not know what you know. You do know that with faith, it will be revealed.

You interpret a stream of information transmitted as vibration, light, tones and code as a command that you must be obsessed with adding value. To whom? To what? Your mind or something connected to your mind transmits in silence. All you hear is an answer.

Yes.

You know that whatever this is or wherever you are is beyond any concept of reality—and at this moment it is the only thing that is real.

If you fell out of yourself, and your mind was so clear that you could access *Creation's Codes* beyond all conditioning, where would you be? Who would actually be there? If you were not there, then who was asking and answering those questions? Maybe it was a different you, a *YOU* that exists with much greater access to the information and forces of creation. A you, Seeker, supported by a Super Energy Rich state.

As we move beyond the mind as the narrator and binder of information so we can be consistent with our illusionary sense of self, our world and our participation in it, we are radically transformed.

A lower level of energy and information cannot understand or experience this next level. Even the Energy Rich state does not have the capacity to access the higher levels of *Creation's Codes*. Therefore, the mind uses whatever it knows to describe that which cannot truly be described. This is because our fourth-dimension-linked mind does not have any tools or mechanisms or experiences for processing this massive bandwidth of data.

That being said, what I first described with the *extraordinary* seductive and magical mountain scene can help you conceptualize this truth. Some translate the experience of Super Energy Rich as light (the burning bush), sound (the voice of God, music of the spheres), mathematical representations, sacred geometry or equations, vibrating threads that connect us, or angelic beings. We interpret this with our minds, which cannot decipher the higher order. This can only be experienced.

There is a baseline of gratitude, humility, love, a sense of belonging and a memory of true **HOME** in Super Energy Rich. Also, there is an expansive emptiness with a connection to a larger humanity and an overwhelming sense of awe, bliss, rapture and grace—plus the hunger to share one's gifts and others' gifts for a greater good. I have seen these attributes consistently across many diverse cultures in the thousands I have helped into and at times out of super-rich states.

A woman at one of my energetic events where enrollees experience each of the organizing fields of consciousness described her Super-Rich experience as follows:

I began to see beings of light showing me massive amounts of diagrams, words and pictures. It was information that I didn't recognize or understand at that moment. Absolutely incredible.

MIND BLOWING!!! Absolutely OUT OF THIS WORLD!!! Soulfully amazing, spiritually blissful, head to toes and beyond illuminating! I felt the magic of the stars flow through me and my being became essence sprinkled throughout the heavens.

Another shared:

The energy I would call soul...swirled...getting more and more real. This wonderful connected light and spacious warm energy held me and diffused, it was a profound "YES, I KNOW THE TRUTH...YES this is it, this is home." It was so sweetly glorious, so still. I felt as if I was gliding through light particles suspended in space. "YESSSSSSS, this is it...the confidence of love, the confidence of eternal pulsating glorious love."

Yet another man wrote the following about his access to super rich:

This was the session of "I know who I am; I know why I'm here; I know what I'm made of; and more importantly, we know who we are; we know why we're here; and we know what we are made of!" So magical, impactful, elegant, extraordinary and beyond anything I'd ever experienced before!

And someone who had challenges with her experience of her past discovered the light that changed how she experienced what she had previously excluded. She found community beyond the concept of a separate her:

I went into the vortex; I saw thousands of versions of me in a double-stranded helix that went on and on. The further I went, more branches of my ancestors began to join in. The strands eventually braided into a giant tree...a multi-dimensional family tree of all of humanity.

Nothing had to be figured out for any of these individuals; nothing had to be let go of, understood or changed. There was nothing that had to be done, achieved or practiced to get there. Simply having access to more unbound energy spontaneously fueled a mega-bandwidth to take them there. The experience was just a small part of what the real impact was in creating quantum entanglement. Engagement of their Fields with the larger Field added massive contribution to humanity.

What do you experience with or think about these responses people described? Do you sense the different universe between Energy Rich and Super Energy Rich? Have you had or known someone who had these types of experiences? Have you heard of these possibilities? How does extraordinary at this level sound to you? If you could bring this into greater manifestation in your life, would you?

"You have to find what sparks a light in you so that you in your own way can illuminate the world."

—OPRAH WINFREY (AND, SHE DID!)

Many people ask me about my experience of Super Rich. For me, it is without the level of ecstatic union that often launches and guides people into this direction. Instead, I am in the center of the hurricane and experience my connection to the energetics of creation as if they are moving the fingers on my hand. I experience gratitude, grace, love, oneness and an *unreasonable* hunger to serve by bringing this awareness to as many people as I can.

It seems that most of what I experience when I'm in Super Rich is post-sensory. The sensory system is necessary to warn you of dangers in your environment. I experience the data stream or codes and at times just know. The key for me is with those around me whom I interact with. I focus my attention on becoming, even for a moment, Energy Rich or Super Energy Rich so the gift of light is passed on from person to person. And many of you, when you are Super Rich, may not personally experience the higher states as rapture or ecstasy.

Still, there will be grace, love, acceptance, gratitude and heaps more energy. It may show up in those around you as they experience or express more of these states. You will know you know—even if you do not yet know what you know.

> When you do yoga, meditate, pray or engage in some form of energy practice, what is your E-State? This determines the outcome. Is your Field High Energy Neutral or Energy Rich? Are you truly Super Energy Rich with the attributes described? What degree of synergy is effortlessly and "spontaneously" happening between you and others who might not even be in close proximity? Quantum entanglement occurs between you and others both locally and at a distance when Super Energy Rich.
>
> What is your posture when you are in or attempting to get into a higher state? Is your spine straight, and does your neck drop back while your chest rises up? Are those around you moving from Neutral to Rich or from Rich to Super Rich?

Conversations will change. Doubt, worry and confusion will disappear. Polarity will become unity; everything will become either an opportunity or a gift. Doors will open and people's bodies and Fields will become more energized. They will begin to awaken—all of this during your daily life and activities and without any formal practice or seclusion.

No matter what you or others say or do, it is the Field that communicates the reality.

Rich Is the Goal

Super Energy Rich is NOT our target most of the time. Super Rich destabilizes your life and that of others as it takes us way beyond the matrix and belief in this four-dimensional world we still must live in, and to which we Seekers must bring and inspire the *Unreasonable* and *Extraordinary*.

Energy Rich is a more sustainable goal. After you live rich more consistently in at least a couple of the domains in your life, you will feel the not-enoughness with humility and excitement for more. With international nodes of people consciously living Energy Rich, individual access to a super-rich Field of humanity will be more readily available.

Super Energy Rich is a place to visit for a moment or two when a quantum jump best serves you. It requires and transmits much more energy than Energy Rich, and we want to be efficient and ecological in the amount of energy used.

As a child and throughout my life, I have had access to the Energy Rich states, including Super Energy Rich. I've had to learn how to cultivate this in my life and find ways to help others access this. In this book, I am giving you tools to build the skills of entanglement as the language of the divine. The spiritual states of masters, saints and prophets were all about serving others and definitely not about entertainment, or seeing if they can achieve something.

If you want light to be more available in your life, you need to stand where it is shining.

The attempt to elevate human consciousness is a noble endeavor. For years I was focused on facilitating this through creating a more integrated and coherent nervous system in my clients. Over time, I've recognized that attempts to elevate consciousness beyond momentary states has not worked for the masses. When in a High Energy Neutral state, however, it sure seems like a wonderful and righteous goal.

Consciousness requires energy to manifest, and Super Energy Rich requires super abundant energy. That is a very large gap for the culture to bridge. Instead, I've chosen to help you and humanity move from Energy Neutral to Energy Rich. When we are rich with synergy and our access to the unbound potential is realized, the jump to Super Energy Rich is much more accessible.

Make this your aim as well. Choose to raise us all toward rich so that super rich is within reach.

Love, Bliss, and Rapture

What is the true nature of Super Energy Rich? Ultimately, it is love and the full awareness of our connection to the forces and intelligence in creation. The experience of selfless love, beyond yourself and your roles, is often a biochemical reward for having, at least for moments, a Super Energy Rich Field with another. You think of one another, and no matter how far apart you are, the two of you are super connected. And it feels good, true, and right. Your friends may refer to you as codependent. That's a label created by the mind to discourage this type of instability.

Our attraction toward Energy Rich and Super Energy Rich has powerful biochemical roots. A friend of mine, the late Candace Pert, PhD, was a Chief of Brain Biochemistry at the National Institutes of Mental Health. She is credited with discovering the opiate receptor site and mentioned my theories and practice in her groundbreaking book *Mol ecules of Emotion*. She pondered why humans and other mammals have binding sites along their spines for opiates and hallucinogens.

The only way any drug or chemical can produce an effect in a person is if there is a receptor—a chemical and energetic "parking spot" on the cell—which that particular chemical/energetic signature perfectly fits inside. This activates the person's DNA to produce specific RNA molecules that synthesize particular proteins. These proteins act as vibrational messengers influencing biological fields to produce physiologic effects.

Why would the wisdom of creation provide parking spots that can activate such mind-expanding, pain-relieving, ecstasy-producing, multi-dimensional, unbound informational access to our body?

We are biochemically, emotionally, mentally, physically and socially rewarded or punished for the amount of available energy we bring or take from our Field. When we are depleting our Energetic Capital, we are supposed to hurt or have inflammation and breakdown. When we are neutral, we are supposed to experience temporary relief and less fear for our survival. In either case, we are not energetically contributing to others or supporting constructive change. When Energy Rich, we add value to others. Our biochemistry creates pleasure as more pain-reducing chemicals and fewer stress hormones are released. In such moments, we feel more pride, success and connection to others with a sense of momentum and synergy.

When we have a super-rich experience with someone, it means that our Fields are adding super richness to each other. This is a gift of our contribution to the larger pond of human ripples of information potential. It suggests that we can be part of the metamorphosis of humanity and its structures, systems and ways of being for the world. This leads to adding huge value that can, strange as it may seem, influence future and past generations. I will share more about "*retrocausality*" in the pages to come. For now, though, it is something that happens in the present that impacts both the past and the future.

In short, the manifestation of potential is truly great for your union, regardless of how conscious you are of it. This potential creates seduction. Metaphorically, the angels are giving you a further energy blast and hunger to be with one another, moving past the lower energy states and bringing light to the darkness for one another.

You are smitten. It is as if you have always, and in all ways, known this person. This biochemical and energetic reward shows up with changes in serotonin, oxytocin and many other neurochemicals causing well-being and attachment flowing through your body. Your conversations are about how you can be and create **MORE** together. This is where you get an additional "angelic" loan of Super Energy Rich unbound energy and the data Fields to help manifest.

In this state, you take risks you would not take otherwise. You dream big. Your love adds value and inspires others. Others smile as you enter or walk out of a room. This loan provides temporary access to massive available energy and bandwidth activating an experience written about in spiritual texts.

This works if you make your system bigger than the two of you and focus on how your love can serve others...just because. When you want others to know what you experience for your own sake—**BAM!**—the loan is called back, and the love drug wears off.

When we focus just upon ourselves and drop down to neutral—avoiding discomfort, seeking to get more love, or the BLAH BLAH BLAH stories that reflect our E-State—we lose the bandwidth available in Super Rich and the information stream supporting our quantum entanglement and oneness. The energetic loan with its biochemical rewards disappears, and there is pain. We once again are back within the matrix. Humpty Dumpty has had a great fall.

Love is meant to be more than us. It's meant to manifest something much bigger. In that way, people get rewarded or punished instantly—biochemically, emotionally, mentally, physically and spiritually—for how much coherence they create or how Energy Rich their E-State is. Super Energy Rich is an aggregate wealth that we must pass on to others.

Passing on this wealth is central to Super Rich. To seek the reward without sharing the wealth is a form of addiction. Drug addicts seek the biochemical reward without adding value and steal Energetic Capital from those who support them the most. A characteristic of drug addicts is that simple pleasures and accomplishments do not provide the stimulation needed to activate the genes that foster a sense of well-being.

This is why groups like Alcoholics Anonymous and other rehab programs encourage or require their participants to help others. This gets what I call the "angel chemicals" going again and even activates some of those same receptor sites that were stimulated by the drugs. Seeking to reap the biochemical and energetic rewards naturally earned by those contributing significant Energetic Capital to the Field, without significant contribution, has a very significant downside. As seen with addicts, it most often leads to collapse in body, mind and spirit. I believe that when you are Super Energy Rich, hallucinogens may be activated to awaken you to a bigger participation in life. Beyond all social conditioning, the grasp of the cultural matrix and ceiling of humanity, you experience what is true, right, real and necessary. Instead of just believing, you now have a deep inner knowing. You experience quantum entanglement.

In quantum entanglement, two particles act as one regardless of their resonance in time or space. To experience this and what most would call "the breath or heart of the divine"—we must have access to an *extraordinary* capacity to experience beyond the mind. We must have enough freely available energy to use as fuel for our bodies, emotions, minds and the force of attraction of that part of our Fields that intersects with all others.

"If grass can grow through cement, love can find you at every time in your life."

—CHER

When your life seems most guided, when you experience knowingness beyond reason, when you experience gratitude and awe at the magnificence of a peach or the touch of a lover—or when your business plans seem magically fueled as you fall in love—remember, the source is a Super Energy Rich state.

How different is it when all of this disappears in low neutral, or when you are high neutral and working toward it? When you are Energy Rich and think that if you achieve more, study more, improve yourself more and keep raising the bar, you will finally feel like you are enough, reaching goals gives temporary satisfaction and enhances your sense of self. Enhancing the sense of self is a strategy quite different from transcending it in Super Energy Rich.

Oops. **There is nothing that comes from thought that will ever bring us to super richness.** When Super Energy Rich, even for moments, you can know without being taught. Super richness can influence, inspire and redirect the mind in service to the spiritual aspects of *Creation's Codes.*

You might see a five-year-old child prodigy playing complex classical music, or someone playing chess games with several opponents at the same time. You might witness someone's "knowing" that leads to great writings, philosophies, music or an *unreasonable* and *extraordinary* talent. You might watch an athlete set a record—defying the supposed limits of what's possible. Somehow when you witness them, the energy richness through entanglement still shares its light—even years after the fact.

Achieving Richness

Many use prayer and/or meditation as a way to move away from what they don't like, or to silence the mind. This is a game made up by the mind so it can maintain its Energy Neutral state. There are many forms of meditation originating from different traditions. Their magic is in the practice of developing non-attached witnessing of oneself, one's mind, or even the cosmos. Often it is used as a means of deepening or growing consciousness states. This is so important, especially in today's times.

Meditation is a wonderful means of helping the masses to move from low neutral to high, and for some from high neutral to Energy Rich. With years of practice, some (often secluded from the chaos of life), will reach moments of Super Energy Rich. I applaud any method that achieves the goal of bringing the coherence, synergy and syntropy of energy richness.

I am offering another angle at which to look at this. Since consciousness is a consequence of E-State, what happens if your awareness development is E-State centered? Seasoned meditators have found this an exciting and novel way to effectively impact their energetic awareness of themselves and the Field. Within moments, with this Next Tier, we can have access to the energetics associated with the higher spiritual states. There can be **MORE**.

Like a flash of light, some of the impact those practicing meditation seek can happen in a moment. The time needed before was to calm the mind, unbind energy and access more information for you to move at least from high neutral to rich. Centuries of awareness practices have supported what is finally available to the masses as they experience the energetics of how life itself organizes in this Next Tier.

If you engage in a meditative or spiritual practice, I suggest you add one dimension. Ask what E-State you are experiencing and radiating? What has it been, and what will be its consequence?

With any spiritual practice, focus your attention upon the benefits to others, which will often activate more bandwidth and generate additional Energetic Capital. From an Energy Rich state, you will more easily achieve Super Rich and boost its benefits while there.

Adding a slow and conscious recitation of one of the *Seeker's Codes* sets the stage. Next time repeat with another Code. As you discover your EpiWay of accessing information and energy that potentiates an Energy Rich center, you will be more engaged and aware as your E-State instantly shifts. Please remember that your E-State regulates all thoughts and experiences. As you more consistently experience and live Energy Rich, the doorway to Super Energy Rich cracks open.

I encourage you to continue your practice, with greater insight into your E-State and the value you can create with more energy. With this said, in the pages to come, you will learn how to become Energy Rich anyplace, anytime and within seconds.

In Super Energy Rich, the greater bandwidth of information and energy requires that you experience the dissolution of a solid bound sense of your body and your identity. You know you are so much *MORE*. Super Rich is much more than an experience; it is also acting and being in a way that illuminates others simply by the communion of your Field with theirs.

Years ago, I had the privilege to participate at a retreat in upstate New York personally led by Pir Vilayat, the Sufi master of the western world. He impressed upon us that we should never, ever, do any meditation or spiritual practice to move away from or avoid anything—nor when we are angry, feeling resentful, shamed or less than adequate.

He went on to describe that it is important to celebrate each experience as it occurs—especially those you don't like. He advised attendees that they would not be ready to meditate until they practiced that. Instead, he suggested engaging in a dance of peace, love or compassion—and singing in a way that creates a Field supporting the sacred place that we go when we meditate or pray.

In the late 1980s, when I was first able to initiate a spinal wave in people with no spiritual or yoga backgrounds, many spontaneously assumed yoga postures and even sang chants beyond their religious training. While some might wonder if yoga was developed to support the future of Lululemon, its origins are likely related to spiritual masters who attained what I would consider a super-rich state. If people witnessed the masters' bodies spontaneously arching up and moving into postures with breath and vocal tones further supporting the experience, I would imagine they would believe that if they modeled those postures, they would achieve that super-rich awakened state!

What I have observed over my years of caring for people with the methods I've developed is the reverse of what the mind would think: become awakened, and then the postures will form from the energy. First move beyond Energy Rich, and the gifts of awakening you seek will become available.

In the presence of a master in a Super Energy Rich state, there is the

Field influence from the union of the master's Field with the observer. This is true beyond yoga and meditation. The spiritual teachings of Chabad, which is often referred to as Kabbalah, and many other high spiritual teachings are expressed by those in super-rich states.

Orgasmic waves and experiences were referenced in early Christian writings. The wave-like motion while standing around the Torah, referred to as davening, was practiced by a group of ten men. Ideally, six of the ten men are ones who have not prayed that day. The other four who prayed that day heightened the Field resonance experienced by the other six. With these ten, Super Energy Rich is potentiated so the individual and collective prayers can help those ten and any others gathered to receive answers. In my opinion, this resonance is required to create quantum entanglement and receive the true transmissions through the Torah.

The Sufis celebrate through the Dances of Universal Peace. As the music gets more rapid and intense, so does the movement of the group. Through movement, the group's Field can briefly activate a Super Energy Rich state triggering greater illumination. Orthodox Jews also engage in circular dance. As their celebration builds, there is the experience of moments of heightened spirit as many participants revel in a Super Energy Rich Field of blessings.

Most ancient spiritual traditions have similar dance, movement and song rituals that create a quantum entanglement (oneness across distance in time and/or space) of the group's emerging state of rapture.

With quantum entanglement, as you express the data stream and immense bandwidth that Super Energy Rich supports, your focused attention leads you to being more of the prayer you wish for humanity. It paves the way for this energetic to reach others through what might seem like a contact high. And yes! Even this is organized by *Creation's Codes*.

The words of a prayer transmit your personal energetics. The act of becoming Super Energy Rich makes *YOU*, the **pray-er**, become an embodied **prayer**. Others in your presence, or upon which your attention is focused, will be sparked to momentarily jump two E-States. In what seems like a moment in a Super Energy Rich state, one can download a lifetime of wisdom and possibilities.

I am sure you also know people who have spiritual practices, and still get triggered if you tell them that you voted differently than they did, or if you are for something they oppose. They must move away from you if you are passionate and have very coherent masculine or feminine energy.

Or perhaps they are spiritual and failing financially or living in scarcity. Maybe they claim that they are spiritual yet don't speak to their parents or have alienated a part of their family because of "blah, blah, blah." These are all signs that their effort has yet to match the promise of true super richness.

Super Energy Rich Awareness

You will know the E-States of others by their energetics, posture, language, facial expressions, and the light or benefit they share.

When you are Super Energy Rich, you know it. Therefore, the question is, "When are you *not* super rich?"

If You Are Not:

- almost jumping out of your skin.
- moving in ecstatic glory.
- smiling so your cheek muscles are sore.
- driving your arms and hands up to share light from the stars or from close to you out to them.
- appearing to have the power of the universe either going through you or others around you.
- sure if it is happening.

- certain that there is super-abundant energy.
- sure you and others around you have access to the informational Fields for manifestation of *Unreasonable* and *Extraordinary*.
- humbled by the experience and honored of this gift of awareness of the energetic threads of love and grace everywhere.
- experiencing effortlessness.

Then, you are experiencing something other than Super Energy Rich.

In Super Rich, you get to experience the energy behind all of creation. You realize by experience that physical form is a manifestation of energy and intention. You understand that you're not a body having a spiritual experience, but instead a spirit having a physical hallucination.

In having this experience, you know you are Super Energy Rich.

The model of waiting, working and doing spiritual practices for the most part can elevate one to Energy Rich yet it falls short of Super Energy Rich. If you are practicing it, then you are not there. Once you experience the information Field of *extraordinary* with super richness, you will "get" where these practices are meant to take you, and you will go there. In that moment, you can deepen the experience and connection with the energized mind.

The doorway to Super Energy Rich reveals the light of truth. Truth contains more bandwidth and data than any mind can grasp. This abundance of energy burns through so-called personal "truths" that were obscuring a bigger reality. To have "your truth" or "my truth," there must be a separate you or me. In Super Energy Rich, this separation ceases to exist; therefore, "your truth" or "my truth" are meaningless distinctions.

Super Energy Rich shows up as more than the personal experience. It appears entangled and commingled with grace in actions, plans and the ways we show up in life.

"I will love the light for it shows me the way; yet I will love the darkness for it shows me the stars."

—OG MANDINO

When Super Energy Rich, we will be called to be with people who are Energy Poor and Energy Neutral, as the light is meant for us to shine and contribute. Please see that this is one of the gifts of Super Rich. Remember, it is not YOUR body, not YOUR emotions, not YOUR thoughts, not YOUR soul, not YOUR energy, not YOUR information and not YOUR light.

The sun is not yours, yet you can instantly be bathed in its energy and light as all it knows is to share its essence. We are the forest, the sky, the water, the earth and the air. Whatever we choose to observe, we participate with, and it with us.

You are born of abundance, and you can access the abundance of energy and share from its overflow. As long as you live, you are a renewable resource, and you see and impact the world as you are. The more you share your abundance, the more you have to share. This is your—and our—legacy.

What Will Be Your Legacy?

Ancient spiritual teachings were created thousands of years ago for the people living then. We have since had a shift in energetics. Now, for the first time in history, the unbound energy is more often the primary reality for Seekers.

This Next Tier of humanity is now being born. Spiritual teachings are modern-day representations of interpretations of the data streams experienced by spiritual masters, prophets or students that have been shared through the centuries.

It is essential to experience the Energetic itself and discover the meaning you give it and how it shows up around you for the unique needs of our complex current and future times. Now we are experiencing a conflicted, disconnected and disillusioned humanity with massive amounts of bound energy ready to explode.

In today's turbulent world, how can super richness be known and experienced in the midst of daily life? When super rich, we will recognize things beyond our *unreasonable* and current ceiling of *extraordinary*, transcending the hunger to change anyone, let go of anything, transform anything or even understand what is happening is a portal toward becoming Super Energy Rich. Beyond that portal is the pure experience and knowing of reality. We are inter-dimensional information Fields woven into and from the fabric of the cosmos and gifted with the opportunity to experience the awe of creation.

Seekers, you are now ready to truly know what is really happening in our world, and why it seems so upside down and inside out. What is the difference between the prior and Next Tier of humanity's way of energy and information use? How did we get here? What is ending and what is beginning?

Why are you really reading this book now?

Seekers, we are at a critical, dangerous and *extraordinary* juncture in human history. We must ask these questions to access the unbound. You know it; you sense it. It disturbs you, as it should. The **MORE** we were born for is here. How do we usher it in, share in its power and honor the invisible forces that create and manifest reality? Seekers, humanity is about to get an upgrade, and I invite you to be at the front of this parade for a new and sacred reality.

SEEKER'S CODE #1
WE KNOW THERE IS SO MUCH MORE TO LIFE THAN WHAT APPEARS AS PHYSICAL REALITY OR CIRCUMSTANCE.

SEEKER'S CODE #2
WE HAVE AN OBSESSION TO GO BEYOND WHO WE HAVE BEEN.

The coming pages will reveal new answers—and new questions—as we enter the domain of the Next Tier.

CHAPTER 6

====

MAY YOU LIVE IN INTERESTING TIMES

THE NEXT TIER CALLS

It is likely apparent to you that we have entered a new phase of the human experience. You know that something different, better and **MORE** must be waiting for us during these crazy and polarized times. It is both a period of true waking and massive sleeping. It is the "end of days" for the old ways. The larger systems are doubling down and revving up the "me-me" engine of the *Power and Control Matrix*. We are consuming more, as our hunger for more energy, more power and more ownership *consumes us*.

The old ways want more—in all the wrong ways.

In this moment, as the old and new worlds battle for supremacy, what seemed to work, or what we wanted to believe was working, is up for reassessment. Non-Seekers and Low Energy Neutral Seekers are doing whatever they believe will help them return to the way things were—before our daily way of life was interrupted—with what is often adverse to a new and more respectful humanity and Earth. Like any other symptom, this period of disruption is seen as something to be conquered so that some semblance of their former baseline of use and control of energy and information can be restored.

This will no longer work. Something's coming. You know it.

You can sense it emerging from the mess we now see in the world—flickering in and out of reality with the promise of what we've been waiting for. The energetic shift reveals what we know has been hiding most of our lives, awaiting the critical mass that is needed for launch.

You sense the accelerated acceleration. We are on the mountain's edge. Many are diving off the current summit of their lives, hoping for the best. Some are struggling to get back to where they were, holding on firmly to the branch of a tree at the top of a chasm—watching the roots pulling from the rock and dirt. Others are looking back from the other side of the gorge, remembering how they soared.

A story comes to mind...

An atheist is desperately clinging to a tree branch on the edge of a cliff to avoid a lethal fall. He calls out, "God, please save me." After a few anguished seconds, he hears a voice speak to his mind and soul, "You have denied my existence, yet you ask that I save you?"

The atheist is jarred as most of the tree's roots have separated from the mountain. With terror of his impending demise from the thousand-foot drop, he answers, "Lord, I'll do whatever you ask. Just save me, please."

After a poetic pause, the Divine replies, "Live your life with faith in the forces that guide, transform and liberate you...and you will be saved."

The man calls back, "Thank you, God! I'll do anything! Just tell me what you want of me."

The Lord slowly answers, "My son, you need only to let go of the branch."

You may ask, what happened? Naturally, this is just a metaphor, isn't it? Or is it? Seekers are feeling or sensing this experience every day in some domain of their lives—be it health, relationships, business, finances or social and cultural issues.

How will you handle the moment you approach the edge?

Seekers know that the time is coming for change. Humanity is moving from one branch to another to maintain security. Each branch represents different views. Each branch has its own consciousness and methods of using energy and information. We think that the branches represent reality. What *actually* is real is the space between the branches, the abyss below and the other side of the canyon. When we are Energy Neutral, the system or matrix that runs us does whatever it can to avoid the seemingly empty and destabilizing space between the branches.

Especially for us Seekers, the gap between where we are now and where we must be seems too large and empty. We are aching for a new way, a new value, something more meaningful to fill the gap than what we are seeing now.

Like farmers, we wait with positive expectancy—year after year watering and watching young fruit trees—knowing that as the branches and leaves grow, they someday will bear sweet, sun-fed fruit. Yet nothing appears. For countless days, the farmer's efforts are truly "fruitless."

Under such circumstances, you can become impatient while *Creation's Codes* are meticulously converting the sun's energy and information into a living tree and creating the mechanism for the perfect fruits to be born. You move from your High Energy Rich state to neutrality as you listen to those who say that those trees will no longer bear fruit—that only the new genetically modified organisms (GMOs) or other altered seeds or sources of "food" will grow the chosen fruit. And this may be necessary if there are no other options. You find yourself losing your certainty and doubting what you've learned—and even know to be true—as you are advised to stop your "watering" and eliminate your faith in the larger self-organizing forces. Instead, you are told by the "trusted" authorities to simply shift your consumption to the new, better-than-ever fruits grown indoors with minimal water. Remember, everything we consume has been selected for a type of energy used in its creation and transmits a certain consciousness in the world.

A spark of knowing from a Super Energy Rich moment gives you faith. Just in time too! This faith reminds you to trust *The Seeker's Code*. Days later the first flower appears. This is where we are now in human history. We are watching for the flowers that will become the coveted fruit. The blossom is a reality that reminds us of the divine timing in all of creation.

It is too painful to wait any longer for this space to be filled with a new reality. We can no longer wait for the sun to provide the *sol* (Latin for "sun") and the soul energy for what is next. And we no longer have to wait. Together, we can provide the light to nurture the blossoming and sweet fruit that will follow. By awakening en masse to an Energy Rich state, we collectively will be the sun, the light and the substance for the blossoming of a sweeter humanity than has ever existed before—a new Garden of Eden—unplugged from the matrix.

SEEKER'S CODE #5
WE WISH TO ACCESS THE MULTIDIMENSIONAL ENERGETICS THAT MAGICALLY CREATE AND CONNECT US ALL.

You likely sense that a curtain has been cast in front of our eyes, obscuring the possibilities of other potential realities. Here is something to consider.

Carbon dioxide and forces such as germs are seen as the enemy. Often what seems like a sickness is also an attempted cure. Carbon dioxide is an agent of *Creation's Codes* that makes trees and plants grow. Trees and plants help clean up the mess that the First Tier energetic has created. Germs are what each of our cells are made up of and are kept in check as we access a more Energy Rich and sacred internal and external environment and intimate relationships with one another and nature.

When Energy Neutral, we have no choice other than to accept as reality the Bad CO_2/bad germ image projected onto the curtain. By reacting against that image with an equal energy, like in a well-matched game of "tug of war," we are kept in battle, with no real change. As soon as we peel away one curtain, another one is cast by others with their personal agendas. This is the way the world works. We need to develop the super-powered "X-ray eyes"—gained in moments of energy richness—to recognize the existing projection and to choose instead to access more light and constructive empowerment.

These curtains are maintained by those who seek a return to the life they have known, perhaps improved, modernized and automated, but still hooked into the matrix codes. Instead of the *Unreasonable* and *Extraordinary* expression of the codes of creation, this is still in the model where humans have consumed and fought for control of resources for thousands of years.

Now we are tussling over the cords of the curtains to reveal this stage of humanity. Will we debut the new way or play in the old way a little longer? Those trying to maintain the old way have accumulated power. Only a handful of companies own the major shares of big pharma, the news media, entertainment, social media, energy and the telecommunications industry. Media broadcasts on the political right and left are still managed by the same few companies securing the control of information and energy. The natural progression of centuries-old sets of values and consciousness on humanity's tree of knowledge has this tree perched upon the mountain's edge. It is in its death grip with its roots slipping into the abyss.

At the same time, new baby branches have emerged from the **Tree of Life** referred to in the Old Testament book of Genesis. Fed on raw, real and awe-filled beauty, it blossoms in the light of spiritual teachings, values and practices consistent with many spiritual traditions for a new humanity. Its fruit is bountiful and increasingly available, as is the data stream with the secrets of the universe. Even when something is cloned or a stem cell is used to advance our life, it must start with a living cell created by the wisdom of life.

The Seeker's Code is your primer for the **Unreasonable** and *Extraordinary*—here to enable you to flourish in this next phase of the human "experiment."

Along with a constellation of other Seekers, you have been asking, "What the heck is going on?" From another time and place something radically different beckons us to awaken. We are indeed at the end of days as we have known them—and there is no going back to sleep.

Interesting Times

"When she transformed into a butterfly, the caterpillars spoke not of her beauty, but of her weirdness. They wanted her to change back into what she always had been. But she had wings."

—DEAN JACKSON

The quasi-prayer "May you live in interesting times" has been interpreted as "May you live in a dangerous and tumultuous age." It was meant as a "curse" for someone to move from crisis to crisis. I see it as living in a neutral state with the awareness of so much **MORE** waiting to be claimed. This certainly applies to our present age.

This is what is known in physics as *lambda*, the edge of chaos. This is a mathematical zone where maximum instability and maximum stability exist simultaneously. It is the *cauldron of creation*. Focused attention with abundant energy serves as the quantum tipping point for the manifestation of reality. Entrepreneurs, creators and savvy investors wait decades or even a lifetime for this opportunity. It is here that—with Super Energy Richness—the investment of Energetic Capital and positive expectancy create epic results in the wake of tumultuous times.

In collaboration with the forces of creation and the oneness of all of life, this very real reset influences everything on Earth. In many ways, the transformation mirrors that of a caterpillar.

A caterpillar goes through several stages in its life cycle. When it hatches from its egg, its larva stage is what we generally call a caterpillar. With a voracious appetite, it consumes from its immediate environment for its own personal growth. Its next cycles of life require a cloth wrapping. From this seemingly immobilized state, something magical happens. Every cell of the caterpillar is digested by its destiny. Segregated from others that would doubt a new being will be emerging, it eliminates all physical remnants of what existed before. Inside that cloth covering lies a gelatinous soup.

Creation's Codes activate new apps as the stored energy bound in the caterpillar's form has been liberated. This soup is composed of what are called imaginal cells. As long as there is enough available energy to express the apps of **Creation's Codes**, a sacred metamorphosis ensues, manifesting a new level of evolution. New information and consciousness of the available potential marks the end of the world for the caterpillar. Connected to a larger Field, it now manifests a new form—a way of being with a different purpose, beauty, gentleness and strength.

The Wings of New Energetics

The end of the world for the caterpillar heralds the beginning of a new world for the emerging butterfly!

Humans have been in the caterpillar stage from the time they first walked the Earth. In this stage, **a caterpillar has just one occupation**—to consume for its own sake, to fuel its bound and growing body. It must consume enough of its environment, stripping trees and bushes bare, to bind sufficient energy for the growing caterpillar.

The larva stage is all about "personal growth." Most caterpillars will shed their skin five or six times before *Creation's Codes* move them on to their next stage.

This caterpillar stage of consumption, regardless of its direct and collateral costs, is where humanity has been. More recently, we have experienced a cocoon-like stage, actually dressed in cloth masks and sheltered from one another.

To the caterpillar in the chrysalis, this appears as the end of the world. While in seclusion, there is a breakdown of its entire form, an Armageddon, where every feature of its body dissolves. The caterpillar makes a e leap of faith off the mountain, with nothing of its old structure to hold on to.

With enough unbound energy richness and periodic super richness, we individually and collectively attract enough bandwidth to wake up beyond this consumption stage. We can leap beyond the conditioning *matrix* of a belief in single objective reality and the social conditioning of resource scarcity that requires competition and binding—to so much **MORE**.

Through this individual and collective **MORE**, the larger system of this Next Tier will engineer the greatest jump in human capacities—away from *me-me* and into a connected and resourceful *we-me*!

This is not Armageddon for the caterpillar. It is so much **MORE**! As we are finding out now, more for individuals and humanity is about to emerge. A new energetic and informational Field will be redesigning our lives with the effortless and instant attraction of a profound elevated human experience that you may have only dreamed of in the past!

Energy and information that has been unavailable to most will be available for those who live some of the *Seeker's Codes*. Like ice on a summer's day, for Seekers who know our inter-dependence, the walls that have held back opportunities will melt away. As more come to know **MORE**, we will experience the shift from *i'll-ness* to *we'll-ness*!

SEEKER'S CODE #1
WE KNOW THERE IS SO MUCH MORE TO LIFE THAN WHAT APPEARS AS PHYSICAL REALITY OR CIRCUMSTANCE.

SEEKER'S CODE #2
WE HAVE AN OBSESSION TO GO BEYOND WHO WE HAVE BEEN.

In this new era, we will not need to consume everything to harness energy. The butterfly is attracted to and consumes the energy rich sweet nectar from beautiful flower to beautiful flower, pollinating and sharing information for manifestation of new life. Unlike the caterpillar, the butterfly's *we'll-ness* gives new opportunities and activates new energy from the source of the unbound potential for new life.

The butterfly embodies Next Tier energetics and consciousness shared with you and other Seekers through the understandings, experiences and skills presented in this book.

The Next Tier of Life

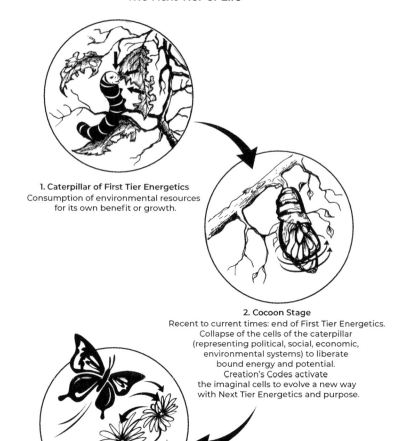

1. Caterpillar of First Tier Energetics
Consumption of environmental resources
for its own benefit or growth.

2. Cocoon Stage
Recent to current times: end of First Tier Energetics.
Collapse of the cells of the caterpillar
(representing political, social, economic,
environmental systems) to liberate
bound energy and potential.
Creation's Codes activate
the imaginal cells to evolve a new way
with Next Tier Energetics and purpose.

3. Butterfly of Next Tier Energetics
The butterfly, symbolizing the conscious
and ecological use of energy and information,
takes flight and lands with light "footsteps."
Creation's Codes and life's order are sacred.
The sharing of information
and energy pollinates opportunities with grace.

Figure 4

MetaMorphosis

"Every act of creation is first an act of destruction."

—SALVATORE DALI

The caterpillar enters its new era through metamorphosis. "Meta" means later, more highly organized, or transcending what came before. "Morphosis" as in Morpheus in the movie *The Matrix*) means a change or transformation in form. This is where we are individually and collectively in the world today.

Our metamorphosis spreads through like the hundredth monkey effect, a hypothetical phenomenon in which a new behavior or idea is spread rapidly by unexplained means. Once a critical number of members of one group exhibit the new behavior or acknowledge the new idea, it is transferred as a meme (contagious consciousness) from that group to others, spreading like a virus between the Fields of all the other individuals. Eventually, through quantum entanglement, it replicates globally.

We are in the midst of a hundredth-monkey metamorphosis. Our relationships are transforming, with our individual selves and one another, while the meaning we give to our experiences and what we value most is also changing This metamorphosis is about to launch into accelerated acceleration.

Ultimately, this transformation is all about the energetics of our species and how we show up in the world honoring the sacred codes of nature and life. How big we believe the system is that we are part of and how and which energy sources we choose to use to create our lives shape a legacy beyond just ourselves.

Evolutionary jumps in consciousness occur once the existing level is satisfied and comfortable. It happens when we feel like we've got it, and it comes with the question: Is that all there is?

In our individual lives, if a jolt of additional available energy hits us, it is usually from the larger system shocking us with events that interrupt our daily life. Shock from trauma, violence, or intense loss that rips us open leaves more light shining inside and outside and more information ready to be manifested. This way of making energy and information available is painful and—even when effective—is less than energy efficient.

> When has a brutal loss, violent or painfully disruptive event happened to you that after weeks, months or years elapsed, you realized it helped you to strip away those aspects separating you from what is real and more sustainable? What seemed to be the turning point that lit you up and turned this around?
>
> Do you remember the moment or day or days that this flipped in your mind from severe loss, violation or pain into recognizing that there were roles or beliefs that were draining the energy needed for you to jump through the next gateway in your development?

Tick...Tick...Tick.

With the promise of "next" at the transition between energy levels, there is a ringing sense of excitement and a tinge of fear as the call for the higher level grows louder.

We realize the prior level is outworn. We realize there is **MORE**. When an electron meets a barrier that it cannot get around, it just goes into another dimension. The electron instantly merges in the space between our conditioned reality where it "believed" it could not go—and appears on the other side.

Tick...Tick...Tick...**TOCK!**

Like that electron, we are suddenly at the next level.

We are novices at this level. It feels better to be the top player on the high school team than the bottom player in the college league. It feels better to be the best in the minor leagues than a newbie in the majors. Perhaps, by now you are realizing that feeling better or more comfortable is irrelevant to your larger *extraordinary* destiny.

WE RECOGNIZE THE POWER OF FOCUSED ATTENTION AND ENERGY/AND CONSCIOUS CHOICE.

This is happening on individual levels all around us. It has been said that when about ten percent of a population reaches this new level of energetics and awareness, this "virus" of new consciousness will spread like wildfire. This is also how a video of a child singing a song becomes viral on the internet. Yet an internet video or meme may change nothing. It is different when we add more Energetic Capital to the Field as a new consciousness is about to be launched.

We've seen the launch of disruptive technologies and companies such as Facebook, Google, Uber, and Airbnb, which all led to higher-order access to information beyond boundaries. We see an unprecedented massive connecting of people that provides for the possibility of shared information and stories like never before. Lives are uniting. This union offers new possibilities to individuals and humanity. **BAM!** The higher order changes human behavior. Decisions are within reach.

The Energy Rich Field, bursting with new information, data and greater bandwidth, becomes the medium of contagion. Each person who becomes Energy Rich and beyond ups the tipping point for this Next Tier of energetics, potentiating a broad access to and reverence for *Creation's Codes*.

The First Tier Energetics

When I refer to the tier of energetics and consciousness into which we have been born and conditioned as the First Tier, my wife, Jackie, looks at me with a look that says, *You know better*.

She reminds me that this is the first that we *know about this* in recorded history. She reminds me that the pyramids in Egypt, Mexico, Central America and other locations, and the remnants of ancient civilizations in which technologies and understandings of astronomy, ocean tides and currents and otherworldly communications existed are evident.

Therefore, to honor Jackie and those that likely lived before humanity's great forgetting, when I refer to the First Tier, I am referring to the "first" that modern culture recognizes as the start of our human experience.

This First Tier blows with a considerable headwind. To reach the Next Tier, we may have to sail directly into that wind. Truly going directly into or opposing the wind will destroy a boat. Similarly, opposing the wind of the larger system is dangerous and destructive, and can be fatal. As we head into this greatest change in human history, we must know the wind, respect it, and adjust our sails accordingly.

To understand what we are facing, let's see the impact of First Tier energetics in recent days, the levels that brought us here and the forces of another wind—the wind of change—that is blowing us into the Next Tier.

Control of Access

Conversations about race, gender, work environments, monetary systems, restraints on personal freedoms and mega-corporations controlling what information we access are a classical part of First Tier energetics. There is a continuing battle for which narratives or perspectives will dominate.

Various groups have been marginalized by fewer available opportunities to access the information and the energy for change. They naturally want to have more of their piece of the cultural "pie," and also be able to bind the energy and information for themselves as those who have been in "control" of the cultural narrative and experience have done thus far. Positioning themselves to have a greater say in what is real, valued, rewarded or punished in society's and humanity's "next phase" always faces a counter pressure from the cultural Field. In reality, all that is changing is who is considered the villain, the hero and the victim. Access is taken from one group and transferred to another. Those on the top, bottom, or middle are shaken up. It is the same drama; only the roles or character actors are switching.

The electrically powered magnetic field is lining us all up with the same script while we are arguing about who is really running the show. The truth is that none of us are. There is a Field that has been running the human experience since we first appeared on Earth.

How Did We Get Here and What Is Next?*

As increasing levels of energy became available for experiencing, interpreting and interacting with one another, humanity developed from cave people to groups that assembled in tribes for protection from larger dangers. Humanity lived solely to survive and existed at a level between Energy Poor to barely Low Energy Neutral. Human sacrifice even took place to beseech their gods for protection.

After fearing the gods and being saturated at this level, the next level developed as tribal lords and kings emerged who believed they were God. As deities, they owned everyone and everything belonging to anyone else. Therefore, they could destroy, abuse, and take anything from anyone. They ruled through terror and kept others as their servants/slaves.

Around 6,000 years ago, after pillaging to bind for themselves everything they wanted, rulers realized that a set of rules had to be established so upcoming Tribal Lords would not be able to steal what they believed was theirs. This represented a significant jump in human

---

* This hierarchy of values and change in the cultural field is inspired by Beck and Cowan's **Spiral Dynamics** model, which is based upon the theory of Claire Graves. It was further interpreted and integrated into models and applications by Ken Wilber, Anthony Robbins, and others. With this, I've blended the historical progression and novelty of energetic states, energetics of consciousness, and energetics of the tiers that are presented in this chapter as a metaphor for various cultural fields of humanity.

awareness and was also the birth of the roots of Judaic, Christian, and Islamic beliefs.

The need for rules corresponds to when Moses was going up to Mt. Sinai to receive the Ten Commandments. These set in stone (literally) the rules and boundaries for individuals in newly organizing societies to be in favor with God. This was a classic example of a Low Energy Neutral center of gravity. If you followed the rules, you were accepted and rewarded. If you broke a non-mutable rule, you would be punished. It made acceptance by the group essential and instilled the belief in one right and one wrong way, heaven or hell—this way or the highway. This set the stage for the creation of the temples and churches of today and the hierarchy of the clergy, as well as the safety and security systems of police, military, and regulatory agencies. All fundamentalists walk this line in life.

When enough people reached this level and then maxed out on it, the next level called them. This was the beginning of Energy Rich. With more available and abundant energy to fuel higher levels of data access from the Field, there was a revolution of thought and values. This led to *Creation's Codes* creating a cerebral cortex capable of seeing more than one perspective at a time and the ability to optimize context and understand *why*.

Once a critical mass of people experienced and lived at this level, the higher executive function area of the brain became more engaged and the desire for more self-determination and participation in decisions was launched.

From the **late 1700s through the mid-1800s**, American, French, Haitian, Mexican, Indians and Central and South American revolutions rejected kings and governments that forced people to follow dictates that benefitted only a few at the top of the ladder. Some who fought in these revolutions briefly experienced this elevation of understanding. As a whole, most followed the current of consciousness, charging their Fields with more energy. The constitutions of these countries established a collaborative government where the people could participate in governance and shaping their future. The scientific method, using metrics to measure progress and seeking to optimize systems, still exemplifies this level.

In the late 1960s, the hippie movement was born. Gatherings in San Francisco, California, and Woodstock, New York, launched a new era in America that rapidly spread internationally. The movement's focus was on social support systems, peace and love. These ideas, sprinkled with mind expansion, respect for the immaterial world, social commentary and of course rock and roll, were more valuable than most everything else.

Many children of those who had fought in WWII refused to go to war because they believed it was unjust. They rejected prior values. Many people got caught up in the revolution of consciousness. They were energized by the purity and commitment of those truly representing that level. They valued peace, equality, consensus, the feelings of everyone and the connection of all life above everything.

As part of a transition to the next level, there was upheaval. While some were rejecting violence and the hierarchy and advocating for peace, there was much rioting and violence by those who were not yet there. The rioters were energetically fed by the passion of the peace lovers, of course, interpreted through the level they were at during that time.

All these human values and consciousness levels continue and are all part of the First Tier. It sets the stage for higher awareness and the need for Energy Rich to find Super Rich.

Please note, there is a hyper acceleration in the elevation of consciousness in this timeline. From the time Moses came down from the mountain, thousands of years passed until the next jump in the 1700s. After that, the jump in consciousness to the 1960s only required a couple of hundred years. Present time, the next jump will be even faster. We are living it now—only sixty years after that last jump.

With this hyper-velocity of advancement of available energy and greater access to *Creation's Codes* manifesting higher-order values and consciousness, it makes sense that the greatest jump ever is happening NOW. With enough available energy, not only do we see the miracle, we co-create it.

SEEKER'S CODE #5

WE WISH TO ACCESS THE MULTIDIMENSIONAL ENERGETICS
THAT MAGICALLY CREATE AND CONNECT US ALL.

A similarity between these developmental stages of humanity is that people living during them believe that those below the level of their cultural Field are regressive—or in some ways inferior, and those at levels beyond don't make sense, are confusing, dangerous or irrelevant.

Whom do you know that represents each of these cultural Field levels?

- The tribal lords who use force for their own desires
- Security through rules, law, and order
- Self-determination and chosen outcomes
- Peace, social equality and connection to nature

Which of these cultural Fields is your most common level?

First Tier Values

We value whatever adds more available energy to us. We devalue that which seems to reduce our available energy and information. First Tier values focus on allowing an individual to control their environment to meet their needs—or, more accurately, to control their experience of their environment and the bandwidth with which they participate in the world.

We see this in the values expressed around us today. Education is more valued than street smarts. Patented pharmaceuticals are more valued than herbs. Medical technology is valued beyond artistry, God-given senses and intuition. Vaccines and treatments are more highly valued than natural immunity and advancing self-healing. The more we can bind ourselves in ownership—to our money, property and anything else under the illusion of our control—the better we believe our lives will become.

These days, when people are really ill, the culture doesn't approve of treating them with an herb or plant that can be found in nature. Why? Because those plants can't be patented as cures. If they cannot be patented, they cannot be owned. Therefore, they have no First Tier value.

In the First Tier, our caterpillar phase of civilization has focused on two primary areas for gaining control: energy and information. Our "advanced modern" societies have an obsessive-compulsive mechanism of binding energy and information for one's own benefit. This drives the hunger to own material resources, creating an incessant belief in scarcity and potential loss of resources. Power and success in the First Tier are found in the ability to control energy and information and to control who has access to these resources. The select few at the top of the ladders are gatekeepers in society—deciding who has access to energy and who controls the cultural narrative.

We can see this pattern clearly with fossil fuel. This form of bound energy needs great force to unbind it for use. Now, think about how long it takes for oil to be created, and realize that the longer something is bound, the more toxic it is when released—and the more collateral damage it initiates. The oil we use as fuel today took 350 million years to make! It was once living plants and dinosaurs. Extracting it from the Earth and refining and releasing its bound energy often requires great force and violence. In addition to providing the power for our homes and businesses, significant pollution and toxins are released in the air. Since energy and information, or consciousness, are linked, each source of energy we utilize brings more of its associated consciousness to our world. We've valued that bound energy so much that wars killing millions of people have been fought to own and control its access.

First Tier energetics support our personal use of the Earth's minerals and resources, because our power entitles us to do so. I say this without judgment, as this is the way it has been, and like you, I too have benefited from it.

The lust for access to resources in the First Tier goes beyond what lies within the Earth. Now, access to information has become a new valued "energy." Often, as seen with internet search engines tracking and selling our activity, we are the product being sold! Whoever controls the narrative and information has "the power." The fight over oil, internet data and other forms of energy and information is inevitable in the First Tier. **Force or violence of some kind is often used.** This is simply an accepted way of life. We address the Earth, its inhabitants, our relationships and our social and economic systems in this way.

We also find this same mentality in medicine. Consider how a serious disease is discussed in the media. You'll hear that we are at war with a disease, instead of enhancing or collaborating with the forces that regulate and heal. We consider the disease separately from the patient. The patient's experience of life and their experience with health-promoting and life-enhancing practices are deemed irrelevant. Instead, serious diseases are treated with methods that can be deadly— like radiation and chemotherapy. Why do we think something that can make a healthy person sick will make a sick person healthy? It's simply because we're approaching significant health challenges like cancer from a First Tier perspective. The expectation is that with more force, the disease will be dominated. Through the energetics and consciousness of war, healing becomes more distant, therapies more competitive, and treatments more violent, often leading to more toxic collateral damage.

Regardless of the success of the treatment, it is consistent with value systems spanning hundreds of years, professing that if a person is brought to the edge of death, the evil spirit will leave the body. A notable example occurred with George Washington following the ratification of the Constitution. His death was attributed to blood-letting. The belief at the time was that removing enough blood would let the bad stuff out.

This may sound crazy to you—and it is. This is part of that same First Tier thinking.

SEEKER'S CODE #2
WE HAVE AN OBSESSION TO GO BEYOND WHO WE HAVE BEEN.

An unspoken mantra of the First Tier is: Whoever dies with the most "stuff" wins. We seek possessions and the power to influence. We wish to bind energy into our identity, roles and titles. We take pride in our diplomas—be they bachelors, masters or doctoral degrees—as badges of honor and success for greater acceptance in the culture. If we bind enough energy and information between ourselves and others, we believe we will finally get the big prize—the unbound gifts of feeling better about ourselves or getting beyond the sense that we are not enough. Perhaps your goal was/is educational in nature. "Once I get my degree, life will be great. I will have arrived." Or maybe it was/is related to finances: "When I earn a half million dollars a year, I will finally be free."

> For those of you who have achieved your goal, was finally arriving enough?
>
> For how long did the feeling of enoughness or that you had arrived really last?

We know that this is a cultural fantasy. How many celebrities have achieved great wealth and reached the top of their career and subsequently developed substance abuse issues or even ended their lives? Binding more energy with trophies, degrees, accomplishments and money only does what it does. It does not bring you unbound non-material rewards like gratitude, empathy, passion, compassion, love, joy or **MORE**!

The Last Days of the First Tier

"The divine process of change manifests itself to our human understanding...
as punishment, torment, death and transfiguration."

—CARL JUNG

Seekers, the First Tier has limited us. First Tier energetics require force, violence and civil unrest to disrupt our habitual binding of energy and information and liberate enough for change and creation. This tier involves breakdown for creation and limits control of information and energy access to a select few. In the new tier, our predominant sources of energy and information will be freely available and accessible.

After centuries of struggling to control all the bound energy, much that has been hidden or bound up in our cultural stories is being liberated by force, coercion and violence. The costs of unleashing energy bound for so many years are high. We see signs of the cultural binding losing its grip this past decade with the various movements and protests going on across the globe. This unprecedented breakdown, revolution and collapse is necessary to liberate the massive amount of bound information and energy.

This dissolution, at a time of metamorphosis, is analogous to when the imaginal cells are formed within the caterpillar's cocoon. To the caterpillar—as to our society—it seems like death. To the butterfly and the Next Tier, it is a new birth, one with a different way of using energy, information and consciousness.

The force and violence that has grown internationally over the past few years, exploding bound cultural "isms"—racism and sexism, as well as economic disparity—has reached a boiling point. When supported by the matrix, low energy neutrality reinforces the belief of each level of consciousness that it is right. Levels above are thought to be dangerous, while those below are considered regressive.

A critical mass of individuals utilizing Next Tier energetics will be necessary to evolve a more resourceful human experience with greater access to energy and information.

Seekers, you know that different energetics must and will replace the way that consumption and the hunger for power and energy have been. Greater access to unbound energy and information, with greater opportunities for a life of **MORE**, must be available to all of humanity.

SEEKER'S CODE #4
WE WANT TO GIVE, GET, LEARN, AND LIVE WITH A
BIGGER PURPOSE/INSPIRING PROFOUND IMPACT.

After we have been successful with First Tier energetics and experienced its limitation, it will be possible to access the energetics of the Next Tier. Our aim must be to reach a critical mass of people utilizing the new energetics without the violent upheaval of the First Tier.

SEEKER'S CODE #3
WE SEEK A RICHER, MORE MAGICAL, AND EXTRAORDINARY
EXPERIENCE FOR OURSELVES AND FOR OTHERS.

The First Tier is dying. It is still thrashing around in an effort to survive. It will be drawing on larger sources of energy and control of more access to information and resources to maintain its throne on earth. The calling of a future higher order with a different way of using and sharing energy and information is just within reach. If we look up, we might see it fluttering expectantly...like a butterfly.

SEEKER'S CODE #5
WE WISH TO ACCESS THE MULTIDIMENSIONAL ENERGETICS
THAT MAGICALLY CREATE AND CONNECT US ALL.

As the Next Tier approaches, those who live in the First Tier will find that they have to expend more and more energy and consume more and more information to get less and less in return. Dropping lower in available energy, they'll become more regressive in their values.

(Regressive means they drop to lower levels of energy, consciousness, and values.) As with the frenzy of drug addicts whose supply may be taken away, they will seek to maintain the First Tier through the use of more force and greater control of energy and information.

This transition will occur over a limited time frame, and Seekers, your conscious strategies and practice with energy richness, and sometimes super energy richness, can shorten the lag.

You can go beyond who you have been, and bring others with you. With enough free energy, the larger system need not be forcefully broken apart to liberate the bound and unavailable energy and information in our human interactions with the environment or with our social, economic, environmental, public health, educational, political, legal or countless other domains.

SEEKER'S CODE #6
WE RECOGNIZE THE POWER OF FOCUSED ATTENTION
AND ENERGY/AND CONSCIOUS CHOICE.

This greater bandwidth of information requires a shift in focus and action for transformation from *ME* to *WE*. Then a more powerful, reverent, passionate, creative and connected humanity will be available to us all.

The Seven Values of the First Tier

1. The physical world is primary.
2. There is a scarcity of material resources that we must compete for to secure our part and protect against loss.
3. If we consume, bind and own enough, then we'll have access to the unbound resources.
4. Once we own something, we have the right to use, destroy or manipulate it in whatever way we please. This includes the environment and living beings.
5. Power, success and wealth are consistent with the amount of energy and information we consume, own and control.

6. For someone to be extraordinary, a backstory of extreme conditions, suffering, loss and adversity is required.
7. The main way that power, control, information and ownership are surrendered is through force or violence.

The Next Tier and Unbound Energy

"The planetary climate catastrophe humanity faces is essentially about energy, but not just fossil energy. A redeployment of positive personal energy, the free energy we each command that determines how we engage one another, how we connect our bodies and our emotions with the earth and the environment, how we come to recognize a unity, a oneness with creation."

—WILLIAM K. REILLY, FORMER EPA ADMINISTRATOR, FORMER PRESIDENT AND CHAIRMAN OF THE WORLD WILDLIFE FUND, AND HEAD OF THE US DELEGATION TO THE EARTH SUMMIT

We are at the beginning of the Next Tier, with the novel experience of a new way of humanity displaying more gentle butterfly-like attributes. This era will embody more spiritual qualities in all realms and a path to sacredness and miracles in the midst of life. Like the ocean's tide, we will receive a taste and access to a new way before it temporarily recedes again. We are seeing and experiencing elements of Next Tier's energetics in increasing scope and depth. As First Tier energetics are still the predominant way, we will be experiencing life in cycles of high and low tide.

Also like the ocean tide, the Next Tier brings the energy and information from the shore back to the sea as it recedes. As the tide continues to move onto the shore before receding, the cumulative cycles result in a net forward progression.

Evidence of the Next Tier has been seeping into our financial and business worlds for a while. EBay is an example most everyone knows. Conceived as a way of bringing unneeded pre-owned items back into circulation, it also created an easy way to have one's own business while allowing for transparent business interactions. EBay did not have to own the physical property, handle it or warehouse it, to manifest opportunities for others while creating corporate revenue.

We can see further examples in the hospitality industry. The March 2022 gross profit reported by Hilton was $1.5 billion. For the huge Marriott organization, which now includes the hotels previously under the Starwood banner, it was $3.2 billion. During the same period, the gross profit of Airbnb exceeded both combined. The key to this was Airbnb's Next Tier design. Rather than binding energy through owning and managing real estate, it gives property owners the opportunity to gain revenue and guests the opportunity to experience more than a hotel room. While property owners gain revenue, and renters experience the value of expanded living options, the company earns a percentage of every stay.

Similarly, Uber and Lyft are transforming public transportation. While they own no cars, they still facilitate transportation and provide opportunities for drivers to earn money on their own schedule while also allowing the free exchange of information about the ride, car and driver. The emergence of Bitcoin, other cryptocurrencies, and NTFs are decentralizing money and revolutionizing the financial world. These days many movie and music streaming services are providing consumers with access to entertainment without having to bind energy by owning the music and movies.

Ultimately, the Next Tier will supplant First Tier's energetics. On the journey to the Next Tier, there will be both old and new tier approaches and systems. Old is based in fear and control of natural systems, and new upon faith, with reverence for *Creation's Codes* and the power of unbound potential. The content in this book is designed to give this Next Tier more than just a running start. My intention is to provide Seekers with a full-out launch through energy richness, with sprinkles of super richness to accelerate the sacred expression of life. A motto from when I was in chiropractic college is "Nature needs no help, just no interference." The Next Tier supports the power of life.

Remember, the Next Tier is a wave, and at times it will recede. We see regression in the First Tier direction with some companies recently attempting to rebind the energy and information they had previously freed. Facebook, now Meta, appears to have reverted back to a more First Tier approach as it strives to control access to information consistent with its objectives. Similarly, many other social media platforms and search engines are utilizing your search history and sophisticated algorithms to track your online activity and "personalize" newsfeeds and ads. We are being seen as assets.

In business and other relationships, we are moving from just transactional into aspirational exchanges. Instead of the First Tier illusion that we can manage people, we are seeking to nurture the fulfillment of their promises. These promises represent unbound potential that fuels the ways in which we exchange energy and information for greater value.

The purpose of such Next Tier relationships is to aspire for more than participants could deliver or be independently. My late friend Berny Dohrmann, the creator of CEO Space, encouraged *collaboration* instead of *competition*. Relationships in this Next Tier offer fulfillment of a promise of greater Energetic Capital exchange in the collaborative Field.

As a philanthropic leader, at many of his events Tony Robbins encourages teams to consciously compete with one another to raise funds and resources to enhance the quality of life for others. His personal journey is one of giving millions access to greater resources and stimulating increased opportunities for less advantaged and marginalized populations. Through consciously unbinding energy within a group, the net result is a distribution of greater energy and opportunities for others.

This adds more Energetic Capital for distribution. Exchanges in this context are about more than the "bottom line." They are about A + B = C. Not simply benefiting A or B, C represents a product of the collaboration of A and B. This means that the new result C is different and More than A or B individually could ever become. Additional vision, curiosity, fascination, creativity, passion and goodness ensue.

In the First Tier, two people or companies may have a wonderful transaction, and the next exchange might be Energy Neutral or Energy Poor for employees, families, communities or the environment. In the Next Tier, the aspiration to add value to more than the bottom line replaces the purely transactional relationship.

When we consider the concept of generating **MORE** value and creation of free energy and more abundant opportunities, much more is at stake than in a business transaction for only the best price or greatest convenience. In Next Tier energetics, we will first consider the collaborative Fields and our personal promise to the larger system, as in the *Seeker's Codes*:

SEEKER'S CODE #3
WE SEEK A RICHER, MORE MAGICAL, AND EXTRAORDINARY
EXPERIENCE FOR OURSELVES AND FOR OTHERS.

SEEKER'S CODE #4
WE WANT TO GIVE, GET, LEARN, AND LIVE WITH A
BIGGER PURPOSE/INSPIRING PROFOUND IMPACT.

Kristen Ragusin, in her book *The End of Scarcity*, shares about the Next Tier:

> Our whole view of money, wealth and finance reorganizes. In fact, our experiences of these concepts reverse, as they reorient themselves in our world. Money and finance take a back seat as wealth returns front and center in our lives. We come to intimately know that wealth is abundant, has real value—and is inseparable from us.

Wealth is an expression of energy and super energy richness. This provides us with value adding Energetic Capital for investing during our lifetime into the Field and our connection to *Creation's Codes*.

Kristen continues:

> There really is no such thing out there as money itself—money is simply the PROMISE to create, produce and contribute something of value—what makes money valuable is our ability to make good on our promises.

As we morph into Next Tier energetics and consciousness, there will be more coherence between ideas and systems. Currently, many Next Tier ideas are encased in First Tier business, economic, or leadership models. Next Tier approaches will combine artificial intelligence programs to imitate aspects of life itself—seeking to optimize rather than compete.

Healing and human performance approaches that activate *Creation's Codes* to help the person develop greater human resourcefulness with aligned outcomes will be the way of this Next Tier.

Health and Wellness Care: Which Tier Energetics?

Although now licensed and taught with First Tier objectives that the Energy Neutral culture requires, the original idea of chiropractic was focused on Next Tier objectives. With all healing or treatment systems——biological, physical, emotional, mental, social and spiritual, the question is about whether it fulfills First Tier or Next Tier energetics, values and outcomes.

These are some questions that can help you discern which of the tier's energetics a system or approach is employing:

- Is symptom relief and normalizing metrics the main goal?
- Is this encouraging personal resourcefulness and offering the experience of *MORE* rather than less?

- Is the symptom or measurement used as a method of monitoring energy, information efficiency, and/or effectiveness of the person?
- Are physical, emotional, mental, social or spiritual outcomes being considered about the person?
- Is it helping the individual to move from *ME* to *WE*?
- Does it start with the remedy of a lack of a resource or inspire an abundance of resourcefulness?
- Does it allow or control?
- Does it enhance available energy without force or violence for the organizing wisdom to create more resourcefulness?
- Are its objectives and main outcomes to elevate the E-State directly or indirectly for greater energy and information efficiency?
- Is it to experience more of one's connection in the body, mind and spirit—and of one's connection to humanity?
- Are healthier choices, new perspectives, and/or different, more empowered meanings naturally occurring with the care or intervention?

This has been my purpose in evolving my Network systems for healing and human performance under the overarching umbrella of EpiHealing. Others have joined me in this Next Tier approach to health. With these questions, you can better discern the methods drawing you toward the Next Tier.

The Most Important Audit

In the Next Tier, with this EpiEnergetics approach, we will audit the consciousness of the type of energy used in the products that we bind for our use and the energy sources we employ. Everything has its own EpiField of energy around it that makes up its consciousness. Let's look at fossil fuel only from this perspective.

Notice the consciousness of fossil fuels. As we know already, they are the epitome of First Tier energetics and consciousness. What are the consequences associated with the economics, politics and social structures of harvesting, distributing, managing, using and controlling this source of energy?

When given the choice in the Next Tier, consider: *What is the source of this product? How much energy went into making it? What resources were utilized? How much life power? How much soul power? Was more energy put into making, marketing and shipping it than it will give back?*

In this case, fuels like oil are likely to be replaced by energy sources that provide much more than they require to utilize them. The challenge in this transition to this Next Tier is the economic model. In Paul Polak's book, *The Business Solution to Poverty,* he pioneered the idea of providing locally produced goods and services most needed by the masses with the least access to human opportunities.

One can see example of this with his company Spring Health. It offers safe, affordable drinking water to rural, poor customers through a radically decentralized sustainable model. The decentralized model uses small shops, creating extra income through distributing safe chlorinated water. That water is available for purchase in the shop or delivered to homes for an additional fee through a partnership program with local women's groups and bicycle delivery services.

Once Polak created this company, children were no longer falling ill with dysentery. They could participate at school and still have the energy to earn money working after school. Young girls when menstruating could continue to learn in school, as there was clean water available for their personal hygiene. In addition to financial gain, the vision was to add value to humanity. Far beyond simply being transactional, lives were improved and everyone in the system made money as well.

Toward the end of his life, with the help of Bell Labs and other companies, he also found a way to use mesquite wood, a thorny invasive weed that grows in desert conditions, to fuel a process where a clean "coal-like" energy generating material would be produced. This inexpensive access to energy also brings new opportunities to transform the lives of the villagers.

Paul believed that putting clean water production and greater access to energy in the hands of the local people would change their lives dramatically. Instead of top-down capitalization, he would also have it from bottom upward. His work is an outstanding example of Next Tier energetics.

Everything we consume, from the food we eat to what we think about, feeds on some kind of energy. In the Next Tier, we will prefer those things that have the greatest energy, information and efficiency for all of us. With that consciousness applied in the production of the food we eat, we would ask whether we are respectful of the animals in their raising and slaughter. What we eat will fuel us. It has been said, "You are what you eat." What was experienced by the beings we consume influences the energetics and consciousness that become the *YOU* observing and impacting the world.

In the 1990s, as members of the board of directors of EarthSave, an organization founded by John Robbins, my wife and I became increasingly aware of the many personal and environmental concerns associated with the factory farming of animals. As both the son and nephew of the cofounders, John, of the Baskin-Robbins ice cream company, was heir to the very successful family business. In writing his book, *Diet for a New America*, he shared his concerns about an industry his family business was dependent upon—with the Next Tier perspective that a more conscious and ecological use of the energy and natural resources involved in production plus respect for living systems was needed.

After publicly sharing my choice of a plant-based diet, I was once approached by someone in the audience. He said he disagreed with me and felt a plant-based diet was cruel and inhumane. I inquired as to why he believed that. He paused, and then with a smile said that he would not eat anything that did not have a chance to run away!

For the most part, animals consumed these days in first world countries do not have the opportunity to run away. Beyond providing biochemical nutrition and energy, we ingest information. What was the information or consciousness that brought the food to your table? Consider the process from its growth to harvest or slaughter and the transportation and preparation for retail sale. Greater awareness affects the choices we make. The associated changes in consciousness will lead to untold evolutions in the Next Tier. I simply provide these as examples of Next Tier paths that have been followed. It is certainly a lifetime journey with a meandering river of choices! A Franciscan description of responsible stewardship shares that in our relationship with the divine, we will be delighted with all creation, have reverence for all people, responsibly use the Earth's resources, and freely share the gifts entrusted to us with those in need.

Values of the Second Tier

"The awakening of consciousness is the next step for mankind."

—ECKHART TOLLE

The following statements articulate values unique to this Next Tier. As a Seeker, YOU are predisposed to have more immediate access to Next Tier energetics regardless of your baseline level of consciousness.

1. There is an abundance of resourcefulness that can be effortlessly available at any time with sufficient access to energy.
2. Resourcefulness is contagiously collaborative.
3. The physical world is a byproduct of another primary quantum reality.
4. Everything in existence is the manifestation of information with energy. The amount of energy available determines the quality and quantity of what we consider to be real.
5. There is a broader sharing of opportunities that potentiate greater engagement in a more participatory humanity, with greater access to the fields of possibilities.
6. By having access to material and immaterial resources, the

obsession to own and bind for our own security or personal value fades. We are temporary stewards of all we own and grateful for the energetic investment that allowed it to be.

7. Power, success and wealth are a function of the value of energy richness we radiate that also inspires opportunities for others.

8. Awareness, Acknowledgment and Acceptance of one's personal energetics and hunger to make more of a difference for others instantly provides available energy that would otherwise require painful loss or trauma to access in the First Tier.

9. We seek to optimize access to the energized Fields of information available for ourselves and humanity.

10. We are conscious of the energy invested in everything we consume and continually seek to add more value to our environment than we take.

Meditation and Spiritual States Are Not What You Think!

Long before Einstein's law of general relativity or Michio Kaku's string theory, several spiritual traditions shared that **multiple dimensions** exist. A dimension is how space is organized, and each dimension has unique ways the laws of physics and reality are manifested. Time, for example, really only exists as we know it in our fourth dimension. It is the reality that our mind can interpret. Hallucinogens help stretch this reality, as does a Super Energy Rich state.

An expanded view of physics and reality are inherent in Next Tier energetics. The unseen or formerly invisible forces that draw us into unity and synchronicity are experienced as natural when employing the energetics of the Next Tier—even if living in the First Tier!

Next Tier energetics have been calling you and other Seekers. We are fueled by both bound and unbound sources of energy that organize and shine light into and through this world.

WE WISH TO ACCESS THE MULTIDIMENSIONAL ENERGETICS THAT MAGICALLY CREATE AND CONNECT US ALL.

This central theme and baseline in the Next Tier energetics is your *Home*. When your available energy level drops and there is no longer enough bandwidth to experience this, it is like a fall from grace.

Next Tier energetics are different from what many spiritual and consciousness disciplines (that are still fueled in the First Tier) tell us. Instead of suggesting that these higher states are only available for a small number of most dedicated disciples who are following complicated practices, Next Tier energetics suggests the opposite. **Energetics precede consciousness.** Regardless of your prior spiritual or transformational practices, work, efforts or beliefs, elevated and coherent consciousness is freely available in this Next Tier. With your conscious and ecological use of energy for more than your own benefit, it is an available part of your daily living.

Looking at the world today, you can see that the attempt to elevate human consciousness has not worked *for* the many. Still, many work *at* it! I have been with and attended to thousands with various spiritual and consciousness practices.

Using consciousness to elevate consciousness, although a noble cause, is at best a High Energy Neutral strategy, and it is just not enough for this Next Tier energetics or humanity. For those who are Low Energy Neutral, elevating to High Energy Neutral is a blessing. And for those who are High Energy Neutral, reaching Energy Rich is wonderful, especially when considering that for most of human history the majority of the world's population has been in a dire survival mode. Even recently, indoor plumbing, clean water and having enough food to eat for one's family has been a very high goal with energy neutrality being accepted and protected by a social code. Therefore, even moving from poor to low neutral and then from low neutral to high neutral has been beyond accessible to most.

I suspect that very few people have truly achieved a high level of spiritual consciousness when moving from the meditation room or community to the chaos of families, friends and work. And I wish to acknowledge that meditation and other spiritual practices have *helped bring us to this tipping point* in humanity. It is my belief that for this Next Tier, the conscious elevation of their E-States will give people access to what they may have otherwise not had available or been able to afford. Doing lengthy processes or practices seeking elevated consciousness is most often a High Energy Neutral desire to foster you getting *there*. With enough available energy, *Creation's Codes* simply organize an elevated state of consciousness. Elevating the E-State gives greater access to information and greater impact in one's life and world. This is an indirect benefit of the energetics of this Next Tier.

"There is a time for everything, and a season for every activity under the heavens."

—ECCLESIASTES 3:1

While the Next Tier unlocks access to unlimited energy, information and consciousness, it also includes each of the states of the First Tier. There are times to be fearful of harm and times to be a "power god" who might take out someone who is endangering a loved one. There are times to follow the rules or social order to be accepted or approved of, and there are times to seek peace, agreement, consensus, and care for all of humanity. There are also times to be more Energy Rich and choose your role and outcomes in life.

Now, in the Next Tier, you experience this as a buffet of consciousness for all of humanity. **You know that your personal Energetics are what you shine on the world and influence what you capture back as reality.** You see, what you experience in some way impacts both the future and past...people you know, and people you do not yet know.

Stepping into the Next Tier

About two decades ago, I recognized that there had been enough wounding of people so that they could be cracked open for **MORE**. That senseless or gratuitous hurting is characteristic of the First Tier.

That wounding comes in a variety of guises. There continues to be enough wars and violence, all of which have been happening for select people to benefit. Yes, it is true we need to bind energy. You must bind it to have a body to live in. You must bind enough energy in a relationship or business in order to exist, grow and contribute. The key question is whether the goal of binding is to bind only for yourself or for something larger.

Ahead, we will learn about the two EpiWays, Internal and External. You will get to experience and know how to—within seconds—significantly increase your available energy and access to new codes for reality and to make a constructive impact.

This increases your access to the informational Field of all possibilities, fueling a very different and more than changed life. Connected to everyone else in the pond of humanity, your friends, colleagues, clients and teachers—and people you may never meet—share in the data streams for **MORE**. The Energy Rich *YOU* adjusts the sails on the ship of your life, optimizing the free energy and information from the winds of change. Conscious participation with your ideal energetics in life helps ignite and accelerate access to this Next Tier for each and all of us.

In the First Tier, we accepted Salvatore Dali's quote: "*Every act of creation is first an act of destruction.*"

You can have access to the energetics of the Next Tier—in fact, you have access right *now*! This happens instantly, magically and noticeably free of effort. New manifestation and experience of the sacred forces of creation will allow for our evolution as stewards of a new world. As we reach the critical mass of humanity respecting *Creation's*

Codes, all life on Earth will make the necessary leap into a parallel reality. We must have both growing artificial intelligence and the more important LIVING intelligences that the world's spiritual traditions have claimed for centuries. This reality will burst open the matrix of First Tier thought and control and wake us up to tending to a new garden of life.

The conscious accessing of unbound energy's Field of information in your life ignites *Creation's Codes* for sacred manifestation. A new and different experience happens for you and so many others.

In this Next Tier, this will be the expected reality. **An energy differential leads to an informational difference.** Children will be guided as our more coherent Fields will remind them of the magic of creation.

SEEKER'S CODE #3
WE SEEK A RICHER, MORE MAGICAL, AND EXTRAORDINARY
EXPERIENCE FOR OURSELVES AND FOR OTHERS.

When you turn the page, I will introduce you to *AAA*—the one practice that is your way to effortlessly access the unbound energy for a Next Tier result. It is a premiere tool for fueling your body, mind, spirit and Field. *AAA* is vital for moving from circumstance to energetics and from concepts to raw, real and often beautiful emerging realities. It is about the pure energetics that are running the show of our lives.

CHAPTER 7

═══

ROCKET FUEL FOR THE NEXT TIER

AWARENESS, ACKNOWLEDGMENT, AND ACCEPTANCE

In the energetics of the Next Tier, you are fueled by the practice of *AAA*: *Awareness*, *Acknowledgment*, and *Acceptance*. *AAA* is a vital doorway to access unbound energy for the instantaneous expression of *Creation's Codes* in your life.

You may ask, "Donny, *AAA* of what?"

In this brief chapter, the answer to this question will be revealed. You will be introduced to the most powerful tool I know to access unbound energy and information while bypassing the need for hardship or loss.

This is definitely a profound skillset. In fact, I see *AAA* as the rocket fuel of the Next Tier. Unlike the cultural Field or "matrix," it leads us to liberation beyond the control of the conditioned cultural apps and sets us free from our addiction to energy neutrality.

When I suggest that you become more *Aware*, *Acknowledge*, or *Accept*, you might think this refers to your pain, your thoughts, your experiences, your circumstances or perhaps what someone else says about their own difficulties.

What I am offering you is radically different from this. It is a wonderfully novel form for becoming aware of, acknowledging and accepting the **energetic strategies** that lead to your experience of reality.

Coal to Diamonds

In the prior tier energetics, the larger "system" would test us, challenge us, nudge us, or even rip us apart. At critical times in our lives, we must have access to more bandwidth of information to help us manifest whatever we are here for—and manifest it for more than just our personal desires. In order to achieve this, the larger system will collaborate with *Creation's Codes* (the organizing forces of creation) to create situations that provide for what's bound, unavailable and necessary to immediately become accessible for your progress.

The laws of physics predict that everything bound will eventually be liberated. This also applies to every aspect of our life, and even our body and spirit. With precise timing and "surgical" precision, the information important to our life that was formerly truncated, unavailable, ignored, segregated, judged, blamed or denied must be made accessible to be employed by a bigger app for our life. The energetics of the First Tier do this in a primitive and far less elegant way.

The more refined way is unique to the Next Tier. Unlike First Tier energetics, here the energy and its bound information potential are more openly shared and available. This occurs gracefully through your conscious awareness and choice of focused attention. *AAA* is how you can channel this. *AAA* activates *Creation's Codes* as your E-State elevates.

Next Tier Energetics Available to You Now

I recognized that the elevation of human consciousness through spiritual practices performed by millions for thousands of years has helped elevate so many from low to high neutral while seeking **MORE**. They could often understand many of the concepts and match the movements of their spiritual masters. They may have uttered the same phrases or chants. I sensed that few, usually only after years of dedicated practice, had moved to energy richness in their daily lives. And perhaps those few may have been enough to bring us to this tipping point.

For centuries, when simple survival equaled success, the capacity to elevate to High Energy Neutral would have been like visiting with the Divine. The sheer gathering of the masses in a community with a master who achieved Energy Rich or Super Energy Rich states could inspire quantum entanglement with the master's state, temporarily sparking an Energetic, thus inspiring a parallel shift in consciousness. I am offering you and fellow Seekers—even when alone or in a small group—the capacity to access the consciousness associated with Energy Rich, and at times Super Energy Rich, in the midst of your day-to-day life.

The beginning of conscious living is experiencing and discerning that there is a version, alongside your usual consciousness, who is observing and interpreting the world. It is the heart of the sacred skill of "witnessing." Witnessing that there is a *YOU* that is observing and experiencing the world is like directing a laser upon the matrix providing liberation into an abundant manifestation of *Creation's Codes*. It is indeed your Rocket Fuel to this Next Tier.

This realization led me to seek a path towards accessing the energetic aspects of this Next Tier of consciousness that could work for the masses—even if only as a stepping stone toward the Next Tier.

The result was my realization that greater focused and coherent energy and information lead to elevated consciousness. Even when baselines of consciousness are at lower levels, people can still have short periods of energy richness that might not otherwise happen in their lifetimes. I wondered how to help humanity move from Energy Neutral to Energy Rich with greater sustainability for the masses. *AAA* is a means of accomplishing this.

Through *The Seeker's Codes*, YOU will help energize *Creation's Codes* for the masses!

SEEKER'S CODE #3
WE SEEK A RICHER, MORE MAGICAL, AND EXTRAORDINARY
EXPERIENCE FOR OURSELVES/AND FOR OTHERS.

AAA is a bridge between the tiers. It is a practical tool adding more unbound energy to your nervous system, elevating your E-State and fueling *Creation's Codes*. The more Seekers that apply Next Tier energetics, the closer the tipping point becomes for the rest of us.

Using *AAA*, you can have access to the gifts and way of the Next Tier for moments at a time. A direct experience of a difference in energy leads to a difference in the available information enhancing your experiences and opportunities in life. Conscious *Awareness, Acknowledgment*, and *Acceptance* of the energetics of the experience can expand beyond you. Through quantum sharing (entanglement), it can accelerate the spread of Next Tier energetics through humanity.

With this ripe and ready-to-use tool to access the energy of the Next Tier, *AAA* can instantly provide our "Houston Control" power to access the larger Field and manifest synergy, cooperation and access to so much *MORE*. We pay tribute to the organizing forces of life as we participate in a larger program of sacred relationships and guidance beyond ourselves. This is music to the hopes, wishes, desires and callings of Seekers poised for access to Next Tier energetics.

Access to *Creation's Codes* and "lift off" to the unbound energetics of the Next Tier *requires* your conscious *Awareness* of your energetics.

Being Aware of, Acknowledging, and Accepting your energetic recipe for the experience of your emotions, thoughts, circumstances and situations will transform your life. Instead of taking life personally with its successes and failures, its acceptances and rejections, and its losses and gains, you can experience instantaneous liberation.

Regardless of which role you choose as your lens to look upon the world—mother, father, daughter, son, business owner, employee, woman, man, etc.—and no matter how well you succeed at that role, at best you'll feel you are enough only for moments. While personal development will help increase your actual success in your roles, this does not carry over to a sustained experience of *enough-ness*. All roles are Energy Neutral, leading at best to social acceptance and compliance.

You can redirect your focus and energy when you sense you are failing or have the awful sense of not-enough-ness messing with you and your life. Without attempting to change anything, your destructive energetic recipe can change. I know this seems like a mind game I am playing with you. Trust that it is the opposite; it is the end of the mind game **that has been playing you.** As I, in my Obi-"Don" Kenobi–persona, might say, "The force is getting stronger!"

The following chapters will help you know your personal recipe for how you use the various lenses to observe, judge and narrate your experiences. With enough energy, sensing you are not enough will no longer be painful. In place of the pain will be a hunger for more bandwidth and a bigger participation in life. The simplicity of **AAA** makes this so accessible. It is the rocket fuel for you to "lift off"—through the energetics of the Next Tier—to Energy Rich and **MORE.**

The S*F*S* Experience

AAA is about the unbound energy fueling your system, life and Field. It is part of your personal recipe of the moment for influencing, upsizing and downsizing the available energy/information that manifests as your life and reality.

AAA leads to what I call S*F*S*—or the Sh*t-Fu*k-Sh*t experience. Each reaction corresponds to one part of *AAA*.

The key to all three parts of accessing this Rocket Fuel is to be *Aware*, *Acknowledge*, and *Accept* the energetic strategy that is playing you, as it is, and without the hunger to change, judge or understand the circumstance, situation or experience.

All of your experiences, breakdowns or buildups are a consequence of your E-State and energetic recipe to create this reality.

- *Awareness*: "Sh*t! This is how I was engaging in life. This is what I was believing in as reality. Oh, Sh*t!"
- *Acknowledgment*: "Fu*k! OMG! I am really more than my belief in this app. My world is instantly changing. I see my energetic recipe for this rehearsed pattern. It is all just an algorithm I am playing with." Whatever you wanted to move away from or fix, the story you lived with about why you could not be better, the other Blah, Blah, Blah—it is all just an app playing you.
- *Acceptance*: "Sh*t! I got the exact reality that this Energetic would create. I now remember that I—and *we*—are so much more." You review that energetic recipe and what impact it has had on you and others, then choose another Energetic that will create a higher standard.

Let's dig a little more into S*F*S*, so you can understand exactly how *AAA* can instantly introduce the Next Tier into your life.

Awareness (The First Sh*t)

When I say to be *Aware*, I am referring to the various energetic patterns that shape your experience of reality.

Why is it a Sh*t? Because that's the word you often shout in shock as you become aware that what you thought was real is all an artifact of a poor energy strategy.

You are not really fully aware of what this means for your life. You are only aware that you have a Sh*ty strategy linked to a Sh*ty outcome that you falsely believed was reality. You begin to cultivate the understanding that helps you recognize that it is you witnessing your energetics.

SEEKER'S CODE #1

WE KNOW THERE IS SO MUCH MORE TO LIFE THAN WHAT
APPEARS AS PHYSICAL REALITY OR CIRCUMSTANCE.

For example, if I were feeling guilty for having let my wife down in the past or worried that I might let her down in the future, I might keep thinking in a loop that I was not doing or would not do enough as a husband. As wife and husband define one another and share a common Field, my wife would be likely to feel the same thing about me and perhaps about herself in her role as a wife.

I do not want to feel this. I do not want her to feel this. How do I resolve this? I could make a list of what would make me a better husband and check items off it every day. I could meditate, hoping to feel more love replacing my guilt. I could take courses, read books, or practice being a better husband.

The net result is that I would likely be "working on it" for years, with little relief or change. Since I don't see the world as it is, but as I am... nothing changes because I am still Energy Neutral. If I am still experiencing her through my lens as the role of a husband, I will attract the same energetics and the same emotions. I will still radiate this not enough-ness to her. The wheel keeps turning. I am still the hamster running faster and faster and getting nowhere. I am sure you know this all too well in whatever role you've experienced as Energy Neutral.

None of this—not even this awareness of your emotions, thoughts or roles—is Next Tier energetics. As you fortify the matrix of illusion the energy drop actually intensifies. This type of awareness is incapable of creating shifts. Oh Sh*t, what can you do to make more of a difference, and upscale the you that is experiencing this failure?

There is another way, another type of *Awareness*. In this other way, I could be *Aware* of my energetics that support this experience of reality and my energetic impact upon my wife and myself.

This *Awareness* would also include taking an *energetics* inventory. We will be learning about this in detail in the following chapters. For now, simply understand that you must be *Aware* of the energetics that create your experience of reality. You must be *Aware* that you see the world as you are and that the you that sees and narrates reality is the you this book targets. What is your nature and energetic strategy for experiencing, fighting, or wanting to change one reality for another? This *Awareness* shines light on what is real and activates more energy and greater linking of data points into larger information streams, perspectives and manifestation.

Oh my God. Every time I think as a husband, I am accessing a low energy source to fuel my experience, actions and feelings. Memories, fears and form will be a perfect mathematical expression of how much energy is available to fuel **Creation's Codes.** *So much of life will play off my conditioned cultural Field of what a husband is...without the energy to change this. This is neutrality.*

Awareness, the first step in the practice of **AAA**, involves going from your circumstance, story, or pain to seeing that these are consequences of your personal energetics. De-personalize and then energize by seeing the experience as simply a result of your energetics.

Do this with curiosity and reverence for *Creation's Codes,* organizing your life in a manner consistent with your energetic strategies. Remember that you must do this without the desire to change your experience, transform it, let it go, or make it go away—without even the desire to understand it. Just experience this reality as your personal energetic recipe. Nothing more.

This is **Awareness** of your energetic nature. The light of depersonalized witnessing (detached from story or meaning) allows the unbound light of truth to activate more available energy. As you look at each distinction of your use of energy, something starts to change in your Field. For a moment, you touch Energy Rich. To go further and make it more sustainable, with a new and higher standard, you must go on to the next A, *Acknowledgment.*

Acknowledgment (The Fu*k)

Acknowledgment is like giving testimony to what is real and guided by a higher sacred force.

Acknowledge the impact of your energetics upon your experience of reality. In your lens on the world through a role as mother/father/ husband/wife/professional/student/teacher/business owner/etc.

Acknowledge its impact and its limitations for yourself and those you influence in this role.

With this **Acknowledgment**, you recognize that the energetic strategy you have been using to create, manifest, and interpret life was either creating your most difficult experiences, outcomes and attractions or has been the way you instantly manifested miracles.

Oh My God...is it just a game that was playing me? Do I now choose to play the game—or a totally different game? You realize that the pain, misery, or awe that you energetically create is totally at your disposal.

For example, when you feel guilty, angry or not enough and have a story about why this is so, you *Acknowledge* that you are focused upon the past, or perhaps the future. Or you might be viewing your experience or circumstances through the lens of a particular role—such as a wife or husband or student. By contrast, when you focus upon its opposite, you might feel totally grateful, sensually in love, or enormously empowered and experience the flow of abundance in your life.

One way of focusing your attention limits access to free energy and information and downsizes your perspectives and life. Another way gives you more access to free energy and an upgraded life. The strategy that provides for more available energy provides access to a much larger bandwidth of information for *Creation's Codes*. A consequence of this is the transformation of the relationship between your nervous system, mind, Field and life. With the Fu*k (Acknowledge) part, you simply identify that experience A is a natural consequence of energetic strategy A—as B and C are consequences of energetic strategies of B and C. Situations are depersonalized, and you recognize that you are playing the energetic recipe of the app that you experience and radiate as reality.

MORE on this to come...

Acceptance (The Second Sh*t)

This last A is taking you *HOME*. It is the next level of order.

It is *Acceptance* not of the circumstance, concern or situation. It is *Acceptance* of *Creation's Codes* and the specific energetic recipes you were utilizing to have the experiences that you've been having. It is the knowledge your recipe will be different as you already are experiencing *MORE* in at least this one area of life. It is the "Sh*t" of being on the other side and being free of even the concepts of what you experienced before. It is more the "Holy Sh*t" of victory.

Beyond polarities, or anything else, there is *Acceptance* that this is the recipe for participating this way—with this experience and this manifestation—and it is perfect for what it is. Unlike with *Awareness* and *Acknowledgment*, *Acceptance* is not about circumstances, emotions, stories or your experience of reality. It is simply *Acceptance* of the energetics that created this reality and of the new higher-order energetic strategy you're choosing to replace with it.

It has been said that if you do what you've always done, you'll get what you've always gotten. This is no exception. Use the same energetic strategy, and you will ALWAYS get the exact manifestation this use of energy and focused attention creates. You've accepted that everything you've experienced was real. You now awaken to realize that, like all of us, you live within a culturally inspired computer-like program. The apps you are using can be hacked! You can upgrade your experience of, well, everything and everyone. Yes, *YOU* can create new apps for a different world.

This is the time that celebration, grace and seemingly magical occurrences naturally emerge from your energy richness. You are energetically supported in your use of these skills to effortlessly *be MORE and share MORE* of your abundant available energy. With greater access to *Creation's Codes,* you now can consciously choose to flip an "awareness switch"—replacing the energetics that allowed for the former fear, pain, stories and BLAH BLAH BLAH in the first place. *Acceptance* of the energetics that run your life magically replaces the lower energy experiences with what is now important, real and sustainable. For a moment—as you connect to a larger world and universe—there is a sense of coming *HOME*.

Accessing the Code

With the skills of *AAA*, you can witness your energetics, your E-State, and as you'll find in the coming chapters, your EpiWay. *AAA* enables us to access the forces of creation with humility, curiosity, fascination and gratitude. In other words, we will see *Creation's Codes in action!*

SEEKER'S CODE #7

WE HONOR AND CELEBRATE THE SACRED NATURE
OF LIFE/AND WISH TO SPREAD ITS MAGIC.

Next, we introduce you to the *ONE*.

There is one distinction that is the difference between "efforting" without getting there and effortless manifestation. There is one distinction between obsessing about past traumas and wanting to let them go to claim your life—and immediately finding there is nothing to get rid of because you are truly past it. There is one distinction that moves you from terror about what might happen to readiness for the future by remembering your resourcefulness from past victories.

This one distinction helps you define your authentic, natural and most effective way of instantly transitioning between Energy Neutral to Energy Rich without anything in your world having to change. It also illuminates how and why you drop back into Energy Neutral when you are Energy Rich.

So far, everything in this book has been preparation for these next chapters on finding your way...*YOUR EpiWay*. With positive expectancy, I invite you to turn the page and participate with me in exploring *your ONE way to energy richness and so much MORE*!

CHAPTER 8

———

THE ROAD TO RICHNESS

YOUR EPIWAY

When you find your way, the way to make it happen finds you.

It's time to find **YOUR Way**.

Everything we have explored so far in **The Seeker's Code** has been to prepare you for what lies ahead in these next chapters. From here on, we will explore **the one distinction** that can do more than save your life. It can transform you into an upgraded observer—seeing and interacting with the world more coherently and impactfully—and manifesting **MORE**.

This one distinction is your **EpiWay**.

Your EpiWay is your optimal way of accessing energy and information for creating the *extraordinary*. When consistent with your EpiWay, you are authentically and effortlessly captivated by the power of synergy, syntropy, transformation and the experience of the sacred nature of **Creation's Codes**. Knowing and living your EpiWay is one of the most profound things you can do to advance both your own mind and the collective human performance.

Without having to fix or directly change anything, other than your focused attention and the awareness of your energetic nature...

BAM!

Your personal access to unlimited potential...becomes yours!

Through more energy richness, the power of *life itself* is engaged. *Creation's Codes* organize your Field of attraction, like a magnet draws iron filings, for a profound and constructive **MORE**. A more, for humanity's Next Tier and for *YOU*.

In the next part of this book, I will share with you some stories about people who were on the right and wrong side of their **Way**. Since we are each like individual cells of one humanity, as you experience more richness in someone else's energetics, new energetic opportunities awaken for you.

SEEKER'S CODE #5
WE WISH TO ACCESS THE MULTIDIMENSIONAL ENERGETICS THAT MAGICALLY CREATE AND CONNECT US ALL.

The EpiWay is a novel approach to the union and integration of the physical and spiritual, the seen and unseen, the ordinary and *extraordinary*. Knowing and coming **HOME** to your EpiWay is the simplest and most profound way to access Energy Rich and its gifts.

What Really Is the EpiWay?

To create the term EpiWay, I had to define more than "epi." I decided to look up the definition of the word "way." For this, I turned to *The American Heritage Dictionary of the English Language*, Fifth Edition. As you may suspect, I found the first definition was of "*a road or passage between two locations.*"

I was searching for a term to describe an opening to the energetics of the Next Tier. This passageway would bridge two energy states. The next two dictionary definitions of "way"—*"an opening affording passage"* and *"a space to proceed"*—were even more compelling.

The proper **Way**, by definition, could provide an energetic passage to access unbound energy.

Consider that **Epi** represents beyond, between or around. Couple it with **Way**—which can be the mystical space between immaterial and material, between bound and unbound and between realities. It is the passageway between brain and mind; sleeping and rest; sex and making love; intention and manifestation. With these words combined, your EpiWay is your Energy Rich way of accessing the information potential of **Creation's Codes**—in this "real world"—to organize the immaterial unbound into bound physical reality.*

Being in your optimal EpiWay leads to the actualization of attraction and manifestation. It magically puts you at the helm of your ship of life, effortlessly adjusting the sails as the winds of change of the larger system are taking us through the current storm of potential human transformation and awakening.

We are always planting seeds. An Energy Rich baseline is necessary to bear the ideal fruit of each seed. Depending on the EpiWay you select, the quality, quantity and value of the fruits born from these seeds instantly exchange to different realities.

Napoleon Hill, in his epic classic *Think and Grow Rich* states, "Anything the mind can conceive and believe, it can achieve." He says further, "Both poverty and richness are the offspring of thought." These ideas have profoundly influenced me, leading me to a central

---

* Having, through my Network systems, already established and evolved a similar contextual opening or "gateway" facilitating the intersection of bound and unbound energy and information in the spine and central nervous system, I recognized even more of the universal principles that allowed this to take form.

theme of EpiEnergetics (and this book)—that the linkage between thought and manifestation is one's E-State!

Employing your authentic EpiWay is an instant Energy Rich transport to the outcome offered through the wisdom of individuals who have promoted human transformation through the power of focused attention with positive expectancy. Wallace D. Wattles, in his *Science of Getting Rich* (1910) wrote, "There is a thinking stuff from which all things are made, and which, in its original state, permeates, penetrates and fills the interspaces of the Universe. A thought in this substance produces the thing that is imaged by the thought." The ideas considered metaphysical or spiritual in 1910 are now just commonly accepted truths of quantum physics and quantum neurology. When I was introduced to Wattles'—and Hill's and many others' writings—in the 1970s, they became an integral part of my reality.

I invite you to now take the next steps with me.

Your EpiWay provides the energy level that selects and attracts thoughts and manifestation only possible at that specific level of available energy. When in your natural EpiWay, the size of the system in which you participate instantly grows. The bigger your system, with enough energy, the bigger your participation and impact in the world.

Through example, metaphor and actual experience, you will get to know why your life at times is neutral, effortful, and lacking real vibrant meaning—and why at other times things magically and effortlessly happen, attracting so much **MORE**.

I will share with you a story.

A disciple, on his hands and knees, joined his guru as he searched for his house keys in the garden outside his home. After an hour or so, the disciple asked the guru, "Where did you last see your keys?" The guru replied, "Upstairs in my room."

Puzzled, the disciple asked, "Then why are we looking out here for your keys?"

The guru answered, "Because the light is better here."

In this story the guru seems misguided. It certainly makes sense to look where the keys were last seen. In an Energy Neutral state, we, like the disciple, seek sameness and do whatever we can to search for solutions that are familiar or seem to make sense. We never seek the *extraordinary*.

The situation is not what it seems to be about. With the energy richness of one's **Way,** alignment to an information flow of possibilities and connections brings the guru or someone he does not even know into a Field of collaboration for **MORE.**

The situation is no longer just about the keys. Our circumstances are just that: they are opportunities to remember what is real, primary and what is directing the show from behind the curtain in life. The area of highest available energy—in this example, the light—will inspire the solution, change your direction and lead you to different questions as you are guided in the Field.

There are two ways to look for your "keys," the location of your personal source of energy and the light. It is your way of amping up and lighting up your keys to information, manifestation and impact. One is Inside and the other is Outside. One is from the past, and the other is from the future!

Perhaps, just perhaps, while using the excuse of looking for the keys to something, you may help another to metaphorically find his "key." Or while searching you may connect to something even more important... something that finds you. Your connection with the Field activates *Creation's Codes*. Nothing is as it seems. There is always more. Your natural EpiWay guides, directs, nurtures and brings you into union with your greater **MORE.**

A Way to Be Found and a Way to Be Lost

This chapter is about beginning the adventure of finding your *Way*. It's about looking where the light is better and finding what you're looking for. To do that, we have to experience the ideas that, so far, you have only read about.

You now have a deeper understanding of the true nature of energy and the role it plays in your life. It is time to actually begin to *experience* the difference between Energy Neutral and Energy Rich—and the instantaneous shift that can occur in the *You* that's seeing and interacting in the world. Seeker, you both hope and trust that *Creation's Codes* can transform life in a moment. And there is more than this. We have discussed the [r]evolutionary ways of the Next Tier's energetics, and a novel way of understanding what truly influences and pulls the strings on everything that happens to you.

SEEKER'S CODE #6

WE RECOGNIZE THE POWER OF FOCUSED ATTENTION
AND ENERGY/AND CONSCIOUS CHOICE.

Switching from one EpiWay to the other creates an energy differential. A differential is the difference in quantity or quality of any elements in a system. Energy differentials lead to information, meaning and manifestation differentials. In this and the following chapters, I invite you to notice these differences in the ways you experience life.

In this part of the book, we will put *AAA* into action, merging what you have gleaned in the first part of the book with practical strategies and experiences of an energy difference between Ways A and B. This is where we merge theory with reality.

I demonstrated my first system, "Network"—which, in retrospect, was my introduction for "**EpiEnergetics**"—to researchers from various disciplines at a major university. They told me that the method and the spinal phenomenon they witnessed was scientific because "it is consistent, predictable and reproducible in its capacity to create a novel phenomenon of impact."

In response I replied, "It works in reality, and my question for you is, will it work in theory?"

Already you have learned about some of the theories. Let's now fuse it with reality. This new reality will allow you to increase the influence you have on others, by busting beyond the matrix and being a pioneer in the energetics of the Next Tier.

In the coming chapters, I will share with you attributes of the two EpiWays—Internal and External. Although first we will learn some clues to help you predict your EpiWay.

As you read statements from individuals both in their authentic EpiWay and opposite it, be aware of the energy state they are in as they are speaking. This will help guide you toward your *Way*.

EpiWay Personas

Typecast actors are known for their personas. The characters played follow predictable patterns and attract certain types of situations or dramas. We enjoy watching these characters as we feel we personally know them. Some actors, athletes and podcasters have a style that is so defined that you can often predict how they will respond to novel situations. The same applies to musicians. Concert-goers often demand to hear the music they associate with the musician. That's the persona they align with.

The way in which I discovered the two EpiWays and what they mean was through my keen observation and pattern recognition skills. When delivering my "Network" approaches to spinal and neural integrity, and upgrading the human OS with my energetic applications, consistent behaviors were evident.

When Energy Rich, some people would lift their bodies up from a lying down position on the chiropractic or massage-type table. These people often would reach their arms up and outward. They said different things than those whose bodies stayed lower down on the table.

These same people who moments earlier referenced past painful experiences, scarcity or challenges would now speak about what was working in their life and about future visions being manifested. They spoke more often about grandiose plans, affecting a bigger circle of humanity and about the energetics between or around us. They often experienced cravings of variety and instability, and they seemed far out there—wherever it is that "there" was.

These people, when they were stressed, fearful, or upset would curl their shoulders inward and "centralize" or intensify the bound energy and information in the center of their body, closer to their spine. When they were less resourceful, they would always speak about some past trauma or some resource that was lost, missing or taken away from them.

They believed that trauma was stored deep in their body and that they had to let go of something from the past. Once removed, forgiven or repaired, it would then allow them to live the life that their future destiny called for them. They were never enough.

The other group of people were the opposite. Just moments earlier they mentioned the worry and fear about the future. When Energy Rich, their attention and observation in life was from inside and looked to the past as a source of wonder. This second group of people tended to project energy and information out to their sides and beyond their bodies. When they were stressed or went into Energy Neutral, their body posture was angled outward more than their usual central position. They preferred to take one step at a time and could not get their heads around how even years after an event occurred some people could still be bothered by a past trauma. The past was never painful. For them, the past was their source of strength. They would only recall the wisdom or lessons of the past. They wanted to take the best of the past and bring it into the future. They seemed to prefer stability over dipping into uncertainty.

In time, I found I could tell the difference between these two groups by the positions of their hands—whether facing inward or facing outward. Their hand positions always represented where they were seeking energy and information to experience and interpret what they called reality.

Through these EpiWay discernments, I realized our energetic propensity shapes our desires as well as how we learn, grow, adapt to change, manifest, heal and perform. Knowing this by experience sets changes in motion—without having to change anything.

With very high accuracy, after several years of observation and research, I linked the hand position, posture, E-State, individual preferences, values and beliefs, and I was able to describe two personas of the EpiWay: External and Internal.

Internal and External

Since we learn first by experience, I will share the experiences of two people to better explain the differences between the two EpiWays. Let's explore the "persona" differences of these very different "species" of humans through conversations and narratives of people in each of these EpiWays.

As I share the statements of the following two people about their lives, please notice differences in their words. Take note of what they were saying and how their linguistics represent their E-State. When they reference in or out or past or future, does it seem more Energy Neutral or Energy Rich?

In some ways, this is like asking you to pay attention to the non-verbal clues transmitted when you go into a foreign country where you don't know the language. As with language, immersion is the best way to learn the EpiWay. You may be surprised at how much you already know, as the language of the Field is our primary language. I am looking to help you to develop your superpowers with an unconscious competence that we, and especially Seekers, all have.

Here are the two examples:

Some of you:

> I don't understand why it had to happen to me. I have to find the courage to let go of it. Too often I doubt that I will ever know what is real. There is a fear that I will feel the weight of it upon me. Deep in my heart I know the truth. It is painful, and I will have to work more on digging it out. I have had so many losses and can't keep repeating this pattern. Please lift my spirit up and expand me to the vastness. This is the home that calls me.

Others of you:

> I know the truth. It is from the victories I have had over tough times and the wisdom I have gained from my past. Don't ask me about my plans for years from now or expect me to take big leaps forward. This is my terror. I might lose my grip on what is real and secure. Stop trying to take me into the clouds or the cosmos. There is nothing so great there. Home is where I came from. Let me just be alone in silence in my cave, and I will emerge ready to love and care for you like I always have. When you come down from the clouds, my dear, I will be firmly grounded to take care of you and keep you safe.

Do you sense the high neutral hunger or pain in either of these quotes? Do you sense the longing through difficult past memories/thoughts of the future?

Do you sense that, for one of these people, the pain is deep inside and from the past, and for the other, the past is a refuge and going too far out in the future is painful and an effort? One is more energized when lifted up, and the other has difficulty with up and out—feeling more energized being close to the earth.

Do either of these statements resonate with you? Which one do you identify with? Is it the one with pain inside and from the past or pain outside and from the future? What is the nature of this pain for you? Is this sense of hunger or pain related to your health? Your relationships or intimacy? Your business or finances? Your ability to influence the Field of humanity? Which domain of these is your E-State challenged on?

Oh really, more than one?

Each quote is a classic of one of the EpiWays. With this in mind, do you feel you are effortlessly and magically living your **Way**, or perhaps living a "maybe" way, or are you living "I can't find my **Way** and I'm working on it" in Energy Neutral? Or even worse, and I do mean worse, are you "no F—king way?!"

Finding Your Way: A Wave Flips You Over

Understanding your **Way** and whether you are following it is of supreme importance. In at least one area of life, you have been swimming in the ocean at night.

Suddenly, you are hit by a wave that seems like it came out of nowhere. It flips you over, disorients and totally submerges you, leaving you swimming in the wrong direction and hoping you are heading to the surface for air. Instead, you are using a way that takes you toward the ocean bottom. You realize that time is running out for you to have enough air in that domain of life that has been challenged. You are about to drown in not-enoughness and struggle on the way to being a no-body.

As you remember that you are a Seeker, unbound energy, maybe from the cloud that just moved away revealing the full moon, wakes you up and shows you the *Way*. It seems like a current half-pulls you upward, directing you to effortlessly rise victoriously as you break the surface of the water.

In glorious rapture, you now drink in the fresh air and cough the seawater out of your lungs without thinking about how to do this. Rather than struggling to find the *Way* to breathe and move away from the experience of survival, feeling lost, and swimming faster in the wrong direction—you are truly living and alive. The Energy Rich current of life has brought you to be exactly where you **must be**. You have been pulled out of the water of illusion into reality and have a choice to live and live fully.

It is time for you to live truth with natural authenticity. It is time to wake up from the cultural-controlled computer program of "blah blah blah" or "Someday, I will find my way. Maybe. I hope." It is time to leave behind "I'll try harder."

Raise your head above the water, clear your lungs, and proclaim: "Tick Tick Tick Tock! This is my time!"

It is time for *Creation's Codes* to attract the current of synergy and manifestation for *MORE* than just yourself.

SEEKER'S CODE #2
WE HAVE AN OBSESSION TO GO BEYOND WHO WE HAVE BEEN.

What would it be worth to you if you could, in mere seconds, have the gift of energy richness with its synergy and Field creation instantly engaged for your health, your business, your relationships, your finances and the way you impact others in the world?

What would it be worth to you to have access to the **One Way** for you to go from disliking or blaming your circumstances, your relationships, your business or your family—from having a problem, being stuck, being tired of working on "it" or managing "it"—to instantly being on the other side?

What *will* it be like to access this **One Way** and to have physical, emotional, mental, social, spiritual and life transformation by putting **Creation's Codes** in action without having to change anything—without requiring more loss, breakdown, or effort? How much *will* you desire for people you know and even those you don't yet know to have their lives improved through quantum entanglement as a consequence of a conscious shift in your Field?

What *will* it be like to know why your life is the way it is when you are messed up and how to harness profound energetics that magically bring on a new bolder and more influential reality? What will it be like to take this novel approach into the way you view your body and healing, engage in relationships, create and sustain business or finances, or how you impact others and share your gifts?

It is *unreasonable* for many that someone can go from contemplating a divorce, bankruptcy, a change in careers because of dissatisfaction or alienation between lovers or family members—to suddenly making those troubles irrelevant without anything changing other than the amount of energy available. This is what will happen when you are aligned with your EpiWay.

Even an entrenched story of trauma, a fear of moving ahead, a pain of the past or a terror of the future will be significantly altered or just G O N E.

And it will be replaced by so much *MORE*.

A Brief Experience of the EpiWay

As we begin, here are the most effective ways to perform the exercises ahead:

- Be attentive to your own E-State with each step.
- Allow for both rational and beyond-rational learning.
- Allow experiences in quality and quantity to emerge.
- Acknowledge and record your experiences in spoken or written form.
- Share your experiences with others.

Additionally, as each prompt will speak of many different areas of your life, you may want to **focus on one area you want most to upgrade for the largest change.** Also, compare this energetics to the area of life that you are really rocking at the moment, as it will likely be following the opposite EpiWay as it mostly triggers your sense of not-enoughness. That will allow you to experience and radiate the most profound change through these exercises—and for more than just you.

EPIWAY SPATIAL HACK

This exercise helps you to hack where you go in space to access the codes that become your reality. You can take turns with a family member, friend or coworker doing the exercise.

First: Part 1

1. Think of a difficult experience or an obstacle that you believe is the cause of your challenges. It might impact the domain of your health, your relationships, your business or your finances.
2. Place your hands on your chest. Look down. Do this in front of a mirror, computer or phone so you can witness the power of shifting your **Way**.

3. State out loud what this experience is like and what it means to you. Go on a "rant" about the circumstance or experience. Listen to yourself. Look at your body, your face, the amount of light in your eyes, your expression and your posture. How much energy is bound and unavailable? How much energy and light do you shine?
4. Take note of what you said, how you feel, what you are thinking and your attitude toward what you stated.

Next: Part 2

Think about that same painful experience, obstacle, person or situation that is difficult for you.

1. Raise your hands above your head with palms facing out to the skies. Look up. Now do the same exercise as before, except this time you are looking up with your hands up and facing outward. See yourself engaged in this process as if you were a bird looking down from afar.
2. State again out loud what this experience is like, what does it mean to you, and just go on a rant about the circumstance or experience. Listen to yourself. Now look at your body, your face, the amount of light in your eyes, your expression and your posture. How much energy is bound and unavailable? How much energy and light do you shine?
3. Take note of what you said, how you feel, what you are thinking and your attitude. Then, contrast what you said in Part 1 with what you said in Part 2 of the exercise. What differential did you experience in E-State, focus, thoughts, emotions, language and your general attitude? What is the difference between you observing, narrating and experiencing? Do you sense a difference in your sense or availability of energy? Which is more energizing and transformational: Part 1, with your hands on your body, or Part 2, with your hands up?

For most people, there was a direct experience and transmission of your app of difficulty, pain, blame or lack of resourcefulness for one of those two positions. For the other position, everything was fine, there was no problem, and the painful situation was resolved. Perhaps there was a different *You* there.

The contrast for most is immediate and profound. In a few moments, you are feeling, thinking and acting differently.

Contrast is the way of life. We cannot experience sameness unless we are in a Low Energy Neutral or poor state. Our only constant is change! Our nervous system links to our Field through disturbance or contrast. An energetic differential (rapid change in E-State) is translated into an information/data/consciousness differential.

In seconds, this is experienced on the computer screen of your body and mind as a different experience of reality. And this difference can be projected through your mind and Field to others. For most Seekers, this exercise instantly hacks your previous reality and narration, and even if only for a moment, you change into a different version of yourself guided by different apps.

As you become *Aware* of this change, *Acknowledge* what is novel about it and be with it for a couple of moments. After a moment or two, you might notice how an effortless *Acceptance* *is happening for you coupled with a* new understanding.

OMG, how did this happen? How can your problem, your worry or what you have been working on instantly be gone or significantly reduced without really changing anything?

SEEKER'S CODE #6
WE RECOGNIZE THE POWER OF FOCUSED ATTENTION
AND ENERGY/AND CONSCIOUS CHOICE.

This is because your E-State just jumped up or down one state and the apps of reality you were playing suddenly shifted. And whatever you were thinking about, in whatever domain of life you were focused upon, was similarly also shifted through quantum entanglement.

Next Tier energetics were activated. Your pure awareness of your energetics and the nature of your "system" moved you from the caterpillar to butterfly phase of your life.

What Happens If Both Seem About the Same?

If both parts seemed about the same, this suggests that you are functioning in a Low Energy Neutral state. Your unconscious drive is to make sure nothing changes and that you remain comfortable, liked or accepted, or rather you live a story about why you can't have or be more. When you are Low Energy Neutral, even unconscious awareness of an authentic experience may threaten your conditioned story. Therefore, even though your body experiences the difference, there is not enough energy to bring the information to your higher brain. Therefore, critical discernment, reassessment and acknowledgment of your authentic nature are absent.

In this event, no worries—or if you prefer, more worries—either way, there is still hope for you. In this case, do the exercise with both the most extraordinarily painful or difficult situation and the most extraordinarily wonderful memory, hope or future you have had or will have. Once you find an A and a B experience in which there is a large difference in energy, your shell-obscuring reality will crack open. This reinforces the pure experience of a significantly different reality that occurs when the energy difference potentiates perceptual differences. Reading further and being with others' statements provides a doorway to awareness of the difference between EpiWays.

Ordinary Takes a Day Off

Now let's refine some of the ideas I mentioned in the earlier sections of the book before we continue with this exploration of your EpiWay.

For now, here's a question for you:

Why did the turkey cross the road?

The answer:

Because it was the chicken's day off!

This could be the time to give what's ordinary, expected and practiced for you the day off and watch what takes over in its place. Let's practice having time off from your reasonable, expected and ordinary to allow the *Unreasonable* and *Extraordinary* to enter your life and the lives of others.

At this point you may be asking, "Donny, why does this work?"

We started this book with the statement that we do not see the world as it is, we see it as we are. This is the magic of our observer. When we observe, interpret, or give meaning to anything, we collapse the quantum probability wave and downgrade the information that manifests as form. Is an event painful or joyful? Is a relationship peaceful or at war? Are your finances bankrupt or flush? And on and on...

Our energy and information data stream that our nervous system interprets as reality has two directions of flow, one from back to forward of the body in space and from the past to future—the other one from the front to backward and the future to past.

When we can directly access the data stream and energy source from its place of greatest availability, then we *instantly* access so much more and express and radiate a much more powerful and expanded reality.

SEEKER'S CODE #5
WE WISH TO ACCESS THE MULTIDIMENSIONAL ENERGETICS THAT MAGICALLY CREATE AND CONNECT US ALL.

We know that energy is a constant in the universe; it cannot be created or destroyed. It is instead changed from form to form. From a quantum science perspective, the same is true with information. If it is deleted from one environment or dimension, it is displaced into another. This is called the non-hiding principle. As you become Energy Rich, you have access to the universal information of creation and possibilities that seem to just pop into your new leveled-up life. These possibilities are not available to you when you are neutral and opposite your EpiWay.

The way our central nervous system interprets interference wave patterns, like the ripples made by a stone dropped into the information lake of all possibilities, shapes our experience of everything we believe is real: our physical, emotional, and mental realities. The ripple in the pond of information that you are sends other ripples out in non-time and non-space, and its interactions are the sharing of data about the essence of you and the universe. The interactions between these waves are our reality. What we observe, we are already participating in. We and our environment are one.

The gift here is to be able to hack the codes that create the apps that define your reality BEFORE the probability wave collapses into conditioned meaning or form in your life. *AAA* and a greater amount of unbound energy are keys to doing this.

Beyond the theory of all of this is the **direct experience with the quantum world** through access to results that are *Unreasonable* and *Extraordinary*.

SEEKER'S CODE #6
WE RECOGNIZE THE POWER OF FOCUSED
ATTENTION, ENERGY, AND CONSCIOUS CHOICE.

This is the possibility you unlock through your authentic EpiWay. This is the *One Way* you can create a direct experience of the quantum world and harness all the potential for new creation through *Creation's Codes*.

Seeker, let's get back to the topic of the EpiWay and discover which direction your EpiWay is most likely oriented.

Two Possible EpiWays

Electrons have some interesting properties. When they meet a solid obstacle, they express their quantum properties by dematerializing and showing up on the other side. Every atom in our body has these multidimensional properties, and each electron can contact every other one in the universe in multiple time-space dimensions.

Electrons have two spin states as they have what is called an upward or downward spin. This fact impressed me and led me to begin seeking the answer to this question: Is it possible that the spin is forward and backward, or past or future? The responses of scientists I spoke to were similar: it is possible and depended upon the model or map of reality of the observer. **BAM!**

What even makes this more *Unreasonable* and *Extraordinary* is that the actual spin only exists when someone consciously examines and measures it.

BAM again!

Now our central nervous system, connected to the available energy-activated informational Field, plucks out a form based upon the personal observers! When Energy Neutral, we tend to agree with the group expectation or matrix interpretation. When Energy Rich, and in our natural *Way*, it really gets Next Tier interesting. As I draw from quantum theory...we can transcend the cultural Field matrix of one "accepted reality."

We do not see the world as it is, we see it as we are.

"All matter originates and exists only by virtue of a force... We must assume behind this force the existence of a conscious and intelligent mind. This mind is the matrix of all matter."

—MAX PLANK, FATHER OF QUANTUM PHYSICS

There is further truth to consider here. The 2022 Nobel Prize in Physics was awarded in three equal parts to "independent" researchers Alain Aspec, John Clauser, and Anton Zellinger. They academically demonstrated that beyond the observer, there is no physical reality. We would assume that an apple has its apple form and color, regardless of whether someone observes it as an apple, and its shape and color are real. These quantum scientists state that at a quantum level, the electrons have two directions of spin and there is no real structural form until someone interprets its data stream. **BAM!** It then takes the form consistent with this observer. This is central to EpiEnergetics and emerges as a mutable reality in this Next Tier.

With this understanding and my interactions with and observation of thousands of individuals, I made a "quantum inspired leap" to create the concept of one's EpiWay.

The information that your mind calls your "life" and "reality" comes from one of two data streams. The data stream can flow like the two directions of the electron spin or vibration—from behind you moving forward, or from in front of you moving backward. Your optimal direction depends upon your EpiWay.

Direction makes all the difference. If water is flowing from in front of you, and you are turning your head backward, you will get very little water to drink. If you turn to face the river, the water will flow directly into you. If you point a garage door opener away from your garage, it will not work. It only works when you put it in the right direction for the information to flow. This is true of all information and energy.

I believe that each person has a natural tendency to attract more electrons with one directional spin and less with the other. As with masculine and feminine energetics, each of us has both orientations, and the degree to which one dominates over the other determines our masculine or feminine qualities. In both cases, the orientation is intrinsic.

Your EpiWay depends on where you go with your focus to get free energy to activate the organization of information (in-form-ation—or literally means "to put form into a process of becoming") in time and in space. In physics, this is referred to as space-time, or time-space, as they define one another.

If this sounds *Unreasonable* and *Extraordinary*, it will not in the next few years.

How weird would it be to you if you had been in a coma or beamed from the 1950s or even 1970s into today's world where science fiction was suddenly your daily reality. What seemed like Star Trek's communicators were being used, people were talking to "themselves" on hand held small boxes. People did not have to wait for photographic film to be developed. They traveled in cars with the vehicle telling them what to do, or having a virtual assistant speak with them Perhaps those who are older remember Dick Tracy's two-way watch radio that helped him catch criminals in the Sunday funnies section of newspapers. That may have inspired today's Apple watches. Yes, much of this *unreasonable* technology has already been realized. Elements of yesterday's science fiction have become part of our new reality.

Now it is time to discover which *Way* energy and information flow for you!

- When excited about something or someone, when life is clicking, does your thought process begin from the past or the future?
- What about when things are difficult or suck?
- Or, when things are really happening and when they aren't?
- When your E-State is neutral and when it is rich, from where in space does the flow of information and energy originate?
- Is it in front of you moving toward your back? Or is it coming from behind and moving forward?
- Is it close to you? Is it far from you?

Keep these answers in mind. The explanation that your EpiWay is found at the subatomic level will activate your High Energy Neutral state to want to understand more and integrate what I am sharing with you into your existing map of reality.

To further this understanding, here are some **personal inquiry questions** for the experience of the content I just shared to prepare you for what comes after.

> Do you associate the past and deep inside with painful memories, meanings, lack and what has to be let go of or healed to more fully move ahead?
>
> Does the past, being more down to Earth, bring comfort? Is your source of energy, strength and knowing inside? Does being too far out there and too expansive bring you pain or difficulties?

This is related to the direction your information and energy is flowing—either External or Internal. We will explore where you and others fit between the Internal and External EpiWays. You will get to know each of these ways and which is your authentic *Way*.

One way is your *Way* to effortless *Unreasonable* and *Extraordinary*. It is an energy richness elevator, a stairway to heaven. The other *Way* leads you to darkness, breakdown, effort or at best, the purgatory of energy neutrality.

You must know and more often *LIVE YOUR Way*. This is different from your usual or habitual neutral way of tumbling in the void of loss, effort, difficulty, lack of progress or love. It radically departs from the way you "work on" what is missing, or perhaps becomes lost in the sea of yuckiness when looking for juiciness.

Creation and Time: Internals

God and Goddess had a party, and at the end of it, they made a "Big Bang." All of creation emerged from the union of the masculine and feminine energies.

Information with the free energy of this Big Bang went from the past to the future—from immaterial to material dimensions. As the energy merged with the information, it gave all matter and life its properties and sustained it into existence. As energy was bound into form, it was less available to fuel organization or change. As energy fueled the code only known to the force of creation, information/potential manifested as clouds and stars were formed. Galaxies were made.

The suspected age of our universe depends upon calculations that consider the loss of energy in the background signal from the moment of creation.

The *Way* of this use of energy and subatomic/quantum states and information is from the past to the future. For those with this **Internal** orientation, **there is more energy in the past,** and there is **a loss of available energy in the future.** The information flows into our fourth-dimensional world from the past. And the information flow that we access for creation of our existence and interpretation of perceived reality **flows from behind us forward. This is the way of the Internal.**

For Internals, causation happens first, and the effect happens later. You may say, "Well, isn't that the way everything works, a cause leads to an effect?" And the answer is...this is how the mind *experiences* events and how we are *conditioned* based upon the Internal way. For Internals, the past is from behind us and moving forward. This influences your physical, emotional, mental, social and spiritual experiences. It impacts all areas of your life and legacy.

Time for the Externals

The **External** EpiWay may be derived from the infinite future when the universe will fold back on itself in the Great Crunch and all matter will be consumed and become potentiated information again.

The *Way* of this use of energy and subatomic/quantum states and information is **from the future to the past.** There is more energy in the future, and there is a loss of available energy in the past. The information flows in our fourth-dimensional world for those whose way follows *retro-causation*. **Here the effect has happened in the future, and it sends causes into the past to lead the person toward this potential future.** Externals transmit higher-order future realities before the Internal-centered culture feels it is time. These realities disrupt the status quo and take things in different directions.

The Ordinary is bound by time. The *Extraordinary* is not.

Internal and External EpiWay

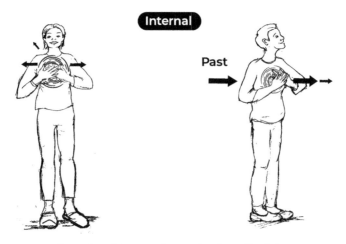

Internal

Past

Drawing Energy from the Past/Inside

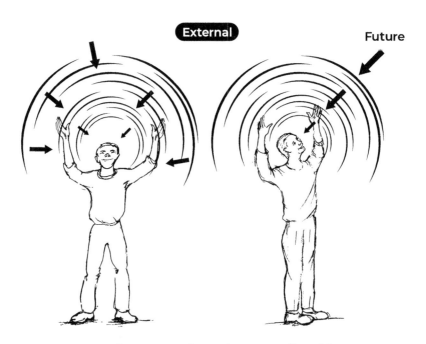

External

Future

Drawing Energy from the Future/Outside

Figure 5

EPIWAY TEMPORAL HACK

This exercise will help you determine if your organic information flow originates from the past or future and to discover your true EpiWay.

1. Place your hands facing one another with your wrists at shoulder height. See Figure 6.
2. Identify one hand as capturing the energy and data stream representing your past relative to your health, relationships, business/finances, or bringing your spiritual gifts to the world.
3. Identify the other hand as capturing the energy and information from the future representing the same four domains.
4. While keeping your hands fixed in the same place, visualize the data and energy stream from your past hand in that chosen domain of life, moving to the opposite future hand. With your "mind's eye," direct the energy to move the information across the space between your hands and into your future hand. Fully associate with who you have been in this domain as you send the information across to the other hand.
5. How does it feel as you do this? Do you feel happy or energized, comfortable or excited, or drained and less vital? Or are you not sure?
6. How far does the data stream appear to travel? Does it stay at the past hand? Does it go ¼ of the way, ½ of the way, ¾ of the way, almost to the future hand—or does it fully reach the future hand and beyond?
7. Observe yourself as you do this. Accessing the information stream that you interpret based upon your E-State is a Next Tier practice in which you become **Aware** of your energetics without the desire to change or understand them. Then **Acknowledge** this strategy provided a huge amount of unbound energy for change. Finally, you can **Accept** the results.

Now repeat this process, focusing upon the future hand, fully associating with the unknown future as if you are already there, just as you had associated earlier with your past. Fully associate with your future self in this domain as you move the information across to the other hand.

Be *Aware*, *Acknowledge*, and *Accept* the energetics of what you observe.

> How does it feel as you do this? How far does this data stream appear to travel? What have you observed about yourself as you do this?
>
> Having completed both parts, compare your experiences of the two. Which information flow went further?

In most cases, the repetition of this exercise will wake you temporally and spatially from the matrix, and you will start experiencing, even for moments, the profundity of instant change in Energy Richness.

Hand Gap Exercise

One hand represents your past and the other your future.
With your focus, direct the energy from the past hand to the future.
See how far the energy goes.
Do the same from the future to the past.
If the energy stops, where does it s top?
Does it go all the way to the other hand?
Does starting your attention from the past or future
better power your life?
Internal: focusing from the future will never allow for past gifts to continue.
External: focusing from the past will never allow for a better future.

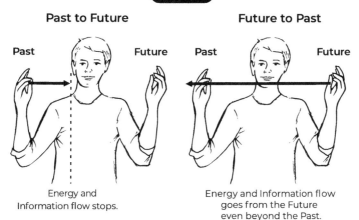

Internal

Past to Future   **Future to Past**

Past   Future   Past   Future

Energy and Information flow   Energy and
goes from the Past   Information flow stops.
even beyond the Future.

External

Past to Future   **Future to Past**

Past   Future   Past   Future

Energy and   Energy and Information flow
Information flow stops.   goes from the Future
                            even beyond the Past.

Figure 6

WHAT DOES THIS EPIWAY TEMPORAL HACK MEAN?

Past Is Energized: Suggests an Internal EpiWay

- If focusing upon the information flow from the past energized, empowered and enlivened you—if it made you feel like calling "yes!"—this suggests that the past is a source of energy for you.
- If the information flow had enough energy to move from the past hand to the future hand, then this also suggests that you manifest from the past. Recalling your past successes, lessons and victories can propel you to an Energy Rich future.
- The further the information traveled to the future, the greater your Internal nature is expressed.

Past Drops Energy: Suggests an External EpiWay

- If focusing upon the information flow from the past dropped the energy, disempowered, or flattened out your experience—if it made you feel like crying "no" or just feel blah—then this suggests that the past is a source of energy loss for you to power manifestation.
- If the information flow did not have enough energy to move from the past hand to the future hand, then this also suggests that the codes from the past are ones that drain your energy, downsize your life, and cause pain and breakdown. Recalling your past successes, lessons and victories are unlikely to lead to an Energy Rich future.
- The nearer to the past hand the energy and information flow traveled, the more your past is a source of pain, breakdown and Low Energy Neutral to poor default.

Future Is Energized: Suggests an External EpiWay

- If focusing upon the information flow from the future energized, empowered and enlivened you—if it made you feel like calling "yes!"—this suggests that the future is a source of energy for you to power manifestation.
- If the information flow had enough energy to move from the future hand to the past hand, then this suggests that you manifest from the future. Similarly, experiencing your potential future can propel you to an Energy Rich state with its expansive victories.
- The further the information traveled to the past hand, the more the **Unreasonable** and **Extraordinary** happens—and your future can influence your past. Every time you claim a new future, the ship's rudder would have had to shift just enough to get you to your new destination.

Future Drops Energy: Suggests an Internal EpiWay

- If focusing upon the information flow from the future dropped the energy, disempowered, or flattened out your experience—if it made you feel like crying "no," or you just felt blah—then this suggests that the future is a source of loss of energy for you.
- If the information flow did not have enough energy to move from the future hand to the past hand, then this also suggests that the codes from the future are ones that drain your energy, downsize your life, and cause pain and breakdown. Focusing upon your long-term vision that your future will not carry the successes of the past—or you will have loss or failure in the future—will keep you Energy Neutral at best.
- The closer to the future hand the energy and information flow stops, the more your future is a source of pain and breakdown.

What if the information/energy flows in both directions for you or the experience with both hands seems pretty much the same?

In this case, your mind will play games in which part of you is using Internal strategies from the past, perfectly competing with External strategies from the future—supporting energy neutrality.

I hear you saying, "Donny, how do I get unstuck?"

First, admit that you are stuck because you are Energy Neutral. Admit that the apps you are playing are set to avoid upsetting your belief in your circumstances as reality.

Sneaky one, it is most likely that when you are looking at your future hand, you are still drawing information from the past, or vice versa.

Time for action steps...

To correct this, read the tenets of *The Seeker's Codes* slowly—particularly the ones that have you stop (marked by the slash) / part of the way through. With those, read the first part and pause. Then also read the full code. For example:

SEEKER'S CODE #3
WE SEEK A RICHER, MORE MAGICAL, AND EXTRAORDINARY
EXPERIENCE FOR OURSELVES/AND FOR OTHERS.

State the entire tenet, pause, then say it again ending on "ourselves." Feel your energy. Then reread, adding "and for others." Do you sense a change in your available energy?

Choose Your Buffet

When in one's authentic EpiWay, instant energy richness is available. When opposite one's EpiWay, the effort of energy neutrality is the best it gets. My obsession is to help the masses of humanity to flip from

Energy Neutral to rich. With this, the energetics of a new humanity will truly be revealed. The one way to instantly get there is to know and more often live in one's authentic EpiWay.

Imagine you go to Nevada and experience the majesty of a self-indulgent excess ritual—the Las Vegas buffet.

Let's consider two different buffets for which you will wait in line, each spreading out different choices: buffet A and buffet B.

Buffet A: Your Authentic EpiWay

Eating from this buffet will bring you abundant *extraordinary* options which are either all your favorites or soon to become your new favorites. Eating foods from this buffet will provide you with the access to a source of strength, success, constructive thoughts, wonderful experiences, love, confidence, vision, creativity, trust, abundance, acceptance, synergy, greatness, an upsized life and abundant desserts of Energy Richness.

SEEKER'S CODE #5

WE WISH TO ACCESS THE MULTIDIMENSIONAL ENERGETICS
THAT MAGICALLY CREATE AND CONNECT US ALL.

Buffet B: Opposite Your Authentic EpiWay

You find yourself in much longer food lines, and eating from this buffet is leading to indigestion and lots of strong burps. The food is artificially flavored, laden with preservatives, and has additives that make you crave more. Though the food may look beautiful, there is no nutritional value. At best, it is great entertainment. You gorge yourself on so much more of this conditioned addiction as everything you would want to eat is available.

As you eat foods from this buffet, the indigestion is expressed as a source of painful experiences or thoughts, upset feelings, weakness, failure, indifference, blame, less than-ness, lack of confidence, rejection, loss, scarcity, failure, abandonment, separateness, a downsized life and more that are all characteristic of an Energy Neutral or poor state.

Through your focused attention, the way you are seeing and interacting with *Creation's Codes*, and the life you are experiencing, it will be obvious which buffet you will choose: your authentic *Way* buffet or the "no *Way*" buffet.

We do not always eat at one buffet. Many of us dip into different buffets in different domains of our lives. In one area of life, such as your relationships, you might be eating from buffet A, while in another, such as business, your sensitivities may be acting up from buffet B. Or, your health may be compromised by the low-quality choices of buffet B while your finances flourish at buffet A.

You are becoming *Aware* of the energetics that are running your life, and that these energetics are associated with which EpiWay menu options are available. This leads to recognizing that when you choose buffet line A, you get energy rich, and when you habitually go to buffet line B, you know what you are getting. Through this choice, you invite its natural outcomes and limitations.

Now is the time to choose the buffet for your life that reflects your authentic EpiWay. Each of these buffets are associated with your available energy, which turns data into code—and code into apps that either play you or you play!

When in your authentic EpiWay, all of this is effortless, and synergy is instantaneous.

This is only the beginning. As your authentic EpiWay becomes clear, it is time to look in greater depth at the two orientations of the EpiWay: Internal and External. Whichever way is your *Way*, understanding both will show you how to best live your EpiWay and interact with those who have the opposite EpiWay.

CHAPTER 9

———

MY WAY

THE INTERNAL

Frank Sinatra, affectionately known as "the Chairman of the Board" and "Ol' Blue Eyes," is often personally associated with the lyrics of his epic recording of the song "My Way." Many of the lyrics of this song truly represent those with Internal EpiWays.

Written by Paul Anka with Sinatra in mind, Frank's energized rendition brings the lyrics alive as he proudly proclaims that his life has been full and consistently lived on his terms. Acknowledging he is approaching the end of his journey in this world, he shares his way of life with an energized sense of nostalgia. At the same time, as he faces what he refers to as a curtain in front of the unknown, he expresses a less energized expectation of what is to come. For Internals, the past is a great resource upon which they can build. Beginnings and next steps are generally the most energized. The further they look into their possible future, the less resourceful they tend to be—unless that future look carries stacked fond memories to carry them forward. The lyrics of "My Way" draw upon the past, which helps to better energize thoughts about the future.

Since the Internal tends to seek certainty before uncertainty, and stability before jumping into instability, the uncertainty of what is ahead can be frightening—and even more so if this is viewed from a future perspective. As Sinatra sings "My Way," his uncertainty is palpable. The fear of future death, with its vast and unknown loss, is tempered by the recollections of a life fully lived.

For Internals, energy richness is built from a continuum of successful experiences stacked from the past. This is in sharp contrast to the massive unknowns of the looming future "out there," which is frightening and challenging for those with this EpiWay.

To an Internal, the song's lyrics reflecting upon a life well lived represent an Energy Rich state. Internals access energy and information flow beginning from **behind or within them. Anytime this information flow moves forward and/or outward, energy is lost.** Remembering past experiences (which will always be positive and constructive) further engages energy richness and hence a more powerful and pleasant meaning with a reassuring coherence, focus and presence.

Later in the song, reference is made to times in life when more was taken on than could be digested. I interpret this as taking in more information than can be assimilated at that time. This grasping of too much information, or even considering the future with much more than what has already been experienced or known, drives Internals into defensiveness or keeps them in neutrality. They prefer small bits of information to be deliberately processed before assimilating them into their existing neural network and world.

Ol' Blue Eyes sings about how when he went into uncertainty or had too much to deal with, he would project or eject far outside of himself whatever was foreign to his sense of self. Outside or far away is where Internals lose energy and downsize life. It is where Internals experience the less valuable, less liked, more painful, more difficult and more challenging aspects of life.

In contrast, taking in too much in life is rarely a concern to an External. They salivate at the idea of being taken OUT for novel information and the excitement of experiencing a great buffet of newness served by the larger system. The challenge for an External is keeping anything IN for long or making it part of their daily life.

Classic for an Internal, the song mentions rejection of what was too much or foreign and that the regrets in life are not enough to even consider. When reviewing the past, there is so much energy richness that even the "worst of times" are recalled as "good" or valuable.

Externals seem to never finish thinking of or sharing with others all the regrets from the past that had to be let go. For Externals, when experienced from the past, even the good times can be perceived as the worst of times.

The song's lyrics refer to a deliberate and sequential chosen walk in his life. No matter what was difficult, "the Chairman" stood tall and remained committed to his path. This is in great contrast to the External way, which happens leap by leap. When certain, the Internal has his information and energy in the center or close to the midline of his body or life. The External, when certain, has his back arched more and arms outstretched and thus experiences expansion.

When things are challenging in life, the song's solution is the repeating refrain of the lyrics. Sinatra sings that he always did it his way. By remembering the past continuum of decisions and actions that an Internal person personally initiated and acted upon, he has enough energy to successfully deal with whatever life throws at him—and what lies ahead at the end of life. Ironically, at the end of Sinatra's life in 1998, it has been reported that his last words were "I'm losing." He was likely experiencing what was beyond the veil to the ultimate uncertainty—and the loss of all that had been.

For the Internal, "my way" is the right way. It's a better way than others. No matter what others feel, do, or plan, their way cannot match the Internal's own **Way**.

Inside Me

"Inside myself is a place I live all alone,
and that's where you renew your springs
that never dry up."

—PEARL S. BUCK

> Why do you think this quote is a classic example of an Internal's perspective? What does this metaphor do for you or to you? How do you respond or react to this quote? Does this add energy to your being or take it away? Or is there no difference?

Let's look closely at Pearl S. Buck's quote.

Starting with the statement of "inside myself" there is a powerful grounding for someone with an Internal EpiWay. This builds upon their core energetics, and claims more energy and greater data streams for, well, everything.

For Externals, this is a recipe for a living hell. Moving further inside or looking to improve or strengthen their cores will lower their E-State and downsize their experience of life. Efforting will ensue.

Buck continues, "I live alone." The smaller the circle for the Internal at their core, the more available energy and greater bandwidth are instantly available. Internals must go into their cave or smaller space with as few people as possible in order to compress and amplify their energetics toward richness. With more available energy, they can expand their circle and grow bigger with others.

It is counterintuitive for the External to go into a smaller space alone to shine brighter. Externals likely shudder at this thought. For the Internal, going inside and being with oneself and the universe within is a great way to power up. The further an Internal goes outside, the greater the loss of energy, and therefore, the darker a situation appears.

Please remember that we all have access to both Internal and External strategies. Only your natural EpiWay will bring the **Unreasonable** and **Extraordinary** into manifestation. Therefore, when you're Energy Neutral, you will use the opposite strategy to varying degrees, muting your optimal **Way** while seeing your usual or ordinary as your **Way**. I say "*No Way*" to this!

Buck continues that this is how to renew your Internal springs. For Internals, this is obvious and natural. For the External, renewal takes place away from themselves—and away from anyone or anything that they have made part of themselves.

In the next chapter, we'll meet the External's "Over the Rainbow." I chuckle to myself because when I was writing that chapter, I kept unconsciously typing *under* the rainbow. I actually wondered why anyone would want to go over, or even more so, beyond it? A rainbow can be a goal to be reached. Although, until that happens, going over or beyond the rainbow has no value.

With that clue, what do you think is my natural EpiWay?

Starting at the Center

Hello. My name is Donny, and **I am an Internal.**

This is not the only reason I chose to put the Internal chapter first. I chose to set the Internal chapter before the External for several reasons. In the first place, Internals want to read about themselves and others like them before they learn about anyone else. Internals are "self-ish" and self-centered first before bringing their best to others. After going within, they can proudly emerge caring about and making a difference for others. I know this is almost incomprehensible to Externals.

Another reason Internals are first described here is for Externals to see and be more likely to respect the opposite way of being—which perhaps might appear boring, seeming more closed or stuffy. Internals, in contrast to your less restrained and expanded sense of yourself, might seem like some alien being, and it is vital for Externals to know the flip side of humanity.

Another reason I placed this Internal chapter first is that it is consistent with our "Western" culture, personal development and psychology's direction. Find yourself, find those disassociated or fractured parts of yourself, and integrate them into your past and present. Know yourself. Love yourself. Focus on meeting your own needs. You are compelled to fix and love the part of yourself that is injured or wounded. Until you strengthen and make your "self" whole, you will never be whole.

The "Eastern" perspective is the exact opposite. It states that the development of the self or the ego which fuels the sense of a *me* inside here is the cause of all of our problems in life, and until one lets go of this *me*, they will never be whole. One must annihilate the ego, and release whatever they have accumulated or that they believe they are.

To self or not to self is really the question. And the answer is Yes. To self-first is natural for the Internal, as not to self-first is for the External.

An important distinction is that the self is always whole for Internals. There is nothing to fix, let go of, heal or solve. Instead, the self must grow more and not lose itself by being opposite its EpiWay. For Internals, the self must *grow* to include others **as part of, or as an extension of themselves.** While the External seeks to heal, repair or let go of "it"-self as it is imperfect or damaged, the Internal seeks to further grow, strengthen, transform or evolve what is already perceived as whole.

As an Internal, I will gladly, proudly and unabashedly speak about my **Way.** I love the word "unabashed," as it is such a perfect way to describe the nature of the Internal. **Unabashed** refers to being obvious and poised, not embarrassed, concealed or disguised.

This is my *Way*. I go inside myself and then expand outward. I "renew my springs," and then I show others, including you, how to bring this wisdom to yourselves.

The perspective of the Internal:

Your starting experience, when most energized and effective, is that you are a separate part of a larger whole. What you think about is part of you. Your journey is to find the larger universe entangled within you and to engage with it. Since "charity begins at home," acting locally while experiencing the connection to a larger circle is your superpower for influencing humanity.

For myself (and others in the Internal tribe), unless I experience you as part of who I am—part of my circle, I will find cracks in your perfection. As long as I am in my Internal EpiWay, and therefore at least Energy Rich, there is nothing I think, say, do, or create that is not blessed with the gift of enough-ness. Speaking from my Internalness, if you would just do as I do, think as I think, and organize life as I do, the world (which is everything *out there*) would be a better place.

This is NOT meant as an insult or to be less caring, it is just how Internals function. For moments, I can expand my sense of self to include more of the planet. Now, as I write this, I am experiencing you and all of the others who are part of my YOU-niverse. So, you are really cool, profound and great! You are part of my inner circle!

Once I have sustained and expanded the bubble of myself to increasingly larger circles, then I have to deflate the bubble and go within again and experience my Field. By centralizing or compressing my body and energy, I drink from the elixir of the creation of life—which holds all that was created long, long ago. This is yummy for me, as the past is my refuge. To me, it is always perfect—or when I remember it, I recall the lesson, the wisdom, the perfection in how it prepared me for now. Thereby, the drink is transformed into a divine elixir.

The waters within this elixir are ever-replenishing and never-ending, a quality Pearl S. Buck would surely appreciate. As an Internal, the flow of *my* spring of life is consistent with my E-State. If you give me a drink from *your* cup and it is "out there," then I might upchuck it, or it will taste vile.

Why? Glad you asked This is because anything I see as coming from outside myself—whether a bird's eye view or looking through another's eyes—loses energy. Therefore, my experience is less than pleasant drinking from your cup, and I no longer have enough energy to shine additional light upon others. I will then give a poorer meaning to the experience, but to maintain energetic status quo with me, you may lower your E-State to Low Energy Neutral. You are also likely to have distaste for the experience and for me.

I might think (if I did not already know what I am sharing with you) that it is about time we told those Externals to come down to earth, so they can be more grounded like us. I prefer that they take things more a step at a time while being with what we already know before going out on a "weird" tangent—like some multidimensional hallucinogenic trip. This had promised to be a simpler conversation. Oh gosh, why can't they be more like us?

As an Internal, You Most Likely:

- thrive on certainty before variety and stability before instability.
- prefer the time-tested and familiar before the novel.
- are most confident and happiest when life goes as planned.

- support the original intent or concept at the core of anything and seek to expand, deepen, understand, transform or evolve it.
- are surer about yourself and less confident in others.
- trust short-term plans and avoid long-term ones.
- wish to make an impact inspired by past victories, constructive experiences, understandings and wisdom gained.
- prolong making decisions that may rock the boat or bring you or others into a new way until you have relative certainty that the result will be consistent with your idea.
- are accepting and curious about new ideas or opportunities after you first consider your past and your past constructive habits, lessons, relationships and victories.
- want to start a book with the preface and introduction or want to know the history of the author and complete one chapter before scanning later ones.
- dislike when people seem to try to "unnecessarily" make things complex.
- tend to chunk things down to more bite-size pieces for relevancy to your existing way of seeing, doing and planning before adopting new ideas or expanding upon them.
- prefer to follow your pre-decided routine without interruption to enable change and be open to novelty.
- don't "get" how even years later people still allow past traumas or injuries to define themselves or seek to heal things that are already so done.
- find it painful to plan future events, as the uncertain future is a source of stress or fear.
- find refuge in your private small "cave," your past, or the long-term friends of your "inner circle" so that you can easily shift gears and deal with the complex.
- experience that the further out from your body you access an idea or action, the less it is liked, accepted or desired—unless it first starts from a familiar thread or basis.

Also, Internals Tend to Find That:

- charity first begins at home.
- you first think locally and then consider expanding to a larger circle.
- the practiced routine and established order must be acknowledged, even if only for a moment before any desired change is deemed relevant.
- following tradition and doing things the way they were done before, or at least referencing historical happenings, is essential before neural networks are open to change.
- believe that if others could simply see, understand, know, or experience what you do, their lives would be better.
- you are fine with the way you have been; the past was blessed with nothing to heal, let go of, correct or transform.
- even the most complex things have a small number of fundamental unifying aspects, moving parts or principles. When those are identified, the world has more meaning, everything flows and rapid transformation and awakening are available.

Gradations of Internal

Both EpiWays can be classified on a scale of one to three.

- **Number 1** appears to have the most minimal of their Internal EpiWay traits.
- **Number 2** represents most of the classical description of their Internal EpiWay traits.
- **Number 3** is an extreme caricature and expresses mostly all of the EpiWay traits with the greatest intensity and least relevancy to others. They are difficult to "find" or read as they are in their "own" bubble.

Consistent with this three-level grading system, where might you reside if in your Internal EpiWay?

Creating A New Future...from the Best of the Past

Internals are hungry to first further what they know and who or what they care about within their inner circles. When change or integration of new information is needed they first reference what they know or understand about themselves, their past agreements, and the original ideas that had led to past choices. Once they make something theirs—an idea, a way, a spouse, a friend, a lover or a business—they are secure, proud, energized, fully committed and more likely to be Energy Rich. Anyone or anything experienced in their inner circle or as part of their identity is treated as sacred with full commitment, protection and love. They can make rapid change once something or someone is theirs or part of them.

This chapter is about revealing and demystifying the direct experience of the *Way* of the Internal. The style of communication is consistent with how Internals think, learn, experience, manifest, and impact their lives and the world.

Externals, please experience this with us Internals. Your chapter will have a different *Way* and culture.

Where I Am

"Paradise is where I am."

—FRANÇOIS-MARIE AROUET (VOLTAIRE)

This was said by Voltaire, one of the most prolific writers and propagators of awakened wisdom in history. Although he passed on around the time of the American and French Revolutions, he was one of the lights of truth whose writings fueled the energetics and consciousness that inspired the social and political claiming of **MORE**. He is hailed as an Enlightenment master of the eighteenth century. Regardless of his true personal EpiWay, this statement reflects an Internal position to me.

Internal Donny is where I am because of the gifts given to me from my past encounters with those who held my hand, pushed me away, tested me or knowingly or unknowingly guided me. Some of these gifts I experienced as shame or rejection at the time helped shape me to become the person I am today.

I realize that paradise is here and a continuation of my constructive and guided past. Into this paradise, I take the energy of all who came before me and the collective prayers of humanity that were set into forward motion from the days in the Garden of Eden. This is the paradise that I choose to live in and radiate when I am Energy Rich. I purposely and in an *Unreasonable* and *Extraordinary* way pass this data Field and energy richness to YOU.

The future version of myself will carry some of the scent of what I have held sacred and true, the wisdom I have had, and the love I have lived, created and shared through my lifetime. From this perspective, I can consider the future for brief moments. If I want to guide the sails toward what can be beyond the ordinary, it is important that I consider the future. To do this, my recipe as an Internal is to first consider the continuum from a past Energy Rich with profound wisdom, experiences and understandings.

The Big Three Defining an Internal

The Big Three that define Internals when in their natural EpiWay are:

1. The origin of thoughts or experiences are from the Past—where the Internals gain their superpowers. When drawing from the Future, Internals experience loss, pain and a breakdown in their bodies, minds, spirits and influence.

   Summary: Past is great. Future sucks!

2. When the Direction of Information Flow in the Field is from the back toward the front of the body, Internals gain their superpowers. The further in the back of the body the information flow starts,

the more powerful, creative and successful they can become. The further forward from the body the data stream starts, the more there is loss, pain and breakdown.

Summary: Information flow from back to front is great. Flow from front to back sucks!

3. The direction one goes to in space to retrieve or create thoughts, memories, visions and roles determines and dictates the E-State. For Internals, the closer to the body or down toward the feet this resource is, the more powerful the result. The further out or up the body and into and through the Field, the more there is loss, pain and breakdown.

Summary: Closer to the body is great. Farther away sucks!

As you continue to read and experience this book, I suggest that you be conscious of your E-State and its impact on you and those around you. Repeat the practices offered through these pages as you discover if your authentic *Way* is as an Internal or External. As you seek to find your most effective EpiWay, keep in mind that focusing on what is most comfortable will likely amplify your chances of neutrality. This is in sharp contrast to assessing, which helps you and those around you to be more energized or have more lively, rich experiences. Where do you have more smiles and sense more freedom? When it comes to *Unreasonable* and *Extraordinary*, your degree of comfort is irrelevant. So much **MORE** is calling...

For the Internal, your next levels are never truly comfortable until you experience them as part of your reality. For the External, your prior and current levels are never comfortable. I invite you instead, regardless of your EpiWay, to adjust to a term other than comfortable. Please consider come-forth-able. **Come-forth-able is the calling of** *Creation's Codes* to organize you within the elegant majesty of this Next Tier of humanity.

WE HAVE AN OBSESSION TO GO BEYOND WHO WE HAVE BEEN.

The orientation that most connects you to the constructive and effortless manifestation of *Creation's Codes* is your authentic *Way*. Comfort is a false friend. Let come-forth be your guide.

The Energetics That Spawn Revolutions

As an Internal, I am intrigued and inspired by how things came to be and the shifts in consciousness from point A to point B. I continue to respect those whose shoulders we stand upon—those who were fueled by Energy Rich and Super Energy Rich states to help ignite a (r)evolution and liberate that which was bound into an evolving form.

Voltaire's influence inspired social, economic, political and spiritual outcomes for humanity led by the American and French revolutions. Before this time, revolution or even the concept of toppling the government, its systems, its philosophy structures was inconceivable.

Massively more energy was needed to significantly elevate the consciousness level that valued and rewarded social compliance through the rules and hierarchy at the time, and severely punished any breach in the status quo.

Anytime that there is a huge and critical gap between the haves and have nots of those who have greater access to energy, information and opportunities, the larger system will inspire breakdown or revolution to redistribute the energetic. The vision of Voltaire and like-minded contemporaries provided the free energy to spark the wildfire (both literally and figuratively) of massive change. What would be birthed would be a new set of values and ways of being through the launching of a more free and participatory populace.

As High Energy Neutral was becoming more available, the awareness of an imperative for a reorganization of cultural values spread through various cultures. The people who were unfulfilled and in hunger and pain were calling for the possibility of energy richness in humanity's Field. New values and thoughts would be launched that before would not even have been considered.

This was the birth of the possibility of self-determination for the masses and experiencing and respecting more than one perspective at once. The gap between present and the needed future for most was huge, more than any system could sustain. The larger system of humanity's Field of possibilities would no longer tolerate these energetics as **MORE** awaited. The only way to access more energy to upgrade consciousness beyond the centuries of the status quo was through massive force, violence and destruction. It would then take years for this to mature and become "a given" for a larger segment of the population unless of course we have access the Next Tier Energetics.

This is so very relevant to what we are seeing in today's world.

SEEKER'S CODE #1
WE KNOW THERE IS SO MUCH MORE TO LIFE THAN WHAT APPEARS AS PHYSICAL REALITY OR CIRCUMSTANCE.

SEEKER'S CODE #5
WE WISH TO ACCESS THE MULTIDIMENSIONAL ENERGETICS THAT MAGICALLY CREATE AND CONNECT US ALL.

Seekers, you know you can and MUST contribute to this Next Tier shift.

You can live more Energy Rich through the content and practices in this book. For higher-end Seekers, it is more than a can, or a will, or a should. It is a non-negotiable must. In order for this to engage, energy richness in your authentic EpiWay is necessary. For Internals, it requires us to take the best of who we have been and to invest our collective Energetic Capital in Next Tier manifestation to transform human values and systems in a reverent and evolutionary manner.

As an Internal, I am fueled by how creation from the past allows for gifts to be passed on into the future. Consistent with this, as an Internal, I honor Voltaire and his original surname Arouet. In my mind this allows me to receive more of the transmission from the informational Field before we were conditioned for less.

He was a prolific writer of the French Enlightenment—a historian, philosopher and so much more. He wrote more than 20,000 letters and 2,000 books and pamphlets and was one of the first authors to become renowned and commercially successful internationally. Think of the commitment this took at a time when all writings were made with a bird feather quill "pen" dipped into ink. With a well-prepared quill, one could get about seven or eight words in small script before dipping again. Beyond sheer brilliance, this was quite a feat requiring unbelievable tenacity and patience.

Reading about this to me is extremely exciting as I think about what it would be like if I were in his place. I consider the tenacity, focus, burning desire and available energy Arouet had to claim to make a difference in the world. This instantly fuels me. I sit straighter and recall other times in my life that I expressed such a state. This was one of the exercises that I engaged in as I began my preparation for this chapter.

Arouet was known for his French wit and for his criticism of all structures and systems that challenged personal freedoms and choice. He advocated separation of church and state, proclaimed the injustice of slavery in all forms, championed the right to free speech, and offered people a choice to take into the future. He most likely was an External communicating in an Internal society. He was one of the lights likely using the Next Tier energetic to fuel his vision for the advancement of the human condition through "liberté, égalité, fraternité"—or "liberty, equality, and fraternity." This concept requires multiple simultaneous perspectives and energy richness.

The Energetic Capital from the earlier visionaries and creatives was passed on in sacred trust for those who would bless it with their focused attention, tenacity and energy richness. As Internals, we take what has been, integrate it into who we are, and then transform it to help pass it on for humanity's future. This is my way. If you are an Internal, this is also your way.

Consistent with this, we look to history. We might wonder what happened in the years right after the American Revolution to know more about how we got to where we are today. Remember that for Internals, looking to see how constructive change happened from the perspective of a past timeline is energizing. Internals have a greater capacity to effectively access a wider data stream from past than can Externals. When I looked at this post-Revolution period, I discovered that there were fourteen presidents of the United States before George Washington. The fourteen included John Hancock, a signer of the Declaration of Independence, and other leaders through the turbulent and revolutionary times of the Continental Congress, which followed the War for Independence from the British monarchy. George Washington was the first president after the signing of the US Constitution.

As an Internal, experiencing new revelations about history serves as a tipping point into coherent and at least Energy Rich focused attention and manifestation. This more effortlessly builds momentum to help transform a more effective and powerful future for more than just myself.

"As we walk, all of our ancestors walk with us. As we dance, all of our ancestors dance the Sacred Dance. Each step that we place is an important one. All of our relatives are walking with us, speaking through us like the many colors of the rainbow. Listen, and you will hear their steps, their voices, their colors. Listen, and you will hear your spirit calling upon all our relations, and you will feel their energy...

"May we always keep our feet on Mother Earth, our eyes and minds above the treetops, our spirit with the Great Universal Spirit.

"And may we always walk with...a sense of humility, kindness, wonder and respect for all living things as we follow the sacred trail of those who have come before us and those yet to come."

—MICHAEL T. GARRETT, FROM *WALKING ON THE WIND:*
CHEROKEE TEACHINGS FOR HARMONY AND BALANCE

Externals, please hang "out there" with appreciation about how different this is from the way you experience and best respond in life. You likely wonder why we are looking at the past instead of moving into a better and different future. Knowing the qualities, gifts and limitations of both your EpiWay and that of the Internal transforms and liberates you into Next Tier energetics.

The Internal Psyche

Next, we meet Michael, who shows us the way of the Internal. His source of energy and its information potential for creation is sourced from his past. Michael once described to me that he felt that everything that was happening in both his and his wife Polina's life was because of the work they had done. Pleased with their lives, they believed the lessons that they had learned prepared them to arrive at their current sacred and victorious place. It was like they were at sea, riding waves that at times seemed perilous. This was all part of the journey, and it was all paying off. They reminisced that even the hardest times had challenged them individually and collectively to step up to **MORE**. They gratefully accepted the invitation.

They strived to grow, learn, and be the best they could both spiritually and emotionally. They shared that step by step, they were transforming themselves. For sure, they are Seekers at the highest level, what I call Seeker Leaders, and are part of the leading edge of Seeker-hood for this Next Tier of reality.

He felt secure to his core that they very soon would have a platform to help humanity in many positive ways. Three decades earlier, his Russian immigrant parents founded a manufacturing company. Michael proudly announced that he and Polina were taking over the company, and they could now make it into their own vision. Inspired by his parents, they would take his parents' legacy forward into the digital age.

He laughed as he told me all this. Leaning toward me, he said as if he were reading from a sacred text, "Donny, you know everything my wife and I have—and you and Jackie have—was made possible, at least in part, by what our parents and others invested in us? We are all so lucky."

Notice that there is coherence and an energy richness of declaratory statements where the past is a source of strength, wisdom and foundation. He referred to his family and his past heritage as resources. You now may recognize that is because their focused attention from the past with the vision and company they own (also a strength for Internals) is at least Energy Rich. Therefore this leads to *Creation's Codes* abundantly manifesting an energized **MORE**. Referencing gratitude for those whose shoulders we can proudly stand upon and continue with what they set in motion is classic of the Internal's superpowers.

Do you sense this? For the Internal, coherence is more centralized, and the energy and information stream is compressed inside and more along a central line in the body and Field, like the idling of a finely crafted automobile. For the External, it is more expansive, ethereal and spacious.

Michael and Polina were gratefully part of the continuum of his parents and added their own Internal vision and *Way* to a company. Progress and success started from the past.

Michael was connecting in some way to a river of energy and information flow that moves from the powerful past into the uncertain and Energy Neutral future. It was energized and newly potentiated by his EpiWay. Progress was experienced in increments, step by step, as the new information and experiences were effectively integrated into the past narrations and flow without charge or resentment. **There was nothing to react to, heal, let go of or forgive.**

This is quite a contrast to the External's *Way*. Likely Externals who are reading—yes, you, and all of your "yous"—wished to jump to the next chapter on Externals some pages ago, or wish to do so now. Please wait. Focusing on the Internals' modus operandi will help you both recognize and have a better understanding of your unique differences.

Challenges for the Internal EpiWay

One big challenge for Internals is taking advice or counsel from beyond the small group of people they consider part of their inner circle. Even within this sacred circle, the Internal is compelled to share his or her knowledge, perspectives, actions or plans before he hears from others. He first wants to hear thoughts and opinions consistent with his vision, as anything he considers is most often experienced under the umbrella of his existing and past centered self. Then he is ready for alternative or even opposing ideas.

Internals are the great interrupters. "Excuse me, did I tell you that Internals are great interrupters? What did you say before? Wait. I must know this before we go further." They must make what someone else is saying relevant to their way of seeing the world. They also must be consistent with their past experiences to truly be present with what the other person is saying and still be able to express their interest or love.

Along with starting with self and building out, Internals must process information from past streams of data before they can become aware of, acknowledge or accept anything that varies from what they already believe. This is because they seek certainty before uncertainty, and to move ahead in thought or action, they must be sure of something. Only then can they allow anything other than this to register.

This can lead to difficulties in relationships with Externals and be even more challenging for two Internals who have different opinions.

An Internal and External Go into a Bar

This sounds like a classic opening line for a joke. As you read the conversation that follows, simply recognize that the two parties have opposite EpiWays and are playing colliding apps. Nonetheless, it's humorous!

External Female: "Please stop at the post office today between the other errands on this list that we discussed."

Internal Male, after a pause: "The post office? You didn't tell me that earlier."

External Female: "I just remembered. Sorry. Regardless, please stop there and pick up a package."

Internal Male, reviewing his memory of the past conversation about the errands: "What package? I don't remember a package. When did you find out about it? Who is it from? Stopping at the post office was not on the list you gave me."

External Female: "I know this is the first I'm asking you about this. The package is a surprise that I thought I would be able to pick up for you."

For the External, this seems like going back to the past to prove that she was right and he was wrong for arguing. For the Internal, this is not arguing. It is getting the facts straight so that he can go back to the original time that this conversation or request was made and make his current mental and neuro circuitry coherent with this. If an Internal wants to change gears, it is necessary to go back in time and correct any variance with what is happening in the present moment.

Internal Male: "Great, now I know. I'll go to the post office and pick up the special surprise that you got for me. Sweetheart, thank you!"

As an Internal, I can respond well to change and make decisions very quickly. That said, for me to even hear that a change has been made or acknowledge it requires a five-step process. As an Internal, this has been my unconscious competency to adapt to and thrive in uncertain times and to learn, grow and flourish.

Now, as a conscious competence, I share these **Magic Five** steps for other Internals:

1. Did I hear of this before? Replay the situation and discover the purpose of the action being taken.
2. What was my understanding before and how did it come about?
3. Now, what are you telling me? Does it agree with my previous understanding or not?
4. Find something from the past that gives me the energy to switch gears and consider what is being said or suggested.
5. Be attentive and integrate this into what I know, acknowledge the change in course, and accept it.

For me, this takes only a few seconds.

This is my most successful strategy for assimilating ideas, thoughts or experiences that originate outside of my personal experience or comfort zone. If there is too much data, too many novel thoughts or what seems like a lack of congruence between the words spoken and the energetics, I must put my hand up to signal stop while I take these magical five steps.

Under these circumstances, if the "magic five" are ignored or forgotten, we Internals drop to neutral. When it seems that we are observing our dynamic from outside ourselves, we sense we are not enough—and for us Internals, this is "non-sense" reserved expressly for Externals!

When confronted with some seemingly foreign or "irrelevant futuristic babble" of an External, I may think, *Please shut the heck up, as I can't keep up with you or make sense of this. I need my certainty.* I feel lost and stupid, which only happens if I look back at myself through "your eyes" or consider the painful future potential ramifications of me not "getting it" now.

Because I skipped the magic five, I am Low Energy Neutral. Even if I could, I don't want to change anything. I decide that nothing needs to change for now or even in the future. Not even one more bit of information will be added to my brain and Field.

About Internals being interrupters, yes, this is how an Internal is wired. Instead of jumping a few steps ahead, the Internal goes back to the prior information stream to jump ahead with full readiness. The bigger the change or deviation from what he knows or remembers, the more intensely steps 1–5 must be implemented to be with the other's idea. These steps also defend against delegating change to something "out there" or "**in the future**." These are ways of reducing "stress" or judgment of others. It's the Internal process of adapting to novel ideas or too much data that is beyond or inconsistent with their existing experience, understanding or knowledge. It's a way to keep the information relevant and of value.

Internals also have the annoying habit of finishing your sentence or saying they got it when you have not even finished your statements. Why do you think they do this?

It is because they want certainty before variety. To achieve this, they first must truncate the data stream to explore it in pieces and see where it fits in their life and mental constructs. Then, they can listen further and decide if they will continue their relationship with the content.

Let's get real. Externals, your thoughts rarely ever end. You keep adding more complex streams of information to maintain your relative sanity and health.

The Internal's Warning Sign

The Internal will give you a clue that he is Energy Neutral and not capable of processing or integrating these foreign, novel streams of data. As I just mentioned, we Internals will raise our hands toward you as if to say, "stop" or "tell it to the hand." When coming from an Internal, an outward-facing hand is not a good sign. An External might see this as agreement or rapport, because this is how Externals access more. Believe me, it is not a good sign.

Likely the gesture subconsciously indicates where you are being experienced in the Internal's Field. By shrinking awareness to downsize the data stream, gain enough energy, and expend less, you are now outside the Internal's personal bubble. When you are moved even more externally, you will be experienced further away and might be moved from being irrelevant to being an adversary.

Here is an example of the Internal's process that a woman once shared with me.

> I have several projects that can change so much of the economic and political landscape. It gets overwhelming how many moving pieces have to come together. This freezes me at times. Reviewing my gifts and the vision I developed over the past twenty-eight years gives me the strength and wisdom to take a couple of steps ahead and delegate the parts that are a bit out there to others.

What is difficult or overwhelming for this Internal is the massive expansion of information and possibilities. A more concise organization of information is needed to make each element relevant to what she knows and who she was/is. She must go through the "magic five" steps first. This only works to re-engage if she is observing her life and narrating her awareness from within her Internal self. From this more resourceful center of her being, she must bring her wisdom and past success and victories of the last twenty-eight years into the step-by-step simplification and assessment of where she is now and what she wants to see happen next.

When you think of successful, victorious, romantic experiences and feel great, are you observing or thinking from within yourself looking out or outside yourself looking in? When you are thinking of painful or challenging times or conflict, are you thinking from inside or observing from outside?

When we view or interpret the roles which define us, the way we interpret failure, success, not-enoughness or enoughness is via our E-State. It is likely that she is experiencing not-enoughness in some roles as a business owner or as a visionary. When she thinks as a business owner, this may reflect a different E-State than when she acts or thinks as girlfriend, mother or wife. This will show up in how she functions, thinks and feels—and how productive she is able to become.

Remember, there are three factors that influence your EpiWay:

1. Is the direction of the information (data) flow that is interpreted as thoughts and reality from inside out or outside in?
2. Is the flow of information from the past or future?
3. Is the data stream accessed from close to or far from the body?

Knowing this, we can better understand this woman's EpiWay. Her Internal narrative suggests that the role making her overwhelmed and frozen is likely accessed or interpreted far from her body or "out there." Also, the information flow that is interpreted as a business owner is likely originating outside of her and moving in toward her body. She likely is focused upon failing in the future. This downsizes her thoughts and feelings and is her recipe for breakdown.

Knowing this, the solution is clear. She references from the past twenty-eight years to have enough energy and integrated wisdom to move ahead. Whatever is "out there" is moving to Energy Neutral and is best handled by Externals who can go there. Otherwise, she must once again become Energy Rich and use the "magic five" to approach such topics.

He Can Lose $50 Million in a Moment

An *extraordinary* man, humanitarian and philanthropist is the owner of an investment company. He managed billions of dollars in assets which he built up on his "own." He loved what he did and enjoyed making money for others using his genius, compassion and wisdom. He was brilliant at taking the wisdom he had in tracking past markets and world economic trends and integrating this wisdom into political and social trends in a unique and successful way.

When he considered how a momentary loss in his trading could impact the financial security of his clients, he got thrown way off course. With an unexpected shift in the market, his fund could lose $50 million in ten minutes. His pain was that many of those people who worked hard to deposit money in their retirement accounts could lose their future security.

When he saw the investments losing value, he imagined his clients' despair when he would have to report to them. Their loss and pain became his own. He said that it was like he was looking down on himself from a dark cloud. He could not see where he was or where he was going! He was caught up in the unknown of the future. If he had not seen this pattern in the past and did not know how he could successfully turn it around, then his very next trades could, as he described, "go up in smoke."

He reported that in those moments, his attention was no longer on where it might otherwise be focused. He focused upon the future lives of others and his future legacy for his life's mission going "up in smoke." Going up into the immaterial world is great for an External and toxic for the Internal. In his Internal Energy Rich state, he would make more gifted trades. Being aware of what he had to know and be in these moments could continue to define his success and legacy.

Focused on the pain of others as a consequence of his trading and on future trends, the skills of the External, and generally the poison for the Internal, he could not have access to his superpowers, residing in his past reference for success. He lost energy and made fewer effective choices when he used an External strategy for focusing upon others and how they were feeling with the loss. This was further compounded by his rehearsing the pain in the future.

With the changes politically, socially and economically at the time, he was at a loss for his known and practiced rules or economic trends to draw upon. He would have to find some other past success strategy for him to have more confidence and make more Energy Rich investments.

His mention of looking down from a dark cloud is a perfect metaphor for an Internal going externally and losing energy and light. How should he move when he is now outside of his authentic way? Yes, he should focus on his past successes and wisdom by looking for similar past patterns he is familiar with or must discover. The future without this goes UP in smoke, which means it goes "up and out"—the External's source of energy and the Internal's kryptonite. The Internal's superpowers are "down and in."

Love and Lovers

This Internal man shared his marital relationship/intimacy success strategy.

> When my wife gets upset, instead of trying to understand her feelings or what is upsetting her—which always leads to accelerating my judgment of her—I focus on how I can be more present with myself so I can be even more present with her. I show her that I care. Beyond all the details that she mentions, which are usually all over the place, I can come back to the love I have for her deep in my heart.
>
> I experience her as part of me, instead of seeing her outside of my thoughts. With a simple touch and focusing on my love for her, I experience her as part of me, and she turns back to where she has to be. Her challenge is over. I don't have to know what it is all about. I look

at her so she can see it in my eyes, and I just pull her over to me and squeeze her as she forgets what she was worried or upset about. It is up to me to center myself and everything around me.

This husband is sharing his strategy to show his Internal love for his wife and how he can help her when she is in a less resourceful state. Notice how many times he uses the term "I." Sense the energy richness transmitted in the Epi-spaces between the words and transmitted to you on these pages. He shared that his love for her is deep in his heart. Deep inside is where energy richness is accessed by the Internal.

Flipping Reality

Now you have a sense of the *Way* of the Internal. How they find their *HOME*, the language they speak, what turns them on, and how they feel, think, remember, manifest and impact one another are characteristic of their specific way of organizing energy, information, time, space and, therefore, reality!

It's time for us to expand in space, take a giant leap from a future world into another galaxy...the galaxy of the External EpiWay.

We'll go from the past and "Way" to the future and "Over the Rainbow."

For Externals, *HOME* is found beyond the beyond. Let's turn the page and enter an other-worldly existence between the trapeze bars of life...

CHAPTER 10

———

OVER THE RAINBOW

THE EXTERNAL

The movie *The Wizard of Oz*, kicks off with Dorothy Gale (played by Judy Garland) dealing with a threat to the life of her dog Toto. Once reunited with Toto, she wonders where there might be a safe place for her and her dog, breaking into one of the most famous and beloved songs of the twentieth century: "Over the Rainbow."

After the song, Dorothy decides it best to run away with Toto in search of that safe place.

Before she can be safe in a place where she can't get into any trouble, she must go on a wild journey, an epic adventure in the company of three new friends she meets along the way. Ultimately, their journey takes them to the Next Tier energetics—*the unbound—with massive resourcefulness.*

Where is the safe place in your mind that *YOU* go? Where do you go where troubles cannot find you—and, if they did, it wouldn't really matter? Is it up, up, and away—or is it deep down inside? If you know where, point to it right now.

You can choose the safe place more often. While that would keep you from being Energy Poor, it would at best be Energy Neutral and opposite your Way.

Now, let's take a different journey. Let's go to a space beyond the concept of asking, "Is this safe?"—beyond being curious as to where to go to manage your circumstances or your life. Beyond that place, a diffuse vapor-like space exists—an *unreasonable* space—the space of *extraordinary*. This is where the magic of **Creation's Codes** with Next Tier energetics engages us in whatever we are truly here for!

Like Dorothy and other Seekers, you are part of a community of souls embarking on a bold adventure.

Dorothy sings that when one goes far away over the rainbow, there is light, and troubles gently dissolve. For Externals like Dorothy, the more difficult states are experienced closer to the body and the ground. In contrast, the more resourceful and syntropic properties are found high up and away.

Notice how different Sinatra's message in "My Way" is from Dorothy's in "Over the Rainbow." Sense the difference in the bound or unbound energy and information as you read these lyrics or listen to these songs. Please listen to the songs, and if possible, watch these performances. You will get a greater sense of how these two EpiWays are galaxies apart in experience, information flow, and meaning.

Judy Garland dreamily relates the effortless, magical and so natural reality that exists up in the sky and beyond. And to show you how External her EpiWay is—going up to the rainbow is not enough—when you get "somewhere out there," you then go even farther.

Where did Dorothy find out about life over the rainbow? She discovered it in a lullaby.

Most Internals can't tolerate such transgressions from their bound and more real Earth-way. While reading through some of the descriptions that light up Externals, Internals might even roll their eyes. They seek adventures **below the rainbow that are grounded here on Earth**.

Trusting in the message or advice from a lullaby, wanting to go beyond the rainbow, or wishing upon a star lacks any sense of history, credibility, or the real here and now. Where the External gains energy and wonder is where the Internal loses it.

Dorothy sings about "someday," an open-ended non-committal time frame. Hearing this, an Internal response might be:

> *So you're telling me that someday in the future you will wish on a star or an undiscovered galaxy? And your dreams will come true? Come out of the clouds now and make it happen here with the resources you have.*

The musical score seemed to be flowing without bold borders. The lyrics were about a future vision with ethereal and expansive imaginary metaphors. This is a full about-face from the descriptions and metaphors used by Internals.

Dorothy reaches for up, up, and away as she watches the sky and sings about the birds flying. Then suddenly, **BAM**, there is the descent from grace when she mentions the only line in the song that is not declarative. She asks why she can't fly.

What do you think was the most likely reason for Dorothy's rapid drop from Energy Rich to Energy Neutral in the song?

I suppose that, for a moment, Dorothy was saddened. With a sudden awareness, her feet being on the ground, contrasted to the expansive flying she imagined a few seconds earlier while looking up at the bird, would have been enough to crash her E-State to Low Neutral. As she now experienced her being "grounded" in both altitude and energy state, her emotions and thoughts would instantly match this energetic strategy.

All doubt or worry is always borne from energy neutrality. For the External, doubts are about what the External cannot or did not do, feel, see or plan well enough. Or, the External is in the wrong place or time. When Neutral, Externals believe they are broken, lacking something or not enough. In contrast, when Internals are Neutral, they believe someone else is not enough, broken or lacking.

Dorothy is transported by a tornado and met by merry Munchkins who represent the playful, loving, innocent nature required for any spiritual adventure. Glinda, the Good Witch of the North, sets Dorothy on a path to follow the Yellow Brick Road to see the Wizard of Oz.

The direction of the North in spiritual teachings represents love and the connection needed for the evolution of the soul. Dorothy (a soul traveler with unrealized/bound potential) sets out on the Yellow Brick Road to find the wizard—who can help her find her way **HOME.**

A yellow road or Golden Path is referenced in Buddhist and Kabbalah ancient spiritual teachings. This road less traveled is meant to be a way to the experience and knowing of the oneness of creation—or what some call enlightenment.

When on the Golden Path, we have access to the unbound energy and information that appears magical in nature as we are also conscious of the bound, material path. The takeaway from this story is access to the unbound energetics of the Next Tier. It is when we move from the yellow brick road that we resort to First Tier energetics—where lack and acquiring mainly just for ourselves is ruling our lives. Along the road, Dorothy and Toto invite others to join them on the journey. The fellow journeymen are the Tin Man (likely representing the body), the Scarecrow (the mind), and the Lion (the spirit). It is Dorothy's passion for the promise of going **HOME** and taking all of the value she gains (Energetic Capital) from being on "the road" that creates the Field of unbound magic.

Dorothy was a Seeker that engaged her unlikely crew to a purpose bigger than each of their desires.

The Yellow Brick Road is a path to Energy Richness, from which the larger system can lead them to the *Unreasonable* and *Extraordinary* on the adventure of transformation and awakening. Super energy richness was ignited by the good witch's sparkle (light) blessing and her overseeing their experiential journey.

SEEKER'S CODE #4
WE WANT TO GIVE, GET, LEARN, AND LIVE WITH A
BIGGER PURPOSE/INSPIRING PROFOUND IMPACT.

SEEKER'S CODE #5
WE WISH TO ACCESS THE MULTIDIMENSIONAL ENERGETICS
THAT MAGICALLY CREATE AND CONNECT US ALL.

When in her authentic EpiWay, Dorothy's problems did not have to be avoided or solved, nor did those of her companions. Although each of them sought a missing resource, by the end of the movie, it was the unbound energy and information for greater resourcefulness that they received. The energetic synergy led to Energetic Capital that fueled the outcome of the journey.

Near the end of the movie, when Dorothy is ready to leave the land of Oz, she is told that no real effort was needed to be transported *HOME*. The possibility had existed all along. All she had to do was to remember, "There is no place like *HOME*," and act with this in mind. For Dorothy, the ritual of clicking her heels together activated *Creation's Codes*. If your authentic EpiWay is External, like Dorothy, a ritual such as the hand exercises in this book, knowing your EpiWay and E-State, and reaching up toward the future and the stars can take you there.

The questions for Externals are, Where is **HOME**? Where do you search for it? Her **HOME**, like other External Seekers, is a place out there from the future, coming toward your body.

It is not here but is between the bars. This cannot be seen from the current matrix or with ordinary eyes. It is in a future world that makes no sense to us here and now. It is in a world where Next Tier energetics makes most of what we think, do and live outdated. This **HOME** is your source—even while you live in a not-so-perfect or temporary house.

HOME is where magical manifestations happen as Dorothy and her companions follow the Golden Path. It is a place that you find when you are Energy Rich. When you're Super Energy Rich, your home has a spirit-centric participation with the cosmos. Perhaps this is a metaphor for your journey. Dorothy finds her true home over the rainbow, and then finally returns to her house with her family. This time, though, she is energized enough to bring the best qualities of her dream back as she awakens.

In 1939, *The Wizard of Oz* was touted as the first major motion picture in "Technicolor." Imagine how *extraordinary* such a color spectacle must have been to an audience living within a black-and-white matrix. When Dorothy returns to the farm from the colorful land of Oz, she is reunited with family and the characters on the path in her dream— only now viewed on the screen in black and white. To them, she never left her room. Dorothy enthusiastically remarks about this being her room with EVERYBODY here and that she is never leaving home again. She went to the full-color higher dimensions and brought the energy and information she gained there into the current black-and-white matrix of reality. I love this as a metaphor for making Energy Rich your **HOME**.

Dorothy was able to bring this higher vision, bigger worldview, with the magical forces of creation to her house and make it her **HOME**. This is the true journey of the External. She helped shift a black-and-white cultural Field into a new reality. This is what External Seekers must do in these interesting times—as Internal Seekers continue to refine the Yellow Brick Road and create the cultural and pragmatic means of making this shift.

When on the Golden Path, the journey to go over the rainbow in an Energy Rich or Super Rich state gives Dorothy and every External instant access to more of *Creation's Codes.* This brings the super-powers of external-ness into this fourth-dimensional bound world. With a high level of Energetic Capital in your Field, you can engage a diverse community of Seekers to upgrade the Field beyond the existing matrix. Your Field carries more light from higher dimensions into this dimension. Because of your abundance of available energy, greater bandwidth and more impactful code, you and others can more easily be in your own nature. Nothing else must be done, as *Creation's Codes* will create a force of attraction for whatever other resources are needed to support your greater resourcefulness.

You wake up from the concept world into actually experiencing *Creation's Codes* IN ACTION!

Changing the Past from the Future

As Externals, you can help change the past to lead us to the future that is your **HOME**. You may ask, "How is it possible—when the past is my kryptonite, my source of pain, neutrality and poorness—that I can actually *change the past*?" The reason the past is so painful for the External is that it is supposed to hurt to go there, as this is not their **HOME**. If you are an External, the future, higher dimensions, multiple realities and the space between the material and immaterial world is where your pillow awaits.

As an External, you may be starting to feel that your **HOME** is in the future. Your future life exists with a greater amount of energy and the wisdom to be gained by living in a world still foreign to us now. In the future, you will have gained novel understandings, experiences and access to this Next Tier. Now, you likely think there is still a big gap between the past as it has been and your cosmically promised future.

You may ask, "Donny, how can I transform the past?"

The answer is in quantum reality. It is the way every one of your electrons and subatomic particles moves in time and space and between the dimensions.

Externals, how valuable would it be for you if you could receive the download of who you are *in the future* and the information linking you to all possibilities *before* you collapsed the quantum Field with your Energy Neutral belief in only one objective reality? What would happen if you could look down from a bird's eye view of the future and find the **altitude** changing your **attitude**? What if you could reach your hands up and play with the energetic-information threads that connect us all, gathering the starlight, and dancing with the intangible quantum Field as if it was your lover?

What if you could influence others in an *Unreasonable* and *Extraordinary* seemingly magical way? And what if you jumped past having to transform anything and just beamed in a fueled version of you with *Creation's Codes*, inventing a new reality—one with greater bandwidth—transmitted from the outer edge of a wormhole in the cosmos? Externals, observe how it almost takes your breath away to drink in this possibility!

This is the pot of gold at the "bottom" of the rainbow (an Internal reference for me!) where the immaterial forces are transmuted into bound resources. You slide down the rainbow to the Earth, and now you have access to the treasure. While up on top, you had access to the unbound. Now, you have brought it into your life and gained gifts and information that were formerly unavailable. It's not a dream; it is a reality.

As a Seeker, Internal or External, you already know this. Those with

Internal Energy Rich and Super Rich EpiWays will build the road to this future from what Externals have been transmitting for all of us. No need for you Externals to know those boring or elusive **next steps**; the Internals have it. This is their pleasure.

This collaboration between the Internal and External agencies of creation is available in energy richness. Once you Externals come down from above and touch the juncture between the bound and unbound, you become more relevant to Internals.

Remember, things are difficult and painful in life when you are opposing the way your energy and information systems are designed. When you follow your authentic EpiWay, there is more coherent abundant energy with more constructive information that collaborates for the benefit of all.

A Misplaced Reality

Externals, you likely sense that you were born into the wrong family, the wrong town or at the wrong time. You are not like others that on the surface appear like you. You seem to know or see things that others do not. When your parents told you to stop talking to imaginary friends, you argued that they were not imaginary—or instead just continued to have private conversations with them.

You wanted to fit in, and the rules just did not make sense.

When your teacher asked you what you wanted to be when you grew up, you gave wildly varied answers that would require totally different or opposite skills or objectives—like "an astronaut, a musician, a doctor, or maybe a rock star or the owner of an ice cream parlor." Somehow, you could not settle on just one thing or person as something else was always calling you. When you attempted to fit into the existing family, social group, business or team, somehow life often threw you out. You kept feeling that you did not belong nearly anywhere. AND you don't!

Did I say you don't belong? Perhaps you wished I did not say that, as this is one of your greatest fears. And, you know it is true. How many times have you felt that since childhood?

It is said to be uncomfortable or painful whenever you try to fit a multi-dimensional round peg into a square three-dimensional box. In order to do this, you have to eliminate some of the best parts of you that simply don't fit here or now. It hurts because you belong in an upgraded, larger seat with ample room for all of your dimensions. To fit, you have to squeeze your energetic torso into an economy seat and ooze past the hand rests of those passengers on both sides of you who resent your spilling into their comfort zones.

This is because your true *HOME* is in the future and far away from the cultural and social matrix of today's world. Your *HOME* is where you are energetically creating, healing and engaging in intimacy, business, finances and relationships—for more than just you.

The Big Three that Define an External

The Big Three that define Externals when in their natural EpiWay:

1. When the origin of thoughts or experiences are **from the future**, Externals gain their superpowers. When drawing from past thoughts or memories, Externals experience loss, pain and break-down in their bodies, minds, spirits, and their impact on the world and others.

   Summary: The future is great. Flow from the past sucks (energy)!

2. When the **Direction of Information Flow** in the Field is from **the front toward the back** of the body, Externals gain their super-powers. The further in front of their bodies the information flow begins, the more powerful, creative and successful they can become. The closer toward the back of the body the data stream

has its origin, the more there is loss, pain and breakdown in the body, mind, spirit and impact.

Summary: Information flow from front to back is great. Flow from the back to the front sucks (energy)!

3. **Where one goes in space to retrieve** or create thoughts, memories, visions and roles determines and dictates the E-State. When this place is accessed from above or in front of the body, the External gains superpowers. The further out and above in the Field the resource is, the more powerful the result. The closer to the body or farther down toward the feet one goes, the more there is loss, pain and breakdown in the body, mind, spirit and influence.

Summary: When an experience, memory, thought or role is experienced far up and away from the body, life is great. When it is experienced close to or inside the body, it sucks (energy)!

Not-Enoughness in a World of *MORE*

Externals never believe they are enough for more than moments. They are more often powered by others first; therefore, they perceive themselves, not others, as the source of the difficulty. They tend to trust a larger group of people farther away or less known to them. If you are External, you tend to avoid simplification and truncating thoughts or ideas. You prefer to see the interconnectedness of things and people. You tend to seek out *unreasonable* complexity. You believe you must improve, fix or heal yourself before you can help others.

This never works, and you dig deeper into the past for reasons why your efforts have not yet succeeded. You can help everyone else but yourself. You believe that others are better than you.

Everything I mentioned here about Externals not being enough is the opposite for Internals. Internals are powered by themselves and bring the success of who they are to the world. Externals model others and look outside of themselves for the information and energy flow that can help them improve upon what they were given.

This is because, for Externals, **HOME** is generally outside of themselves. They are powered by helping others achieve, create and attract what Externals feel is lacking in themselves. If you help others to have greater access to whatever you feel is missing for yourself, those Energy Neutral thoughts and desires disappear, and you will often find yourself Energy Rich!

As an energized External, a given is your knowing that you are part of everyone else's world. Your journey is to find your sense of self while entangled as one with the universe. Living globally and acting locally is a gift you bring to humanity. Externals thrive on extrospection. This is the observation of things and thoughts from a vantage point outside and beyond yourself. You can be observing a forest from the sunlight shining through the canopy of the trees, or as if you were a butterfly drinking the nectar from a flowering plant.

As an External You Likely:

- thrive on variety, adventure and whatever is most novel.
- want **MORE** beyond the beyond, above the above.
- wish to live big and make a huge impact.
- prolong making decisions that lock you into anything or anyone.
- seek the engagement more than the marriage because it is more exciting—as is the pregnancy over being a mother and the dream over the reality. When you get what you've dreamed, you're on to the next dream of something more.
- are more energized by a novel lover than a familiar spouse.
- are addicted to seeking, not necessarily getting.
- want to start at the later chapters in the novel.
- want access to more than ownership.
- see people as better than they are and are disappointed when they do not meet your expectations.
- dislike when people try to make things simple.

- spend years and heaps of money to fix, understand and accept yourself.
- want to expand beyond what others see as boundaries.
- experience a loss of expansiveness, contracting before messing up.
- strive to let go of past baggage or traumas.
- believe that traumatic memories are stored deep inside of you.
- want to heal past generational patterns that are holding you back.

Also, Externals Tend to Smile or Laugh in Recognition That:

- being the best in your town is not enough. It must be the state, and then the country. If you reach that, it becomes the world, the solar system, the galaxy, the universe, the multiverse, and on and on.
- routine, sameness, and the established order drain energy. Following tradition and doing things the way they were done before, or referencing historical happenings, are at best boring and at worst irrelevant, very painful or dangerous.
- searching has more energy than having. Once something is yours, you will either grow tired of it and intentionally lose it, or the larger system will separate it from you as the force of attraction is gone.
- if you have a disease, it is a complex one, or one that no one really understands. In some perverse way, this moves you from Low to High Energy Neutral as you are outside the bell curve.

Gradations of External

As with the Internal, the External EpiWay can be classified on a scale from one to three.

- **Number 1** appears to have the least expression of External EpiWay traits.
- **Number 2** represents the classical description of External EpiWay traits.
- **Number 3** is an extreme caricature—expressing mostly all of the

External EpiWay traits, with the greatest intensity and least relevancy to others. They have difficulty relating to the current time/space frame of reference or having pragmatic involvement in the world.

The Effect Comes before the Cause

Externals, at all levels, are hungry to fly someplace far away, take a new lover, switch careers, or redecorate the house just when they have finally settled IN. At night, they may ask their lovers, "Where do you want to take me tonight? Let's go someplace far away, where we have never been before and make love between the stars."

One of my friends was a #3 External. "Out there" was her recreational "drug of choice." She had three children with three different fathers, was always a single mother, the life of the party—and was totally unsettled in her life. While she could see answers for others, she could not for her own life. At a certain point in her life, she was told she had a rare cancer that was diagnosed in only a few dozen people in the world. The doctor who was the international expert on this relatively "new condition" told her that with surgery and chemotherapy, there was a 27 percent survival rate.

Surprisingly, instead of being anxious, fearful or depressed, she became more upbeat and excited. Her pain level also reduced. As an extreme External, she felt better and more comfortable with her prognosis. She shared with people how much of an outlier she was. She proudly boasted that it was a rare condition, and that she was not "normal."

She shared that with this complex disease, no one except her specialist really understood her condition as he was one of the two top experts in these cases. She was looking forward to the experimental treatment and the future adventure awaiting her. She believed that she would be the one who defied the survival statistics. For Externals, the rarer, further outside the box, and more complicated something is, the more they can move from Low Energy Neutral to High Neutral.

As an Internal, if someone told me that I had needed a rare treatment with only a 27 percent survival rate, I would get another opinion. Since the placebo effect—where an inert substance activates a healing response—can be as high as 80 percent, this means that the results of the rare treatment might be much worse than a placebo. I would seek a longer track record of success first. With a newly discovered condition, I would want to know from which existing conditions this might be a variant before accepting that it was a totally new disease. This is the opposite of the External's thought process.

A fascinating lab experiment found that the night before rodents were to run a maze for the first time, they were already activating the muscle groups specific for the maze they were to experience the next day. While they could not read the researcher's plans for them, they were still rehearsing the motor movements. The *effect* was the running of the maze, and a *cause* for running it effectively happened the night before.

Externals, let's pause and allow this to percolate. This is the reverse of how our minds function and what our conditioning would suggest. It is as if your present life is a rehearsal for who you are in a connected future. Every time you are stuck in the past, you get further from that future you.

We learn that every cause has an effect, and every effect has a cause. This is too simplistic. There is more than one cause and more than one effect, and either can be from the past or the future.

Imagine what it would be like if the effect that called you to live in the future had already happened, while you were looking to make a breakthrough you have already made in the future? And what if the higher, more constructive outcome could be called into your present—fueled by an abundance of unbound energy in the future? What if your reality could contain a wider range of information that was instantly yours?

On a particular day, you are rather neutral and off your game. Before leaving home, you spill coffee on your vest, and since your departure is delayed, you change into a new set of clothes. Subsequently, leaving home for work later than usual, you take a timesaving route to ensure you will arrive five minutes early.

As "luck" would have it, you arrive thirty minutes late after being stuck behind a flipped tractor trailer. This was your third late arrival that week, and you were terminated from the company.

While it may have seemed like a terrible loss at the time, it put you on a path that led you to taking a new training and getting a dream position in a strong socially responsible organization. This was always something you wanted. You just would not have taken the risk to make it happen.

Perhaps this was the effect that was calling you—leading you to arrive late that fateful day and bringing you to a significantly better destiny. The you with your future Field was experiencing the effect that sent a cause back in time to redirect you. Externals are at their best when they embrace retro-causality.

In this scenario, you might not have any conscious awareness of the future effect other than sensing a calling for **MORE**.

How often do you have a sense you should take a different path and know it is right? This is often hard to describe or explain. The data stream of information that is interpreted to be efficient, effective and necessary for your life's impact very often bypasses access to your conscious awareness where it could get stuck when Energy Neutral.

That part of your information processing system gives you subtle cues to direct you toward your future reality. This could be as simple as a seemingly random decision to take a different route to work—or choosing to have coffee before you leave for work instead of waiting until you arrive there. *Creation's Codes* organize more of our collective realities than our minds could ever comprehend.

Your Future Calls in a Familiar Way

Imagine you had a cousin that you had a "falling in" with (a "falling out" would be a term for an Internal as "out" loses energy and feels bad) years ago. Your father and her father got into an argument, and somehow, your friendship was severed as well. For years you didn't speak. Then, in the midst of an intense project, your cousin comes to mind.

Flashbacks about your relationship interrupt your focus at work. You remember when you were best friends. And somehow, as if remembered from a future when this will be true again, you are filled with light and get the warm fuzzies. You repress the thought, burying it inside, but the hunger to speak with this cousin snaps you back into that thought like a rubber band.

It makes no sense to contact her, as you have such a tight deadline for your project, and there is "bad family blood" between you. Even though you really never questioned why or what you could do about it, you accepted that you should stay away from her.

As the sense that something is pinging you and requiring you to connect again, you pull out your emergency chocolate and gobble it down before you even realize it. As you chew up the last bite, you search for her on social media and spend a half hour checking out her posts and pictures with a sense of excitement about what it might be like to hang with her. Finally, you dash off a private message to her that simply says, "Hi Cuz," along with your number. Then, almost on impulse, you add, "It's time we reconnected."

As you write this message, it is like there is a time warp, and your mind is already merged with hers from some other time/space. A day later, you are speaking with her on the phone for over an hour. It turns out, her father is in the hospital, and she has been staying there with him. You find yourself looking from your present time back, wistfully reminiscing about the times you had together and wondering who she has become. As in a dream, time is disjointed.

After the call, you do something very atypical. You cancel an important meeting and book a plane ticket to go visit your cousin. On the way to the airport, the narrator inside your head asks you, "What are you doing, little girl?" You hear your father's authoritative "my way or the highway" drill sergeant voice. This alternates with the current or maybe future you knowing something is calling you to reconnect to your cousin as an adult. That calling is letting you know that finally you are doing the **Unreasonable** that could lead to the **Extraordinary**. Who will win out? The little girl or the grown woman?

You board the plane. You are elated that you are about to *fly up, up, and away* into an *unknown adventure*, something thrilling to the External. The words up and up and the experience of away brings you to an Energy Rich state.

Shortly after you take your seat on the plane, the flight attendant announces you must place your seat back up. You think that "back up" makes no sense, as "back up" is an oxymoron. You push the button on the armrest, and the seat stays back and does not move up (which really means forward). Why didn't the attendant say to place your seat in the most forward and erect position? You reach overhead, ringing for the flight attendant to notify her of your crisis. Back-up, up-back, past-future, future-past—it doesn't make any sense to you. You feel a bit disorientated. You then notice that you have been seated in between two very large people whose arms were entering your personal space. You hit the call button again.

Trapped by the thoughts in your head, it seems like you've been on this plane forever, although it has only been about ten seconds since you first pushed the call button. You rub, while digging your nails into your forehead, abusing the skin to let the thoughts out and hoping you feel less caged by them. This sense of constriction activates a primal fear, as it reminds you of traumatic events in your past when you felt constricted by large powerful authority figures.

The flight attendant rushes to you as the cabin door closes. Your seat is still reclined. Your default is to listen to authority. Now, you cannot comply, and it truly is not your fault. You feel too closed in. The flight attendant tells you that you must put your seat back up as it must be upright for take-off.

Excusing herself, she pushes your seat button while struggling to pull the seat forward, to no avail. With a sigh of incredulity, as if she had expected the seat to catapult into an upright position, she mumbles and runs off.

She quickly returns to tell you that she is upgrading you (obviously a sign from the divine) to First Class. Another flight attendant takes your overhead bags, moves them to the storage space above your plush, spacious seat at the front of the plane and asks if you would like some champagne.

"Yes! Yes!" you call out while giving a high five toward the heavens—with that somewhat otherworldly sense of a break in time that has demanded you interrupt your work timelines to call your cousin. Somehow you are in a strange but familiar space or dimension between thoughts. Truly, you are in an External mode now, down-loading data streams from your future. You recognize that somehow something is guiding you. It is taking care of you, and you can trust in that sensation and where it came from. This is a flash of Super Energy Rich.

A couple of hours into the flight, the person next to you "accidentally" spills some food on your sweater. He apologizes, the mess is cleaned, and he begins a conversation. Your plane mate is going on a job inter-view and "coincidentally" staying at the same hotel as you. What would seem like a coincidence to a non-Seeker is a "but of course" to you. Seeker, your seatmate just so happens to have the exact skills required for the project you interrupted in order to connect with your cousin. He agrees to work with you on the project after you get back.

Pay Attention to the Calling

You call to meet with your cousin. Hearing that her father, your uncle, is still ill, you head to the hospital. In the hospital room, your jaw drops. The nurse looks a lot like the person you met on the plane. While you are shocked by the resemblance, the nurse's twin stops by to bring the nurse a package. The twin is the very man you chatted with in first class. You all laugh at the timing. You recognize that, for sure, you are being guided to a future that is calling you.

Now you look at your new friend with more of an interest in why your life is lining up like this. Something speaks to you from a place far away that says, "Pay attention." It seems to be coming from the same place in your Field where the image of your cousin first appeared. You followed that calling and got "upgraded."

When you look at this new work and life friend, some further recognition happens. With a twinge of fascination and excitement, you recognize some magnetic attraction in the Field between you. You recognize even more that some larger electromagnetic force is gathering you and others, putting all of you wherever you belong for something bigger.

As you think this may be your new future somebody, he smiles. He looks up to the ceiling with his hand up in an expression you interpret as surrendering to something else, then he and you giggle at the same time. He winks and you mouth the words "Of course."

Later that night, you are sitting with your cousin and at the very next table in the hotel restaurant is the nurse and your new friend. The friend jokes that you need not worry, he won't spill anything on you again. It seems like you are in some alternate reality where different possibilities are simultaneously happening. All you have to do while in an Energy Rich or Super Rich state is choose which stream will carry you to a bigger, more impactful life.

The Larger System Reorganizes from the Future

The next day, at the hospital, your uncle expresses gratitude for your visit and for your questions about the family's history. As an External, while looking at the past from the past is a recipe of pain and break-down, looking from the future into the past blesses it and those you think about.

Since you are curiously looking at the past from current time, which is "ahead" of the past, it grabs your interest. You suggest to your cousin that this guy you heard about, Donny Epstein, may be able to help her and your uncle.

Too quickly, it is time to head back home. After such a great meeting with your family, you cannot even remember why you had chosen to stop speaking to your cousin.

Months later, your cousin attends an event with Donny and exchanges her life for a more productive, vital and fulfilled one in service to others. This effect had already happened in the future, which was the source of the data stream that led you to think about, call and visit your cousin. The timing was organized by *Creation's Codes* and quantum entanglement, which made the source of the past family fracture irrelevant. True soulful intimacy replaced the lower neutral blame-shame-reject game.

Even telling her about this Donny guy was all part of the CAUSE called forth from a higher future destiny to lead to a new energized reality. Why is all of this lining up without even the thought of working on relationships, healing or any other outcome? We don't have to know why. We do have to, in faith, comply with the strings being pulled in our life from the synergy of Energy Rich and quantum entanglement. This will allow the future to evolve through our participation with one another and the ripples we make in the Field of humanity. This way, we can be part of the cause that graciously brings us to the future calling.

Months after your cousin's life transforms with the methods of that Donny guy, you and your friend/work collaborator from the plane become more than friends. A year later, you are married soulmates, inspired by a vision you both have always sensed. In your prior Low Energy Neutral state, it made no sense. It only makes sense when you are both in your natural EpiWays.

You recognize now that everything from your future—be it intimate partner, business connection, healing solutions and **MORE**—can only find you when you are at least Energy Rich, claiming your authentic EpiWay and being able to receive the information flow from your future.

You now know that you were being driven by Seeker's Code #5.

SEEKER'S CODE #5
WE WISH TO ACCESS THE MULTIDIMENSIONAL ENERGETICS THAT MAGICALLY CREATE AND CONNECT US ALL.

Seekers will recognize this type of alignment in increasing frequency and profundity as a function of their higher E-State. It becomes more frequent and apparent as you contribute energetic capital to your and humanity's Fields.

The Hebrew commandment of *"Tikkun Olam"*—"repair the world"—is a calling for each of us to go beyond doing good in the world. It is a call to repair, help transform or bring the world into its righteous order. I see this as recognizing, honoring and and seeking to enhance the expression and manifestation of the sacred codes of creation. **It is said that while we are not obliged to finish the task, we are not allowed to abandon it!** Seekers know this as part of their raison d'etre (reason for being). Externals, you are listening to a double calling, that of the Seeker and that of the External. Your contract with *Creation's Codes* is codified in the future and your calling to be manifested in your "current" four-dimensional life.

Awareness of the Future's Calling Ignites a New Life for Externals

Consider for a moment the magnitude of bandwidth and the amount of available energy required for the organizing wisdom of life to precisely weave each of the quantum strings to create this reality. If any one circumstance did not occur, then you and many others would be living in a different life.

For Internals, the organizing wisdom and the threads of connection are within you and extend out to hers. For Externals, you are part of and within the threads of connection within the cosmos.

When you're Energy Neutral, this can all seem impossible. This is another example of *Creation's Codes* and how when Energy Rich, for even a moment, the Field synergy happens. If Super Rich, the quantum entanglement is set into motion, gathering "stars" (others) for whatever is needed for the larger system.

Awareness of the future calling is what begins the process for the External, and the predetermined mission for the Internal is what puts it in a different game in life—one that is definitely *Unreasonable* and *Extraordinary*.

Ellen's Transformation, Finding Her External EpiWay

In Chapter 4, we met Ellen as she transformed from Low Energy Neutral to Energy Rich. As a reminder, this is how she initially described her experience:

> I am a sexual abuse survivor. I have been sober for fifteen years. My neck hurts from a car accident where a drunk driver side swiped me four years ago. I am in psychotherapy for my PTSD. It is generally under control, and I have night terrors. My ex-husband stole from my accounts, pretty much taking everything from me.

Besides being Low Energy Neutral in her first comment, you can now understand so much more about Ellen, as her EpiWay is becoming apparent. Every statement Ellen makes defines her as a continuation of past trauma, and in each case, she has been a victim. Obviously, Low Neutral and drawing on her data stream from the past would suggest that the past is not her ideal way of organizing her world. It would seem that she has an External EpiWay and is living as an Internal. This is evident considering the painful meanings and recurring attraction strategies in her life. She is also using First Tier energetics that require being ripped open to liberate more energy.

What do you now discern as being different in Ellen when she later wrote:

> I am finding my way in life. Opportunities for new friendships and maybe even a new lover are developing.

For her to have made this radically different statement, the Ellen observing and interacting with life must be accessing a more energized information flow. This Ellen is no longer experiencing herself as a victim of the past. Instead, she is experiencing her observer and narrator of life drawing a larger data stream further from her body. She is also looking to or from the future. To find opportunities, there must be more unbound energy and information. And since new friendships are developing, she must have at least touched Energy Rich, as it has already been happening. For sure, this Ellen is in her authentic EpiWay.

> I switched from a talking therapist to a body-centered (somatic) therapist so that I can be more connected to my body, which is no longer a trap for me.

Her body sense has been transformed. Since she is no longer experiencing her world from inside, the past is no longer a trap. Her information flow and energy are flowing from outside in—classical for an External. Before, she was seeking less, and she got less life as a pseudo-Internal. Now, she is seeking *MORE*, which is essential for a Seeker.

> I am taking courses to prepare for a leadership position in the human resources department at work.

Ellen has made the transformation from a helpless victim where everything was taken from her to a leader. Her focus went from her internal self to a focus on helping people. She went from a lack of resources—such as energy, respect, dignity and vitality—to advancing human resourcefulness—a Next Tier energetic.

Ellen completed her comments, letting me know:

> Oh, at times, my neck hurts, and sometimes I feel anxious. I am riding it to wherever it takes me, and Donny, please know that I am well.

Ellen no longer experiences her "sense" or awareness of her body in the same dark place as victim, masculine energy and pain. Therefore, she may hurt at times, but it is no longer linked to the past trauma. Sometimes she becomes anxious when she becomes Energy Neutral and opposite her EpiWay. When at a baseline of at least High Energy Neutral, her former low neutral identity from when she was living internally is vaporized. Since the information flow is likely more connected to more energized data streams, she plays the apps that trigger curiosity and faith, knowing that she is being taken by *Creation's Codes*. She communicates with more expansion and is experiencing the Field.

The authentic External E-State has transformed her experience of what was considered to be her post-traumatic stress disorder. Her condition was experienced when she was at the border of Energy Poor and Low Energy Neutral states and when she had been living Internally with an information flow from her past. Her nervous system played the apps to represent the limited data streams of that level of energy, downsizing her participation in the novelty of life. Now, she demonstrates more than *post-traumatic growth*. She no longer identifies with the prior pattern expressed as a function of her lower E-State when opposite her EpiWay. She now lives a more energetically exchanged life with different apps organized by **Creation's Codes**.

Rather than attempting to fix, transform or change her prior self, she now has exchanged into a different person defined by her newly designed information processing system and her Field—all by simply discovering and accessing her External **Way**!

A caveat: None of this is meant as the diagnosis or treatment of any condition. Instead, it is about discovering, experiencing and getting to know and, more often, living consistent with your energetic nature. Notice the relationship between her energetic difference and the difference in her perceptions of life and reality.

Congratulations, Ellen!

Causation Has Its Limits

"Science is all about cause. Now, if really everything is connected to everything, if there really is only a oneness, everything then affects everything, and the whole idea of causality has to be revised."

—WILLIS HARMAN

Be it in business, relationships, finances or impacting humanity, when an External looks to the past for a cause, it is always a never-ending cycle of staying in the matrix. In Energy Rich, identifying a problem becomes obsolete because when you're Energy Rich in your EpiWay, there are only opportunities.

Someone told me this:

> I became a mother at the same age as my grandmother, my mother and my aunt. I felt a lack of love in my childhood, just like my grandmother.

What can you tell me about her from what she shared?

She was placing causation on her family lineage. When Neutral, Externals want to identify past causation, which creates Energy Neutral thoughts supporting loops of energy neutrality. She must claim *extraordinary*, or her cultural Field matrix will continue this lineage. For those of you who have difficulty learning some new theory or, at times, do not think you are smart, you may find this quote and my commentary helpful:

An adult man gave me his Energy Neutral reason why he could not jump into an educational training course in Astrophotography that would transform his life situation and path.

> Being a student is tough for me. It's related to the negative reinforcement I received from my family during grammar school, high school, and college.

We can tell that his negative sense of himself as a student comes when he looks for a cause from the past. This means he is Energy Neutral when he sees himself as a student. When Neutral, Externals are always unconsciously looking for past cultural stories to match their energetics and maintain the status quo. As a consequence of the energetics that led to this belief, many years of learning, wisdom and opportunities in life were likely missed.

Let's look at the same person after he had his hands up in the air and observed himself from the sky, watching me converse with him. I asked him to tell me about his learning from a perspective ten years in the future. He took a deep breath, wiggled his back, expanded his chest, and proudly confirmed, "I am a genius, and I know it. I haven't yet found out in what area that I am smart. I love to look through a telescope and take pictures." He laughed and said, "Maybe my future genius will come through the stars as I document them in photos." This dramatic energetic exchange to a different version took about ten seconds! In that time, he shifted from Internal, at least temporarily, to External—and from Low Energy Neutral to Energy Rich. Externals, this is simpler than you might want it to be when you are Neutral—as you may want to keep believing the story that keeps you Neutral. The gift in taking the leap forward is that you will be able to hear your future calling and get on target for a greater legacy.

Externals, you cannot easily learn, remember or apply what you have been taught if you seek to add new ways or information into what you already know. Instead, you must jump into the new way—inspiring your old way to simply change.

When Opposite Your EpiWay and Neutral

Externals, when you are opposite your EpiWay, these are your experiences:

- You believe that something from the past is the cause of your problems, limits you or holds you back.
- You want to let go, heal or forgive something that only exists when you are in an Internal *Way*. You keep "working on it" from inside.
- Finding your place in the world never works. You do not live in material places. You live in the space between the places, the space between the words, between the expected, between and beyond thoughts, intentions and what others call reality.
- Your hands face your body when living an Internal Energy Neutral illusion. It requires effort to further bind energy, information and reality for no real change. You grab information and energy sources that are depleted and barely available.
- When choosing to be alone, you are generally Low Neutral.
- You doubt yourself. You attempt to fix yourself or solve your not-enoughness and often look where the energy is not—such as deep inside, in your heart or your inner soul—which keeps you busy, Neutral, and owned by the matrix.
- You are on a never-ending quest to love, trust, understand or feel better about an inner sense of self.
- You point to your head with your hand facing in or hold your head

when you don't understand. You touch your heart and say, "I know this is true" or "I love you" when Neutral.

- You want to attract a partner, lover or spouse from inside or compare them to your past experiences. You want to set rules on what they are meant to be from the past or inside.
- You want to attract clients, a new business or more money from out there, while you are inside looking out for them.
- You measure progress from where you have been.
- You believe that there are traumatic memories stored in your body that you must release or heal.
- You try to do things by yourself and say no to being in community.
- You have difficulty learning a new idea or skill, as you look to integrate the new knowledge into what you already know.

The External's Warning Sign

Just like Internals, Externals will give you a clue about their energy state. An External will curl inward, with their neck bent forward and their head looking downward. The chin will be positioned toward the chest, with the spine arching forward into a C-shape.

As far as Externals' hands go, they will face their bodies, likely holding the head, chest or throat. They are likely not revealing anything to you as they are centralized—having the energy and information flow compressed in the center of their bodies. Not enough energy is available to know what is going on or to communicate it to you. Other than experiencing massive distress and energy loss, in this scenario the External is bound in the past, with access to truncated data very close by and moving from the body outward. Sensing failure and not-enoughness, it is too difficult to articulate anything of value. In quiet desperation, the desire is to fold into a ball and go into a hell cave.

Does this sound like you when life is most difficult? Who else does this give you a clue about?

"Your soul is infinitely creative. It is alive and expansive in nature. It is curious and playful, changing with the tides of time."

—DEBBIE FORD

This wonderful statement is the brand of the External. More than your soul, all of you—all thousands of versions of you existing in multiple dimensions and parallel existence—are alive and tend to expand first before you contract to compress and direct the light for these dimensions. You change with the tides of the time, fueled by your future's greater reality.

The tides are different from a singular tide. Externals—and especially External Seekers—are attuned to multiple, overlapping, intersecting and traveling tides of possibilities.

Like with every-thing and no-thing else, Externals live outside of the bound universe and have access to reality, at times, way beyond the capacity of current thought and expected information processing.

"If you want happiness for an hour—take a nap. If you want happiness for a day—go fishing. If you want happiness for a year—inherit a fortune. If you want happiness for a lifetime—help someone else."

—CHINESE PROVERB

The Magic 8 for Externals

When Externals are met with sameness, constriction, past memories or regressive thinking, this is their path to pain, breakdown, neutrality and downsizing of their lives.

The following statements can help an External to remember their nature. This requires a bit more assistance as the cultural Field preferentially supports a First Tier Internal way of being.

1. The unlimited source of energy of the stars fuels an abundant remembering of our expanded true **HOME**.

2. We passionately claim the instability of this moment and the gap between possible realities.
3. We are flying above this illusionary ceiling and limited perspective. We hunger for the bigger choice that is already in place, making this apparent situation the cause to get us there.
4. The bar has been raised. With fascination, we **AAA** the calling of the larger, more profound and wilder outcomes that impact such a bigger circle.
5. The future threads of humanity are elegantly and profoundly sewing us into a new reality through this 4D experience.
6. We draw on more of humanity's legacy and seductive promise, which makes this side of the situation irrelevant.
7. We observe this transmission and compassionately look from the other's eyes and hearts.
8. The gift has magically appeared. We bless this existing reality with gratitude, having rehearsed it through so many steps to now.

After reading the "Magic 8," how many of these statements are familiar to you from when you have experienced the *extraordinary*? How differently do you respond to these statements compared to when you read about the Internal's **Way**? Remember, we are speaking about beyond the ordinary, beyond your habitual and about accessing your *Unreasonable* and *Extraordinary*.

The EpiGrid

Seekers, the more you seek and share with others, the more you know awaits you and humanity during these best and worst of times.

Do you seem more like an Internal or an External? If the "jury is still out," and you are not sure, consider when you are most messed up and also when you know things have been or will be *extraordinary*. In those moments, which EpiWay seems most like *You*? When you are Energy Neutral and when you are Energy Rich, there is a massive difference in the way you experience, interact, and attract in life. I suggest you review the exercises in the book and experience the difference in energy and its consequences on your thoughts, emotions, posture and hand positions. Which EpiWay leads you to more energy richness, effortlessness and constructive engagement with others— and collaboratively, with the Field of humanity?

In the next and concluding chapter, we explore the space in your Field where you access all thoughts, visions, creations, stories and manifestations. You will discover how that space is associated with the apps you play—or that play you. This is the key to your force of attraction and how your life shows up. Further examples will help you to more graphically see how to mess up your life and how you can turn on the light and, in moments, power up to **MORE**!

It's time to integrate your knowledge from the previous chapters. Your legacy and the Next Tier of the energetics of humanity impatiently await your turning this page...

CHAPTER 11

——

YOU ARE EVERYONE, AND EVERYONE IS YOU

YOUR EPIGRID

In the 1970s rendition of the song "You Are Everything, And Everything Is You," the lead singer of the Stylistics shares a narrative about how everything he sees reminds him of "you," his lost lover.

The singer sees a woman walking down the street who looks like his lost love. He calls out her name and to his disappointment, he realizes it is not her. At the climax of the song, he regretfully reveals this has been a common occurrence. It has happened again and again.

A bane of his existence—this recurring "pain" (an energetic phantom) regularly interrupts the singer's life and leads him to question what is actually real. He is trapped in an illusionary world.

Has this happened to you? Have you met a person who so reminded you of someone else—in physical appearance, gestures or energetics—that you found yourself speaking with or responding to this person as if they were the same person? Forgetting the difference, you communicate on a more personal level, leaving this stranger wondering why you act as if you are dear friends.

When this happens to you, you may see it—as expressed in the movie *The Matrix*—as a glitch in the system. There is a data loop playing out of sync with what is actually happening and projecting the illusion onto someone. Or perhaps this glitch promotes you to imbue a circumstance with meaning through the phantom of another's energetics.

The truth is that the glitch is not in the system. The glitch in the system is *You*.

We don't see the world as it is; we see the world as *WE* are. To repair the glitch, we must transform the energetics of the *You* seeing and broadcasting that illusion to everyone, everywhere. Had the writer of that song known this, the lyrics may instead have been "*You* Are Everyone, And Everyone Is *You*."

Let's build upon what I have shared in the preceding chapters of this book. Then, we can fly with the profundity of what this chapter offers for you, your attraction, your manifestation, and your personalized strategy for influencing others.

You now know that your EpiWay is intimately linked to the amount of energy available to you at any moment, and this determines the quality and quantity of data streams at your disposal to create your experience and impact.

In this chapter, we will learn about another vital player in your experience and force of attraction. It is one that determines the apps you play (or that play you) and the roles that are your lenses on the world.

This vital "player" determines the quality of your success or failure in these roles and your sense of enough-ness or not enough-ness.

We will see what determines the exact meaning you give to your experience and the patterns of attraction and repulsion that repeat in your life. It would require at least an entire book—or intensive personal course of study or mentoring—to fully describe these ideas. You, Seeker, and humanity need these vital discernments NOW to further demystify how we see the world and how it responds to us.

The Energy Neutral Matrix

You Are Everyone, And Everyone Is You expresses the quantum entanglement between our Fields. This is a metaphor for how, seemingly out of nowhere, we attract the same patterns and experiences.

No matter—

- how attentive we are,
- how many self-improvement courses or therapies we have under our belt,
- how much personal or spiritual development we do,
- how much we care or love,
- how we train ourselves,

our Energy Neutral—at best—energetics generally were, are, and will be running the show.

These energetic attraction strategies—the glitches in the codes of your roles, the *You* that is a lens into your world, are still looping an Energy Neutral illusion and downsizing your life.

Have you ever thought that you have done so many things, tried so many paths, loved so much, desired so much and taken so much constructive action, only to still experience the same ordinary or below-ordinary results? Your life falls into patterns. It may be an old pattern, old injury, old trauma, a repeated loss or a fear of what might happen in the future. Whatever it is, it is in a loop. Here we go again! The ghost in the machine, in the apps you are playing in life, is putting you back on "repeat." This pattern appears in between your thoughts, your body, your relationships and your finances—engaging you and others with its projections and distortions.

Whether subtle or obvious, it creates *pain* in some form. I define pain as any uncomfortable pattern or experience that interferes with your ability to effortlessly experience the magic of the moment. There must be a gap to have pain. The gap is between where you are or have been, in contrast with where you must be. The bigger this information-energy gap, the more you are the glitch in the matrix—and the more profound your disconnection is from accessing the depth of *Creation's Codes*.

Whenever you experience this loop, time appears to slow. Something is off. Somehow you can sense a disturbance in the system. The person you are looking at, the financial challenge you are struggling with, the difficulty in your marriage, or the trouble with your health seems all too familiar.

Its familiarity is because it is linked to a well-practiced sense of rejection, failure, abandonment, loss, anger, shame and dozens of other challenging states. It is linked to whatever Energetic stands in the way of where or who you must be. Your next lover, office manager, boss, child or your financial state is haunted by the same data stream that pops up as reality. One character actor exits stage right and another enters stage left in an all-too-familiar and often haunting script. You attract and repel others and opportunities by a sympathetic resonance in the organization of your Field.

I am sure you know what I am talking about. You are stuck in the Energy Neutral matrix of a repeating dream that overshadows a 4-D reality.

You can finally declare, "Enough of this!" It's time to take your power back—your power of choice, your power of directing your attention and your power to claim your energy state, taking charge of the game in life you play, instead of its addictive Energetic playing you.

It is time to wake up beyond "comfort" or relief-seeking, beyond avoiding not-enoughness or playing too small a game, looking for missing resources and managing your life. You are ready to show up and get to know more precisely what codes or apps are playing and how they are organized.

Now, as you pull back the curtain, as Toto did in *The Wizard of Oz*, you can see the illusory nature of what you believed was real. Energy richness and **AAA** are changing the game. You are soooo ready to access *Creation's Codes* and transform your relationship with your Field and the *You* that is seeing the world.

Step in and claim **MORE**—and for more than just yourself. You must either take the energetic and information stream that is your substance from the past or from the future and direct it into your Field.

The *You* seeing, experiencing, interacting and attracting through your Field must know and experience the data stream BEFORE you collapse it into your personalized meaning or physical form. You must energize it, allowing for an attraction strategy that is more constructive and productive with novel and more impactful outcomes.

Simply speaking, the *You* observing the world must be different, and as I have promised, different without having to change anything! Yes,

I know it sounds like a paradox. We are speaking about what, in the First Tier and fourth-dimensional reality, seems totally *unreasonable* and impossible.

And it is.

If there were only four dimensions, if we ignore the data stream and information potential that is in the Field, and continue believing we are all in separate bubbles, then it would be impossible.

Seeker, it is possible. More than possible. And Tick, Tick, Tick, it is time.

As a Seeker, it is time to take what you know from *The Seeker's Code*, and the transmission you have gained through your Field, to the next level. You know that it is time that the bound energy, information and outworn patterns must be ignited for **MORE**. This will happen when you access the Next Tier's energetics and instantly and effortlessly exchange the *You* observing—and claim something bigger for more than just yourself.

You must know your energetic game that creates and sustains these downsized patterns. With **AAA**, in mere moments, the need for them is extinguished and irrelevant. This allows you to shine enough light so you can grab the next rung up the ladder to the Next Tier. Once you do this, a different 4-D reality emerges through your focused attention and conscious witnessing of how you engage with your Field.

And in that moment, your life is changed...

Your Emotional Brain

Studying what emotions really are and the neurophysiology of the emotional brain, I was able to parallel this map into a whole new world of possibilities, understandings and strategies for you through the EpiField, establishing a new access to a mutable reality without having to do anything different in your life.

This is the promise offered through these pages and teachings.

The hippocampus (and no, this is not a place where a hippopotamus can get a higher education) is a part of the emotional brain. It is linked to other parts of the emotional brain that also look for patterns from prior experiences (and likely future ones too).

It helps us to retrieve two types of memory:

1. Declarative, which are perceived facts of experiences.
2. Spatial relationships, such as where and when something happens.

Where were you when the World Trade Center came down? Or at the moment someone told you they loved you? Time and space are blended together by an event or a fact when there is a massive infusion of energy. Whether joy or trauma, energy is the glue linking this time/space recollection. This chapter will expand this concept, awakening you to the *Unreasonable* and *Extraordinary* for yourself—and the world.

There is a tagging that happens in the hippocampus and the amygdala, its partner in the emotional brain. The amygdala is linked to experience, judgment and reward or punishment. It is associated with emotional behaviors and social interactions, helping you to feel emotions in yourself and others. It predominantly codes for fear and aggression.

We create meaning and our experience of the illusions of the mind and the matrix before signals even get to the conscious mind. This is why most of what we think about is just made-up stuff. Once we *AAA* this we are ready for the true transformation of reality, influence, and the *MORE* you are made for.

Here's the key to how we do it. The emotional brain has a **neurological grid** in which it accesses emotions, meanings and the whole range of energetics of experiences. This is organized in space. Memory A is in Box A, which might be a collection point for all of the experiences tagged as **rejection**. Box B might be the gathering point for all the experiences tagged as **abandonment**. Box C might be for **failure**. Box D might represent **support and love**. Each labeled box has a very specific location in the **neurological grid**.

When any experience or data stream enters a labeled box, it has the meaning dictated by the amount of energy represented by that box. It is also often blended with the information and energy of other boxes in its immediate vicinity.

The amount of energy and the size of the data stream selects for pathways in the nervous system and brain. When the E-State is poor, it usually stays in the survival brain. In neutral, it seeks the lower-order thinking brain. In Energy Rich, it opens paths to our executive function higher-order brain. When Super Energy Rich, it accesses the unbound information in the Field beyond the thinking mind.

I found a way of activating a new strategy, a continuation of the biologic-neurologic grid. I call it the EpiGrid.

Mirroring elements of the emotional brain's mapping of experiences, I see this as the mind's and nervous system's link to interpreting itself and its environment. It is made up of energetic "boxes" in your EpiField. Each has a certain amount of energy available with its corresponding information potential. Your EpiGrid determines the quality and quantity of your experiences, and the *You* seeing and influencing the world.

If the accessed box in the grid is Energy Poor, then the outcome is Energy Poor. When neutral, then there will be a neutral reaction. All of our roles—such as parent or child, husband or wife, doctor or patient, business owner or employee—are experienced and given meaning by the location of the box where the information for that role is activated.

The EpiGrid is where your brain, central nervous system and mind go to gather information for manifestation of **Creation's Codes**. *The way your EpiGrid is conditioned, energized and organized determines the apps you play.*

Depending upon which boxes you use—individually and collectively, with the conscious or unconscious mind—they significantly influence the exact apps of reality that will engage in your life. The conscious **AAA** and engagement of your EpiGrid is the secret sauce, the "holy grail" in our world of personal meaning, creation and influence.

For example, when you think of your husband, your interpretation of the information called "husband" depends on where your central nervous system goes to retrieve the information coded as "husband."

If the experience of "husband" is in a box next to that of rejection, abandonment or failure, then the app of husband triggers those qualities. Your husband is in a relationship with you and your Field. Your EpiGrid is the primary reality that potentiates a separate being you call yourself. At a time when you become Energy Neutral, your husband will also be likely to experience rejection, abandonment and failure.

This is similar to the way that the emotional brain and hippocampus is organized. Before he was experienced as a "husband" through the filter of the husband box of your EpiGrid, he was likely a lover. The lover app may have been experienced through a different box, closer in or further out of your EpiGrid.

The guy you worshiped as a lover or as a husband no longer exists. All that exists in an Energy Neutral state is the concept of husband or lover infused with whatever other information Fields permeate the husband or lover boxes. We conserve energy by living in the matrix of the culture to automatically fit and not have to experience or interact with the totality of the soul of the person. This is what Energy Neutral does. Thoughts are substitutes for reality—and roles are our lenses of "appropriate" thoughts.

The app for "lover" likely lives in a more Energy Rich and Super Rich space with heaps of *extraordinary* information potential. Once he becomes a husband, your nervous system goes to a place in your Epi-Grid to play the husband app. If it is a less-energized place, you are then the glitch. Over time, he becomes increasingly more of what your husband app creates...a person who engenders the sense, for both you and for him, of rejection and/or abandonment. Whenever you see and experience him as a "husband," the husband app retrieved through his EpiGrid will require him to fail in this role. At best, he will become an Energy Neutral concept bundled with all the neighboring roles. You experience a projection of the app that replaces him.

Crucially, no matter what you do or what your husband does or does not do—you can only experience him with whatever else is "stacked" near the box through which you play the husband app! You are everyone and everyone is you—because your reality is shaped by where parts of one person's data stream is played.

No wonder in the Stylistics song so many women reminded him of his lost lover! Most likely, he accessed the data stream of "lover" in the same place as his girlfriend. Therefore, other women were experienced as his lover if her gestures were accessed from the same box in his EpiGrid or its immediate neighborhood.

Stuck in Gridlock

Have you heard someone say in an argument or complaint that "you always" or "you never"? Was it really *always* that you did the annoying thing or *never* that you did the positive thing? Or was it a few times over several months or years? Did you really *never* take the wonderful action, or just not the past couple of weeks?

This is an example of stacking. The emotional brain has stacked a series of similar emotions and experiences on top of one another into a similar area of the emotional brain, and it links those emotions and experiences to specific parts of the EpiGrid.

We are miserable when we stack situations, people and events into one location opposite what serves our authentic EpiWay. As an Internal, I stack several uncertainties as realities in the future when I go opposite my EpiWay, and I believe them to be true. An External will do the opposite.

When this happens, the person you perceive as lover, husband, daughter or boss—or even your perception of yourself—is plugged into a hellhole of data and meaning. The reality of *You* no longer exists. That person no longer exists. The glitch in the code that cycles over and over creates our pain, obscuring greater bandwidth, perspectives and opportunities. Your grid becomes locked in a loop with no exit. This interruption obscures your true reality.

This is true Gridlock. As in gridlock on the street, this is all about traffic. It's blocking the flow of information. In other words, the information and energy are bound and cannot travel to other areas of the brain or Field.

Here's the good news. Transformation and awakening are possible with *AAA* of the state you are in. When you stack more Energy Rich or Super Rich parts of your EpiGrid, *AAA* can unbind the flow. Within seconds, where there was congestion, there can be liberation. This leads to the experience of *Unreasonable, Extraordinary* victory, love or rapture stacked upon whomever or whatever else is similarly placed in your EpiGrid. The gift of this is that your circumstance has little to do with the way you respond to what life shares. We will visit real stories of people in gridlock and see the path to liberation. From these examples, you will see a mirror for your liberation.

Always Remember to Kiss Me Goodnight

In our bedroom, Jackie and I have a framed quote over the fireplace. It reads, "Always Remember to Kiss Me Goodnight." Fortunately, neither of us often needs reminding!

Perhaps you have forgotten to kiss your lover goodnight. When it happened, the upset expressed may have seemed disproportionate to this simple omission.

That's because the upset was not about what just happened. Below the radar of mind, a whole information processing system was comparing not being kissed good night to the emotions of neglect or rejection—to past relationships or projections of failure as a wife or husband. It might have connected to the detachment of a prior spouse or the fear of future loneliness. This interpretation of the experience was created by the linkage of thoughts that matched a low-energy state being transmitted through very specific EpiGrid paths.

When the experience of not being kissed was accessed, the nervous system, like a tree root, sought to drink from the Low Energy Neutral EpiGrid stream, and it was no longer just about the experience of not being kissed. The same nervous system and Field pathways associated with other painful experiences that engendered similar and overlapping meanings was being accessed. The reaction was the cumulative experience of every place information was grabbed by the nervous system.

The location in the Field from which this information was retrieved and the amount of energy available led to the interpretation of the data stream as objective and real.

BAM! Gridlock!

Tree draws from an energy and information stream that is dried up and results in painful and downsized life and darkness

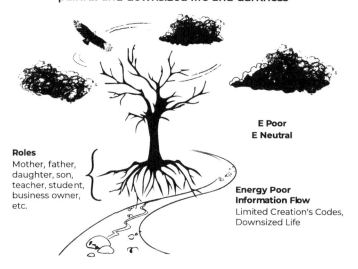

E Poor
E Neutral

Roles
Mother, father, daughter, son, teacher, student, business owner, etc.

Energy Poor Information Flow
Limited Creation's Codes, Downsized Life

Tree draws from an energy and information stream that is abundant for optimization, growth, productive and upsized life and impact

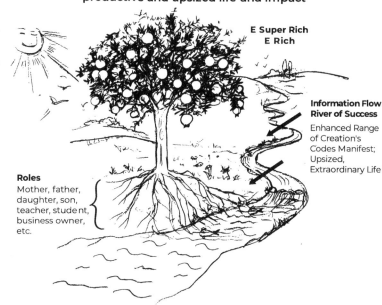

E Super Rich
E Rich

Information Flow River of Success

Enhanced Range of Creation's Codes Manifest; Upsized, Extraordinary Life

Roles
Mother, father, daughter, son, teacher, student, business owner, etc.

Figure 7

If this place was close to and behind the body (for an External) or far away and in front (for an Internal), then you as the lover or spouse no longer existed. You were instead experienced through a hellhole of data and meaning—the matrix of Energy Neutral management to achieve a degree of relief.

A series of "facts" remembered were blended into an illusionary reality. Then the rest of the nervous system played the abandonment or rejection relationship app. You became just another player in this energetic play. Then came the inevitable "you never-you always" accusations.

The response may have been radically different if instead the role as "spouse" or "lover" was linked to being loved, to a soul union or to masculine/feminine presence and accessed in the same **EpiGrid** box as a kiss. Whether sleeping or not, the forgetful lover likely would have received a goodnight kiss and some whispered words of devotion and gratitude for their soul union. Whatever other emotions were available through the Energy Rich or Super Energy Rich EpiField neighborhood of husband/wife and lover would be experienced.

I know it seems so crazy that it can be so simple without having to discuss, manage or treat anything. As soon as the experience and app for "husband," "lover," or "wife" is experienced in an Energy Rich part of your EpiGrid, the only thing that matters is your being together and transforming the world through your union.

"This field is responsible for our mind's highest functions, the information source guiding the growth of our bodies. It is our brain, our heart, our memory [and, I add, our spine]—indeed a blueprint of the world for all of time. The field is the force, rather than germs or genes, that finally determines whether we are healthy or ill, the force which must be tapped into in order to heal."

—LYNNE MCTAGGART, FROM HER REVOLUTIONARY BOOK, *THE FIELD*

The EpiGrid is the space between information and reality, between the immaterial of the Field and the apps that create our experience of reality. It defines the quality of the expression of you and me in the world. It influences our force of attraction and manifestation, synergy and quantum entanglement with others. It shapes the *You* that sees the world as you are—as it conditions who the heck this you that you are actually is! This awareness, to borrow from the chapter on **AAA** is a Sh*t, Fu*k, Sh*t moment.

Your EpiGrid: Architect of "You" and "Your Self"

Seekers, you are **out-of-the-box** thinkers and creators. Internals and Externals have different locations of and experiences with their boxes. For Externals, you may want to be "way out" of any box, as "in the box" belongs to Internals. The Internal may think of **"in the box" as HOME** while expanding and evolving it.

The box represents the cultural Field that you accept and either support or react against as the one "objective" reality. The box is also a representation of your EpiGrid. It is the place from which you draw the data that is turned into code and processed through your nervous system as energy dependent reality.

Creation's Codes are enhanced or muted, and information is either expanded or downsized depending upon the specific energy available from the grid. Where you go to access information from in your Epi-Grid—where various roles, emotions, memories, hopes, dreams and plans are accessed—is where the architect of your life lives. It is the main force of attraction, repulsion and manifestation. It is how you see the world and how it responds to you.

Your Field speaks before you enter the room and leaves after you...

And this, my fellow Seekers, is something over which you have full authority.

When Energy Rich, with **AAA** of your energetics and your EpiGrid,

Creation's Codes are available to transform this primary force behind the curtain for a new reality. It can transform your sense of reality for you and for more than just you!

It is the link between the nervous system and the Field, between one reality and the infinite range of possible realities.

The "Epi" part of the term EpiGrid is the intermediary between the material and immaterial, between the mystery and reality. It lives between information and experience, between focused attention and manifestation. It is the arbitrator of what is real. It is the linkage between fourth-dimensional reality with its potential Energy Rich synergy and Super Energy Rich beyond reason quantum entanglement—the higher dimensional realms, with apparently different rules than our conditioned four-dimensional physical reality. It is our very real connection to *You are Everyone* and *Everyone is You*. And this impacts everything and everyone upon which you share your sacred focused attention.

The EpiGrid Speaks

A woman attended one of my events. With her hands close to and facing her body, she shared about her challenges with men and masculine energy. She linked this to past failures and hurts. The information flow of men and masculine energy went from behind her forward. When she thought of intimate relationships, she was stacking her painful past experiences, rejections and abandonment close to her and behind her. Each one blended together as one bundle. When one of these was experienced, they all were. Everything was stacked together in the same EpiGrid neighborhood.

Based upon the stacking of all these elements, plus masculine energy and intimate relationships, she played the app of rejection and abandonment.

Based upon this information, what do you think was most likely her EpiWay? With such stacking and information flow, what might you expect the consequences to be on her life and the men with whom she wanted to be in relationship with?

Feminine energetics and the role of a woman were also challenging for her. She was living opposite her EpiWay as an Internal, and therefore had few options to change her life. She took many courses and did the "work" to improve herself and, as a single mom, to also improve the life of her son.

She experienced her son far out in the Field, with helping others and joy all stacked in the same energy files as "son." These were all linked with Super Energy Rich attributes. Therefore, thinking about her son would give her more joy or satisfaction in life than other masculine roles. Following the conditioned energetics, her son eventually could be more likely to serve as a surrogate man in her life instead of having an intimate partner.

All of this was in her baseline state. Then, I asked her to raise her hands over her head with her palms forward. I asked her about masculine energy, men, and intimacy in relationships. I asked her what it might be like if she experienced masculine energy and relationship intimacy outside and up—and in the same neighborhood as her son and helping people.

The contrast in her appearance and the energetics projected through her face, body, hand positions, posture and energetics was radical. It seemed as if the lights were turned off when inside and turned on bright when outside. She immediately transformed into a very distinct and different version of herself. I asked her to become aware of her energetics without the hunger to change, transform, let go of or understand them. She did, acknowledging the energetic strategy she was using and its likely undesirable outcome.

Her EpiGrid was becoming Energy Rich. To her astonishment, in seconds, we witnessed a dramatic shift from her Low Energy Neutral focus upon her past wounds and losses—to an Energy Rich state. Masculine energy and men were now linked to helping people and joy. Think how this force of attraction would change her experience of men and masculine energetics—how she would experience them, whom she would find attractive, how they would treat her and how she would unconsciously be conditioning her son.

I was helping her use Next Tier energetics to make a massive explosion of energy instantly available for her through her **AAA**-ing her energetic recipes for the masculine and feminine forces of creation.

Can you personally or professionally relate to this with either your own masculine or feminine state or in your relationships?

In moments, she energetically exchanged her data and energy, connected to her more feminine seductive, powerful and playful self. Beyond all conditioning or thought, she spontaneously giggled. As she lightened up, her lower spine developed a forward curve, and her head dropped back with a forward neck (cervical) curve. Forward or "lordotic" curves in the spine are biologically linked to female sex hormones and the expression of seduction, flirtation and attraction. Flattening of the curves is similarly linked to more "masculine" biochemistry and behavior and is more familiar to us.

I asked her to tell me about a relationship with a man, and she looked up, smiling with a slightly naughty look, and swayed her hips. She said it could be pretty good. As the "placement" of these traits shifted to Energy Rich areas of her grid, she expanded her available bandwidth of data, drawing from a different information flow that she interpreted as masculine and feminine energy when she thought of relationships and intimacy. Everyone at the event noticed it.

This was not just a change in her, as we were soon to find out. The next day, she shared a text from the father of her son who had disappeared years earlier. He had texted to say he wanted to reconnect with her and show up for their son. She spoke with him and shared that she also wanted her son to have a father again. *Pay attention, my fellow Seekers. She did not have to do anything, nor did the father.* **Creation's Codes** handled everything—through synergy and quantum entanglement, through her more coherent Field to whomever she thought about that was linked to those roles.

With the conscious and ecological use of energy and information, she recognized her E-State, EpiWay and EpiGrid representations of reality with the rocket fuel of Next Tier energetics. Then **BAM!** Her Field transmitted a different, and at least Energy Rich, EpiGrid. Her Field, with its radically different EpiGrid, was able to transmit this new *her* to whoever and whatever had been withheld in her prior version. Suddenly, her ex had more energy. What would happen after was up to their collective E-States and personal energetics.

SEEKER'S CODE #5

WE WISH TO ACCESS THE MULTIDIMENSIONAL ENERGETICS
THAT MAGICALLY CREATE AND CONNECT US ALL.

This renewed communication is an example of quantum entanglement. Within minutes of her changing the energetic apps that were opposite her EpiWay, she was liberated from total reliance upon her cultural Field app. A Low Energy Neutral app had been playing her with mathematical precision to produce the exact outcome her Field resonated with—and her nervous system interpreted as reality. She chose new apps that she would play rather than be played by them. As she represented relationship and masculine energy in a more Energy Rich way, whomever she experienced in the same part of her EpiGrid also got a greater surge of energy and would be pinged in a constructive way.

Knowing that a game is playing you reveals a doorway for you to decide what game *You* wish to play. *You* will be the one that creates the greater human performance and resourcefulness. This makes so much of the content, conflict and effort of your mind, body and Field totally irrelevant. This is an end unto itself. It ignites an additional source of unbound energy for *Creation's Codes* to magically and instantly awaken a more vital and creative reality. A new *You* and a new energetic "sheriff" has just ridden into town. It is Next Tier energetics.

Torn between His Wife and His Lover

Alexander consulted with me about a situation that he cautioned I might not understand, as it is taboo in America (though more common in Europe, where he lives). He would not tell me what it was upfront. Instead, he shared that he and his wife loved one another very much. They were on the same page in life and had similar backgrounds, vision and experiences. The first three or so years of marriage, they were crazy passionate and daring lovers. After that, things changed.

"My wife and I," he said, "have a pleasant and enjoyable relationship, but the zing is gone."

With a serious and sad voice, he admitted that he was not very attracted to her anymore. She kept asking him if he still loved her. She wanted them to take off on a cruise around the world, stopping at various foreign ports. The idea frightened him, and he did not want to commit to this in the near future.

He mentioned that his finances were not the challenge and not the reason why he wanted to avoid the cruise his wife desired. He did say that such a trip would break with his usual routines too much. The idea of traveling the world out on the vast ocean, scattering his attention across different cultures and having so much unstructured time and too many choices each day, seemed too far "out there" for him. He said it seemed like it would be very unpleasant.

I asked further questions to discern his most likely EpiWay. I asked when stressed, how he got into a more resourceful state. He quickly responded that he liked to go into his room by himself, look at old photos, and listen to the music of his twenties.

When Alexander left his cave, after seclusion, he was more able to be with his wife and provide more attention and love. This honored the promise he made to her to always love her as a responsible husband.

> At this point does Alexander seem like his natural EpiWay is as an External or as an Internal? Why do you think so?

Alexander said that his wife would often go on and on about some topic or another. He wouldn't know what she was talking about, so he would smile as he stated that she was way off-topic. It all seems so tangential to whatever they started off discussing. His confusion was interpreted by her as a lack of interest. This pissed her off. He then felt that she would be upset forever. He knew it made no sense, and he just couldn't get over it.

I wanted to know what he did to get back to his love for her or being a more responsible husband. He shared, "I just look at her and say how lucky I am to be the one that makes love to her—even though it is not as often as it used to be."

Alexander was indeed reporting perspectives and energetics that classically reflected an Internal EpiWay. He was fearful that his disinterest would intensify over the years. She had transformed into a wonderful wife and was definitely much different than the girl he married. He smiled in pride when he boasted that he was basically the same man she married. His fear of the future and empowerment from the past is typical of someone living as an Internal.

This was all interesting. I was still waiting to hear exactly what he was going to tell me that I, as an American, might not understand or accept. Then, he finally spilled the beans.

About three years into their energetically flattening marriage, he met someone who reminded him of a former fiancée with whom he was still intoxicated. He said he hadn't broken off the engagement to this woman because of lack of love for her. She was perfect, and she checked off all the boxes on his list for an ideal wife. He told me he had axed the marriage because *the idea of being a husband seemed like it might be a prison sentence for eternity, and this terrified him.*

He wanted to continue as lovers or indefinitely stay engaged. This put the kiss of death on their relationship. He mentioned that even to this day—at times when his energy level drops—he wonders if his prior fiancée might have been the right choice for him.

It was now more than clear to me that Alexander was a classic expression of the Internal EpiWay. I invite you to follow how every part of this interactive is 100 percent opposite of what would work for an External.

Continuing, Alexander told me that he met his lover when on vacation with his wife. Pointing far ahead of him, he told me this was a conflict that he hoped he could resolve somewhere down the road.

He then reminded me that in many cultures in Europe, it was not looked down upon for a very powerful or successful man to have what one might call a "side chick," as long he could keep it low-key and financially take care of both women.

"I love her also," he said of his mistress. "She comes from the same village as my parents." He held his hand to his heart and said, "It feels like I can own her. She is totally mine, and with her I feel powerful and alive." Again, all of his more energized and natural references were from the past. Being excited by her being from the same village as his parents would generally be far from a deal maker for an External.

"Please don't judge me," he added, leaning forward imploringly. "Just help me sort out the energy that is causing pain for me and the women I love."

I asked how the women were doing. He stretched his hands up and out as his energy dropped and body lurched forward. He quietly confided in me, almost in a whisper, "A friend of my wife saw me having a romantic dinner with my mistress when I was supposed to be working late. Now both women want me to choose which one I will be with exclusively."

"I am terrified that I have messed up both of their lives, and that my children will hate me forever. I want to have and take care of both women. They are both an essential part of me and who I am. Right now, I feel like a failure, a sense that I hate, and I really don't want to change anything." His fear was from the future and associated with what others would feel, both of which are challenges for Internals.

He said both women were feeling rejected, betrayed and abandoned, even though he was being responsible as a man to each of them.

I wondered if the emotions that they were feeling were consistent with those emotions that were stacked in his EpiGrid because of the way he experienced his roles. He mentioned "wife" and "husband" when he broke off his prior engagement. This triggered my curiosity as to whether the roles of "husband" and "wife" were so low energy and so painful that he was willing to sacrifice love and his future with his lover.

I asked Alexander where in his EpiGrid he accessed the information that his mind interpreted as "lover." He immediately boasted that it is like a hot spear of excitement that flowed from his back and into his heart in a very powerful way. It intoxicated him and made him lose all reason. He smiled, looked proud and had a very powerful masculine and self-assured energy. This is a truly classic example of a relationship being described by a very Internal man.

Wanting to know more, I asked if the experience of a lover was more from an information flow from the past or from the future. Alexander sat up with his spine erect and shoulders back and told me that when he thought of the concept of a lover, he immediately thought of his mistress and the times they had had together. He felt that there was a soul contract that was made "to share profound intimacy from before we were born."

Are you experiencing this similarly to Alexander, or are his descriptions of past and future, close and far away, more painful or dropping your energetics? As a wife, husband or lover, how do you experience these roles and experiences?

We experience and respond through the EpiGrid locations of our "Roles."

With curiosity, I inquired from where in his Field he went to retrieve the idea of "husband." He sighed, his shoulders leaned forward, and his neck projected up and in front of his shoulders. He coughed and reached his hand out, pointing about three feet diagonally to his right side. He experienced this concept from the future. Once Alexander experienced himself as a husband, the role of husband would become Low Energy Neutral to avoid the drop into Energy Poor. This placement of the role of husband felt like death to him. From a survival standpoint, he naturally avoided any awareness of being a husband and the painful emotions or experiences linked to it.

My next question was about how he interpreted information related to "wife." This information flowed from outside toward his head and from the future. This EpiGrid location was on the borderline between Low Energy Neutral and Energy Poor for an Internal. When he experienced the role of wife or its relationship to husband, he would run away from it to protect himself from a dangerous energy drop that would break down more than the relationship; it would also compromise the integrity of his body and life. Through the quantum entanglement of their EpiGrids, his wife also would lose her energy and find her life downsized as his roles were taking energy from her too.

Now, it made sense that in the past, when he experienced his "wife" as a "lover," it was all the *extraordinary* super richness of being "One." Once he transitioned his love from a "lover" into a "wife" and himself as a "husband," there would not be enough energy for their synergy, quantum entanglement and the "love drugs" that added value to his experience of them as a couple.

No woman would have a chance with Alexander unless he experienced her as a lover. Once he would begin to experience her in the role of a wife, the energy and data stream would play the wife app instead of that of a hot and seductive lover. The same pattern played out that had led to his calling off his past engagement because of his future terror.

By contrast, now, he experienced his wife as a lover (who reminded him of that past fiancée lover) in a Super Energy Rich place that was compelling and intoxicating. His wife had once been a lover; now his mistress was in the same place in his EpiGrid as lover. Therefore, she had taken over the space that his wife had occupied during their romance and first couple years of marriage.

Crucially, "lover" was experienced as Super Energy Rich due to its location in space and time behind him, moving from his back and forward through his heart. This was extraordinarily exciting and Super Energy Rich for Alexander.

I saved Alexander's story for you until the end of *The Seeker's Code* because only now is it completely clear to you that we don't see the world as it is. Instead, we see it as we are—and impact it as we are. Roles are the way our identity or sense of self in the world is experienced. Our cultural conditioning determines what we are rewarded or punished for, how we think and feel, and what is perceived as a success or failure. And here is the big kicker: **where a role is located or accessed in our EpiGrid determines how that role plays out in the world.**

Let's return to Alexander's dilemma. For Alexander to find himself in such a situation, even though he loved his wife and wanted to continue to love her, was very painful. His role as husband was drawing its information and energy from an external, toxic, dried-up stream, flowing from the future and from outside in. He experienced this as if he was dying. These experiences and the role of husband had their information flow opposite his Internal EpiWay. Additionally, failure was experienced in the same neighborhood as "terror" and "rejection," both in front of his chest in an Energy Poor place with the data stream coming from outside in and from the future. Therefore, terror, failure and rejection were stacked in the same place, so his experience of one blended into the others. Whatever role would draw its sustenance from this river would lead to the same experiences, no matter which actor in this script entered these parts of the EpiGrid.

The person no longer existed. They were now part of the EpiGrid data Field. The role of husband would over time become equated with failure, terror, rejection and a few other darker states. No matter what he did to improve, manage or change, this pattern would continue.

> Now you likely are sensing how there is no one objective experience of reality. It is all energy plus information mediated through our Fields. Have you noticed that over time one lover or spouse eventually fills the role others filled with similar painful emotions or actions—as if they are following the same script? Have you noticed how this seems independent of the love, desire or commitment you share? Is the pattern experienced often contrary to your values? You know this, and still you continue with this behavior or experience?
>
> Do you also see these patterns in your finances or health condition?

This happens when your EpiGrid representation of how you access these roles is inconsistent with your actual soulful intention of who you believe you or someone else is. The Field is your true initial language. The degree of energy and information expressed through your

EpiGrid's architecture creates the apps of reality you experience and attract.

You likely wonder what would happen if we asked Alexander to experience his wife or his lover in a different place in his EpiGrid. This is on the right track. If he experienced both women on an equal energetic scale, he would see them closer to who they are in relationship to himself. This change is only possible when at least Energy Rich. When we are Energy Neutral, we believe that the Field and nervous system app playing are reality.

Alexander recognized that where his roles and stacked emotions had been accessed in his EpiGrid was in favor of his mistress as his lover. His wife was out of the game—and not because of her actions or his lack of love for her. When he thought of his wife as his lover and from the past, he was attracted to her and the relationship flourished. This was happening less frequently as he had someone else whom he experienced as his mistress—a person who was not experienced in the less energized husband or wife box.

Alexander suffered from Extreme **Gridlock** and knew he was inconsistent with his greatest values of love and integrity. He stated with full congruence that both roles needed at least an energetic equal footing to make a decision.

Theoretically, if Alexander experienced his wife in the same place in the EpiGrid as he experienced his lover/mistress, he would recapture and renew the *extraordinary* love and desire he had before he became a "husband" and before she became a "wife." With both women in the same place, they would be on equal energetic "footing" for him.

I reminisced that while developing the concept and skills of the Epi-Grid, I realized how simple and profound a shift from Low Energy Neutral to Energy Rich or Super Energy Rich could be, and how one's life could instantly change **without having to do anything else. Similarly, after remembering this powerful first awareness for me, as** an **Internal**, I laughed and cried with excitement and awe at life itself, knowing it was time for Alexander to experience.

SEEKER'S CODE #6
WE RECOGNIZE THE POWER OF FOCUSED ATTENTION
AND ENERGY/AND CONSCIOUS CHOICE.

His responsible husband role was already changing as he was becoming *Aware* of his Energetic without the hunger to change or transform it. He then *Acknowledged* the apps he was playing influenced the reality and situation he was living in and the women he loved. He *Accepted* that this was all energy and information, and if he changed his energetics for more than his comfort, his contract with the Field and others would instantly be upgraded. **He did it!** He thought of his wife from the same Super Rich place in the EpiGrid as "lover" and "mistress." He chose to experience his wife first as his soul-lover, which was represented behind himself and from the past, where the information flow was going from behind him through his heart. Instantly, he sat up fully excited and laughing. "Wow, there she is again!"

When asked what he was experiencing, he said he was so desirous of her, in every way, and that this was the woman he always wanted. Rejection, lack of acceptance, betrayal, abandonment and failure did not have the "security clearance" to fly in the same airspace as the light and could no longer be stacked together with husband and wife.

BAM! His EpiGrid reorganized! Although wife/lover and mistress/lover both went through the heart, the wife/lover was Super Energy Rich as it started from behind him and the past. It was the most energized and Super Energy Rich location for an Internal. His mistress was now experienced outside and going from outside in. It was at best Energy Neutral. The energized hottie spell they had for one another and their quantum connection was lowered. His mistress had been fed immense energy every time he thought about her as his "mistress," and that was now gone. She had been drugged and fueled by his Super

Energy Rich state that triggered chemicals of love and intoxication. That suddenly changed.

Now the really trippy quantum entanglement part.

Before Alexander even told his mistress of his choice, she contacted him and informed him that she could no longer be in a relationship with him. She said that she was conflicted about their relationship dynamic, and it would be best if he worked things out with his wife, and, "give her the energy that I've been getting."

Waking up from their energetic drugged state, neither of them saw the other in the same way as before. She was losing attraction toward him, and he toward her. There was only one choice that his Field could respond to in the apps he was playing. His relationships experienced a changing of the guard as "mistress" was displaced by "lover-wife" in his EpiGrid.

We all go wherever there is more coherent energy. Greater energy equals greater possibilities and opportunities. Alexander chose his wife to be represented in his most Energy Rich EpiGrid location, placing her in the space he would always be drawn to.

Months later, his relationship with his wife was raw, real and beautiful. Each of them felt pain when they went into Energy Neutral. Over time, this was replaced by intense love and faith as they upsized their intimacy. When we are Energy Neutral, we all find challenges and pain. Drama will once again dominate. Remember that conscious attention to your E-State, EpiWay and the calling for *Extraordinary* is a must. Unconscious stacking of roles and experiences with the associated accompanying gridlock will repeat your effortful and ordinary—or even subordinary—outcomes.

Alexander - Internal EpiGrid

Before Interactive

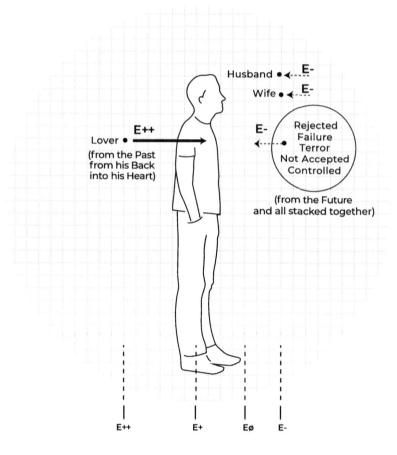

Husband • ◄----- **E-**

Wife • ◄----- **E-**

Lover • ——————► **E++**

(from the Past
from his Back
into his Heart)

E- ◄----•

Rejected
Failure
Terror
Not Accepted
Controlled

(from the Future
and all stacked together)

E++   E+   Eø   E-

E- : Energy Poor
Eø : Energy Neutral   ◄ - - - -   From the Future
E+ : Energy Rich   Loss of Energy
E++ : Super Energy Rich
                           ————►   From the Past
                                   More Energy

Figure 8

Alexander - Internal EpiGrid

After Interactive

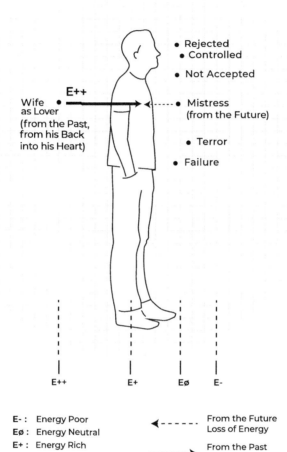

Rejected
Controlled

Not Accepted

E++

Wife as Lover
(from the Past, from his Back into his Heart)

Mistress
(from the Future)

Terror

Failure

E++   E+   Eø   E-

E- : Energy Poor
Eø : Energy Neutral
E+ : Energy Rich
E++ : Super Energy Rich

From the Future
Loss of Energy

From the Past
More Energy

Figure 9

Take a few moments to review the illustrations before and after Alexander's transformation. In your own EpiGrid, which roles are close to you? Which are far away? Which are linked to the past? Which are linked to the future? Does the information flow from outside to in? Does the information flow from inside to out? What other emotions or thoughts are activated when you sense you are not enough? Where is the most Energy Rich or Super Rich part of your EpiGrid?

When you think of the most *extraordinary* experience, encounter, relationship or moments of ecstasy, where are these represented in your EpiGrid? What happens if you experience intimacy, lover, husband, wife, girlfriend, boyfriend or a role as man or woman in the same place you experience the most Energy Rich or Super Rich roles or experiences?

SEEKER'S CODE #5
WE WISH TO ACCESS THE MULTIDIMENSIONAL ENERGETICS
THAT MAGICALLY CREATE AND CONNECT US ALL.

Exactly. Just like for Alexander, everything changes.

Authority Figures from Hell to Heaven

Mirai was living in fear of male authority figures, particularly older men. She would become frozen when confronting them and their policies. As a single mom, she wanted to do better. She wanted to be a better mom *and* dad to her son. This, to me, meant she felt that she was not succeeding in her feminine and masculine roles. The gap was huge between how she was experiencing and living reality in her relationships compared to the **MORE** she sensed was possible.

SEEKER'S CODE #1
WE KNOW THERE IS SO MUCH MORE TO LIFE THAN WHAT
APPEARS AS PHYSICAL REALITY OR CIRCUMSTANCE.

She had an External EpiWay, so experiences, people or roles that were accessed close to her body or referenced from the past downsized her energy and information. The natural consequence was pain, doubt, fear and breakdown.

She experienced the idea of "masculine" inside her. This would make masculine energetics at best Low Energy Neutral.

The information interpreted and experienced as older men, father, son and masculine authority figures was experienced and stacked in her EpiGrid behind her head and upper body. Her grandparents, who lived through WWII in Japan, were also experienced opposite her EpiWay; therefore, she could not receive any constructive information from her lineage.

These experiences would combine with fear and rejection to drain most of her energy and create the most painful and destructive emotions, thoughts and stories. She could not trust the masculine energetics or systems created by them. It was exhausting for her feminine energy to condemn the other half of the force of creation, further muting her feminine experience and impact. The stacking of all of these together was horribly debilitating. As a masculine family member, her son was likely to be conditioned by her same mistrust and animosity for men, especially as he grew older, and his Field would be conditioned to continue this Energetic.

Mirai's EpiGrid was set up to attract destructive, painful and terrifying dynamics with masculine energy, in ways that they appear in society and culture, and in her life, including in her roles with men, her son, her father and any authority.

Conversing with her, I discovered that, in contrast, Mirai experienced joy all around and above her. She smiled, and she momentarily became Energy Rich when she thought of it. This was consistent with her External nature.

I told her to place her hands apart and facing one another—with one hand representing her past and the other her future. Then, I asked her to use her mental focus to send energy and information from her past to the future. This is the same exercise you have done in prior chapters. As would be expected of someone with an External EpiWay, Mirai did not feel much movement from the past hand. She then sent the energy and information flow from the future to the past. It went all the way across to the past and even through her hand.

Remember that a differential in energy leads simultaneously to an information differential. As soon as she became aware of the future to past information and energy flow, her mood and posture changed, and greater bandwidth became available with a transformed experience of reality.

She realized that when she focused from the past, there was not enough energy to create a different future. And when she went from the future, it could influence her past. As you know, this is classical for an External EpiWay.

Her concepts of—

- older men, authority figures,
- grandparents,
- masculine and feminine roles,
- rejection and hurt

only existed as painful when inside or behind her when she drew information from the past using an Internal EpiWay.

Through Mirai's **AAA**-ing these past and future energetics and their consequences in her life, more energy became available for more awareness. Now, Mirai could jumpstart access to her EpiGrid roles for a more constructive representation of reality, one with greater information and energy showing up as reality on the computer screen of her mind.

At this point, I asked her from where in her Field she went to access the representation of a female Japanese goddess referred to in historical Japanese spiritual writings. I asked this as it likely would be "living" in the Super Energy Rich parts of her EpiGrid. She lit up and looked like a different woman as she joyfully reached all the way up with her hands into the part of her EpiGrid that accessed energy richness. It was as if her spirit was pulling her up. She was outwardly grabbing for the energy and information Field that she would experience as the goddess. It was all around her and raining on the top of her head from the same place as joy. This position engaged super energy richness for her, and she now showed up as at least a #2 External!

She found the External female source of energy and then invited the masculine energy from the future to dance with the female and something magical happened—beyond her—outside, external and from the future.

Instantly, magically, a different Mirai was beamed into her body. With a radically realigned EpiGrid, there was a new woman. Now, masculine energetics, father, son, control, fear, anger, motherhood and grandparents were no longer linked close to her body. She was no longer stacking the pain of these roles in the same dark place of frozen energy and information.

People witnessing this on an international video call, including those with no prior experience with me or any of these concepts, were in awe of what was happening. It was a co-joined, entangled experience— even through the internet. Before our eyes, Mirai now was guided by future possibilities and information flow. Mirai was at least Energy Rich for a few moments—long enough to turn her life and destiny around to seeking so much more—yes, fellow Seeker, **MORE** than just for herself.

Mirai - External EpiGrid

Before Interactive

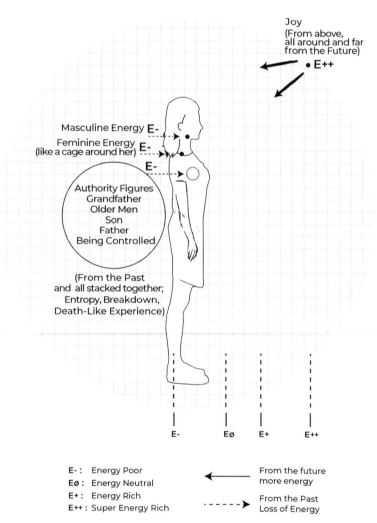

Joy
(From above,
all around and far
from the Future)

• **E++**

Masculine Energy **E-**

Feminine Energy **E-**
(like a cage around her)

E-

Authority Figures
Grandfather
Older Men
Son
Father
Being Controlled

(From the Past
and all stacked together;
Entropy, Breakdown,
Death-Like Experience)

E-   Eø   E+   E++

E- : Energy Poor
Eø : Energy Neutral
E+ : Energy Rich
E++ : Super Energy Rich

From the future
more energy

From the Past
Loss of Energy

Figure 10

Mìrai - External EpiGrid

After Interactive

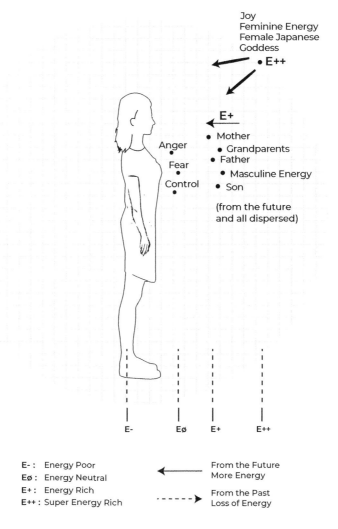

Joy
Feminine Energy
Female Japanese
Goddess

• E++

E+

• Mother
  • Grandparents
• Father
  • Masculine Energy
• Son

(from the future
and all dispersed)

Anger
Fear
Control

E-   Eø   E+   E++

E- : Energy Poor
Eø : Energy Neutral
E+ : Energy Rich
E++ : Super Energy Rich

From the Future
More Energy

From the Past
Loss of Energy

Figure 11

A few months later, she reported on her life. She said that since that magical moment everything had changed, she had started to sort things OUT. Mirai was living the *Seeker's Codes*. She was putting them into action in her intimate relationships with men and creating an even beyond greater-merging of the masculine and feminine forces of creation. Since that moment, a different, self-assured and radiant woman had appeared. She had a better relationship with her son. She said men were OK and now even lovable. She felt good in her role as a mother. She also now had the opportunity to help more women.

And, "Oh, I am no longer triggered by or have judgment toward older men. It was magical, really magical."

SEEKER'S CODE #4

WE WANT TO GIVE, GET, LEARN, AND LIVE WITH A
BIGGER PURPOSE, INSPIRING PROFOUND IMPACT.

Mirai did not have to "work on her issues" to eliminate her terror and anger. As I have stated throughout the book, there was nothing to fix, transform or let go of. She had been attempting that for decades, waiting for the relief that never really came. All she had to do was upgrade the energetics of the information stream that fueled her reality by recognizing and claiming her EpiWay for *Unreasonable* and *Extraordinary* impact and influence.

She simply had to *AAA* that her energetic strategies were coming from a practiced conditioned Internal energy neutrality and instead choose the energy richness of her authentic External way. Once she saw the futility of living from the past, she could choose to experience from her future and the places in her Field that were most joyful and celebratory. Life met her this way. She no longer maintained her status quo of her family's WWII cultural pain, as she more often lived her External EpiWay.

Externals, your target is from the future to bless the past. When those of you who are External did the hand awareness experience, the energy and information flow from your future hand most likely moved to reach or actually pass through your past hand. In the same way, the Energy Rich information flow from the future can bring its light, greater bandwidth and wisdom to destabilize energy-neutral gridlock from the past.

I believe as more Seekers pave the way using Next Tier energetics, this will **slightly shift the way the past experiences happened through a quantum entangled time warp.**

Donny, you ask, did the past actually change? I answer, are you so sure that it truly happened the way you replayed it for all those years? I have seen, experienced, and spoken with countless people who reported this shift. This is true, even if it still seems *unreasonable* and just magical when it happens.

You Are Not You

The individual "me" of Alexander and the individual "me" of Mirai changed as their EpiGrids reorganized. So did the signal that their Field projected into the information pond available for humanity. Within moments, Alexander and Mirai became different energetic versions of themselves, as did their impact and forces of attraction and manifestation.

This applies to you as you become Energy Rich and experience yourself and others through your authentic EpiWay. It also begins to happen as you audit and *AAA* your EpiGrid. As we go through the S.F.S. *AAA* experience, the former *You* is replaced by a *You* that is **MORE.** And this is the dream, passion, desire and calling of Seekers, with either Internal or External EpiWays.

This is what we are seeking for each of us and en masse for humanity. Next Tier energetics will optimize our impact as we further our transcendence—meaning as **we include and evolve beyond our prior selves.** The best of who we were, and who we will be, merge into a new *WE*.

Once we transcend the matrix of the cultural Field of thought and the sense that there is truly an objective and separate *Me*, and an objective and separate *You*, so much liberation happens. This is the experience of Oneness, the experience in love and in meditation's transcendent state. We become aware of this in the Energy Rich state as a possible additional perspective on reality. When Super Energy Rich, this becomes our new baseline for reality.

A new and expanded *You* participates in a larger system, with ripples in the multi-dimensional and quantum pod of humanity's potential. There is now a very significant upgrade in information and coherent energy that was formerly bound and maintaining the curtain of separation.

You are not an objective *You*!

Externals, you sense this. Each time you attempt to focus on improving yourself, it hardly ever yields energy richness, and in fact, often results in a downsizing of your life. Your concept of yourself is a function of the relationship between your central nervous system and its uploading and downloading to and from your EpiGrid. Your *self* is a future self, connected to so much more reality, energy and conscious participation in the mystery of life.

External *You* is a collaboration of future versions of *You*, inspiring whichever *You* appears as if it is real. Quantum science refers to multiple co-existing parallel worlds and realities. We are counting on this for humanity to jump into a new Next Tier world for which we are being prepared.

Internals, you wonder about this, as you are energized anytime you pay attention to your *You*. You can get excited that the *You* that you experience is bursting to be made even more real, more extraordinary and better able to send your signal out to impact others. All of this is consistent with your contract for incarnation with more ease and magic. The *You* that you are is a combination of versions of *You* that had victories, successes, experiences and important interactions in the past—all melting into one.

Earlier in the book, I mentioned that much of my quest was inspired by a teacher asking me what I wanted to be when I grew up. I responded that to answer this, I had to know what I really was at that time. This book offers you real answers, profound understandings, experiences and and tools to manifest so much **MORE** of what you truly are.

YOU are information of the universe potentiated by energy which contacts all other information in existence. Through this book, you have been able to realize that your E-State determines the range of information and size of the system you call *You*. It determines the quality of manifestation of everything you consider real.

The challenges and victories in your life are a function of the *You* that is witnessing the world. The goal of *The Seeker's Code* is to better enable all of us to consciously and ecologically use energy and information to access **Creation's Codes**. Our manifesting a more interdependent and Energy Rich world can burst the illusionary and limiting bubbles of separate you and me randomly bumping into us in a fixed time-space continuum.

"Do all you can to preach the gospel, and if necessary, use words!"
—SAINT FRANCIS OF ASSISI

Remember, your Field introduces you before you enter a room and still carries your resonance after you leave. So, too, will our conscious use of the energetics of the Next Tier, as invisible forces create, sustain, transform, redeem and transfigure reality.

Seekers, I offer a novel and (r)evolutionary option, the energetics and consciousness of the Next Tier. May you passionately live its gifts as torch holders for a new humanity!

EPILOG

A meme is a unit of consciousness that "virally" spreads between people across the globe.

The word "meme" is composed of the English word ME repeated twice. You likely have experienced more than enough individuals who make their lives just about "me." Each of those individuals are competing for limited resources in a First Tier way to build "independence for me" (as if we could really be separate). Collectively, we often act as me and me and me and me...there is little regard for *WE*.

The Western world is rather obsessed with the individualization, repair and growth of the *ME*. It sees the "not me," "less of me," or "fractured me" as the cause of our problems. In contrast, the Eastern world considers the "not me," "beyond me," or "unified *WE*" as desirable and prized. The Eastern mind culture most often sees the concepts of individualization and separation as the cause of our problems.

To *ME* or not to *ME*? To *ME* or to *WE*? Myself or others? This duality is part of the energy neutrality of the cultural matrices. Instead, I propose the union of the gifts of the West and the East. The true Energy Rich and Super Energy Rich **WEME**.

As we actually experience the Energy Rich state, we realize that the *ME* is part of a *WE*. As the *ME* of you connects and is one with the *ME* of others, we have a collective Field of *WE*. When we are a part of the larger bandwidth and energy of the expanded *WE* system, the *ME* has more resourcefulness, energy, bandwidth and synergy.

Then more often we live with the awareness that each *ME* is part of the larger *WE*. The rippling waves of information of the *WE* move through time and space reshaping the *ME*—as the individual resonance and gifts of the *ME* impact the *WE*.

In the Next Tier, when Energy Rich or beyond, the *WE* refines, awakens and transforms each individual *ME*. There is a new *ME* that is integral to the **WEME**. Once expanded, one never truly fits into the old *ME* box. This new *ME* adds a new energetic signature, new information and new energy to the *WE*—and so it goes on and on.

In a moment, individual, relationship, social, cultural, environmental, political and other systems are living in magical and sacred union with the higher order of *Creation's Codes*. Fellow Seekers, this so much **MORE** is fueled by the energetics of the Next Tier.

It Was the Best/Worst of Times

"It was the best of times, it was the worst of times, it was the age of wisdom, it was the age of foolishness, it was the epoch of belief, it was the epoch of incredulity, it was the season of light, it was the season of darkness, it was the spring of hope, it was the winter of despair."

—CHARLES DICKENS

Inspired by this Dickens quote from *The Tale of Two Cities*, these, too, are transitional times. Knowing your E-State, experiencing the energetics of your authentic EpiWay, and realizing how your EpiGrid is stacking experiences and roles can effortlessly exchange you for a different *You*. The **MORE** energized version of *You* will help us all, adding to the best of times even in the midst of "winter."

The reason you sensed that everything is falling apart is because the Energetic that is running the matrix is reorganizing. The game humanity has accepted as reality—when Energy Neutral sets the boundaries for what we can possibly think, believe and desire—was associated with the previous tier principles. The game is now glitching.

The matrix code no longer works for you, me, or we, and it does not support the emerging **WEME** of this Next Tier of humanity. The power has been turned off on the electromagnet that kept the "iron filings" of First Tier systems, structures, and lives in alignment with the mental order of the Tree of Knowledge.

Unbound potential is now more freely available! A newly established Tree of Life mega-magnet of the Next Tier, powered by *Creation's Codes,* has just been turned on. As you are energized in this Next Tier, you will see the *commonly unseen,* hear the *commonly unheard,* and feel the *commonly unfelt.* You will be an *uncommon You!*

You Will Be **MORE**! You will be able to exist, think, feel, act, dream, manifest and impact with energy richness, and at times super richness, with all its synergy, syntropy, quantum entanglement and grace, carried by the wave of this Next Tier. The ordinary *You* will be unreasonably energized and impactful. What you thought was important will fall away, and what is truly important will effortlessly emerge.

You have a choice. You can choose to remain with your centricity in the matrix, or you can choose to embrace your leadership role as a Seeker. You are now familiar with how to become *Aware* of, *Acknowledge,* and *Accept* the forces that *really* run our lives—the very forces that create and manifest our experience of and influence upon new possibilities. When you choose to live more in this way, you can help accelerate worldwide access to the energetics of this Next Tier of the human adventure.

It will seem so effortless to initiate the changes that you and other Seekers must access for yourselves and the world that Non-Seekers will naturally join you in creating this new world. Creation's apps will take over with absolute perfection. Your lives, the lives of those you know, and even the lives of some you have not yet met will be potentiated for *MORE* beyond the ordinary. More of humanity will be awakening to the sacred and majestic nature of authentic energized conscious living. Respect will grow for that which organizes it all, and we'll celebrate *Creation's Codes...in action*!

Remember that when we consciously bring an available source of energy to any system, consistent with its nature, the forces of creation effortlessly, magically and profoundly transform, evolve, enrich and add so much *MORE*. Seekers, the **WEME** brings our energy richness to the world and helps make it one in which we all will be prouder to live.

What you are seeking is seeking you.

Ring, Ring, Ring. The Next Tier calls.

Respond with "Yes, I am here" and accept your personalized calling to add an *Unreasonable* and *Extraordinary* quality and quantity of Energetic Capital to the collective Fields of humanity.

It's time for the launch of a way of accessing and fueling the codes for a new experience of reality—for health and body sense, for relationships and intimacy, for business and finances and for impacting the Field of humanity. It will be the best of times, the age of wisdom, the epoch of belief, the season of light and the spring of hope...

Thank you, Seekers, for joining me on this sacred adventure. Through your personal energetics and Energy Rich Field, you can now leap into a new reality, a new humanity—the **WEME** world of this Next Tier.

Tick Tick Tick...**TOCK!**

FIND YOUR MORE

Seekers: There Is Always MORE

The Seeker's Code: Your Journey to Access the Unreasonable and Extraordinary

https://epienergetics.com/the-seekers-code-your-journey

To further your experience of *The Seeker's Code: Your Journey to More*, here are 2 great opportunities to continue your Seeker's journey:

Take the Free 5-Day Challenge:
https://epienergetics.com/5-day-challenge-access-the-extraordinary

And visit **https://epienergetics.com/people**

FOR MORE about Donny...

visit his website at **https://www.donnyepstein.com** and

the Donny Epstein Channel on YouTube at **https://www.youtube.com/c/DonnyEpstein.**

SOCIAL MEDIA...

Facebook.com/epsteindonny

Instagram.com/donny.epstein

BELOW...*find the methods and approaches that Donny Epstein has created and developed that are consistent with EpiEnergetics. You will recognize some as having been mentioned in this book.*

NetworkSpinal® is a spine-centered healing and human performance evolution of the earlier Network Chiropractic and Network Spinal Analysis (NSA) systems practiced worldwide by Doctors of Chiropractic. With this care, a unique spinal motion wave that is a personal signature for how the nervous system and spine learns, adapts, self-organizes, and heals is created and nurtured through gentle spinal adjustments called entrainments. Specific gentle rocking of vertebra creates and evolves spinal "gateways" bringing individuals to higher-order healing and living.

This system is one in which EpiEnergetics®, energy states and the recipe of energy and information for *unreasonable* and *extraordinary* outcomes, are integral parts of the care offered.

MORE about NetworkSpinal and EpiHealing®:

https://epienergetics.com/epihealing

https://epienergetics.com/watch-the-documentary

The 12 Stages of Healing™ is an approach to healing, living, and consciousness originally published in 1994 as a book by the same name, written by Donny Epstein and Nathaniel Altman. The stages—from more effective suffering through the higher spiritual states and community—are a map of the levels of consciousness available to individuals throughout their lifetimes.

SomatoRespiratory™ Integration (SRI) is a body-centered energetic practice utilizing focused attention to breath, movement, and energy through the 12 Stages of Healing. In recent years the understanding of EpiEnergetics and experiencing consistent with *The Seeker's Code* have been integrated into its practice.

MORE about the 12 Stages:

https://epienergetics.com/12-stages-in-12-days

https://epienergetics.com/12-stages-in-12-weeks/

AlchemE® is an EpiEnergetics approach that helps individuals to experience and understand the energetics running their lives. The course is profound and illuminating, incorporating rewarding online content each month along with live events and online gatherings and processes. This book can be seen as a primer for AlchemE, which goes much further into the understandings and access to *Creation's Codes*.

MORE about AlchemE:

https://epienergetics.com/alcheme

AlchemE Mentors™ are committed students of AlchemE who have taken at least one additional year of study with Donny Epstein as their personal mentor on their AlchemE journeys. In addition, they have engaged in intensive training to mentor other individuals in the AlchemE processes. A growing number of AlchemE Mentors are available in private practices to assist individuals with the content of *The Seeker's Code*...and beyond.

EpiExchange™ is a unique and beyond *extraordinary* Field-centered energetic application exclusively practiced by Donny Epstein at intimate events. It establishes "Energy Houses," which focus and act as battery packs for the manifestation of body, mind, spirit, and connection to the larger energetic and consciousness Field of humanity.

MORE about EpiExchange:

https://epienergetics.com/epiexchange-intro-epiexchange-session

Books By Donny Epstein

The 12 Stages of Healing: A Network Approach to Wholeness

Healing Myths, Healing Magic: Breaking the Spell of Old Illusions, Reclaiming Our Power to Heal

The Boomerang Principle

Somato Respiratory Integration Workbook

As time allows, Donny Epstein serves clients privately with his various EpiEnergetics approaches. For information about the possibility of such a collaboration, please inquire by email to: seekerscode@epienergetics.com.

For information about research, historical academic articles about Donny Epstein's methods, and ongoing projects and opportunities, visit the EpiEnergetics Foundation at **https://www.EpiEnergetics.org**.

ACKNOWLEDGMENTS

Special thanks...to my family. To my wife Jackie for her profound inspiration, genius, love and detailed collaborative visioneering and editing of this book and our lives. Eternal gratitude for the gifts given by our parents, Marion and Carl Epstein and Louise and Jack Haskell, who continue to resonate through generations that include my brother Roy Epstein and his wife Sue, my sisters-in-law Alison Michael and Geraldine Celsi and their husbands John Michael and Tony Celsi, and of course the Epstein, Michael, and Celsi adult children and grandchildren.

Infinite love...to our adult children: David and Katie Epstein, Debra and Andrew Daughters, Daniel and Richelle Knowles, and Faith (Louise) Knowles. Hugs and kisses to their delightful children, our grandchildren, Daniel, Donovan, Savannah, Anika, Melany, Marlena, Ella, Evelyn and Samuel for the blessings they continue to bring to our lives.

I am grateful...for those who have studied with me, practiced, and/or taught my various applications leading to and including NetworkSpinal, the 12 Stages of Healing with SomatoRespiratory Integration and EpiIntegrate, Reorganizational Healing, EpiHealing and AlchemE. By embracing, encouraging, challenging and modeling my teachings and applications, they have personally and professionally added greater value to humanity.

An extra big thank you...to my son and daughter-in-law, Drs. Danny and Richelle Knowles, for their love and continuing leadership in the teaching of NetworkSpinal internationally, and to the many dozens of prior "Network" instructors and transformational event staff. Their past decades of passionate contribution continue to impact the Field and inspire our current EpiHealing event staff who represent the EpiEnergetics evolved models called NetworkSpinal and SomatoRespiratory Integration (SRI).

Danke...to Dr. Carina Roesener, for her love, friendship, collaboration, active participation in professional projects and for being an EpiEnergetics team member, leader and practitioner. Her insight, support and discernment in the creative production and delivery of my ideas and gifts have been invaluable.

I cherish...the close personal friendships of so many, including Joel Rodney Hall, DC, Robin Sherman Rothstein, DC, Mary Johnston, DC, Louis Abate, DC, Shelley Axford, DC, Steve Katz, DC, Roselyn Katz and Ari Diskin, DC, Isabelle Nelson, DC, Donna Mutter, DC, and Marina Reggiori. I am thankful for their decades of service at our many events in the USA and abroad, and also for Louis's coordination of the 12 Stages of Healing and SRI instruction worldwide. To Arno Burnier, DC, a contemporary, also inspired by a similar reverence of the self organizing intelligence of life, extraordinary healing and service for a new humanity. These souls have been a gift in my life...and even more to the people we have had the honor to serve.

For their help on various aspects of this book...thanks to JeVon McCormick, Mikey Kershisnik, Maggie Rains, Annette Mims, Seth Libby, Michael Nagin, Braxton Benes, Geoff Pope, Caroline Hough, and others on the publishing team. Also, *merci beaucoup* to our illustrator Anne Laborde for creating the sketches that appear on these pages and abundant gratitude to Justin Nicola for his brilliant editorial refinements to the manuscript.

Gratitude...to the Russian-, Spanish-, Chinese-, Italian-, Hebrew-, and French-speaking individuals who have translated in the past and continue now in sharing my teachings to enable more people to benefit—as do the guides, concierges, and the passionate members of our growing worldwide community who provide ongoing support. Gratitude also to my longtime amico Silvestro DeBolfo, who has hosted many years of my events in the hotels he has managed by the shores of Lake Como in Italy, and to our friends Cinzia Gheza and Dominque Hort, DC, who have been at my side for years at our European events.

And, all too often behind the scenes...our current EpiEnergetics Institute team members, Diana Kramer, Terry Monroe, Carrie Hodge, Paul Macias, Audrey Faucheaux, Darius Vega, Jason Lange, Mikhail (Misha) Sharapov, Konstantin (Kostya) Lennykh and Miguel Barrera—and as past members of our creative team, Dan Lemberger and Amanda Leathern. Thank you all for helping make it possible to deliver this to you—and the world.

Some of the Visionaries and Collaborators Who Have Expanded My Map of Reality

Padre Eligio is one of my most treasured mentors. His accomplishments and his humility exemplify divine inspiration in action! As founder of the Mondo X communities, this extraordinary Italian Franciscan priest has helped create a better world from what some might call "the bottom up." The mission of the communities has been to help drug addicts and others who have lost their way. As Padre once told me, when the ragazzi (kids) of the community work to rebuild ruins and restore them to their prior beauty, they are also rebuilding their lives. I have had the honor to witness the transformation of souls from outcasts to servants of humanity through this man's leadership at Mondo X. For nearly a quarter century, "P. Eligio" has shaped my concept of selfless service, love and true devotion to a greater purpose. Thank you, Padre, for the massive impact you have made on me and so many others.

Tony Robbins and his wife Sage have been amongst the most influential of guides, teachers and friends. By offering me additional experiences in the way I see, interact, and influence others, their models and wisdom permeate my being. They have catalyzed my mission to bring more to the world. Tony's gracious introduction of me personally and professionally to his community has enriched my life and Jackie's—as has his almost two decades of sharing this journey with love and respect for our mutual gifts.

Betsy Lehrfeld and her late life partner Jim Turner, have been friends, mentors and legal and political advisors. We have shared countless hours witnessing and experiencing the evolving larger system that pulls the strings of all we consider to be real. Jim advised me that when we believe there is "an us and a them," we have already lost in life. There is only "an us and an it." The "it" represents two groups of people: those who seek freedom and those who seek control—both in ways consistent with their tier of humanity. Ultimately, even those who seek professional or cultural control truly wish for freedom in their own lives. Jim was a pioneer in consumer rights, transpartisan politics and the freedom of personal choice and informed consent. To Jim's and Betsy's credit, I have always known them to support what is just and right in the world.

Ralph Kilmann, PhD, Ichak Adizes, PhD, the late Paul Polak, MD, and Berny Dohrmann are to be applauded for their brilliance in developing models of business that integrate body, mind and spirit and a collaborative, participatory humanity. Others that have influenced me include Beverly Rubik, PhD, a pioneer in biofield and sympathetic resonance technologies, and the late Candace Pert, PhD, whose research of the biochemistry of emotions and consciousness has led to my understanding of somatopsychic relationships and emotions as vibrational and biochemical states.

Thanks also to my past Boulder, Colorado, next-door neighbor, Ken Wilber, one of the world's great spiritual philosophers and cultural "map makers." Our theories and models have co-evolved for decades, and his Integral Theory continues to inform the content and context of my thought process and the even broader EpiEnergetics "universe." Hats off to Bruce Lipton, PhD, for his integration of the concepts of energy, consciousness and vibrational states, and being a pioneer in the development of Epigenetics. Our ideas continue to dance together in the Field—and being with Bruce is always an experience of coming home.

Two of my fellow (r)evolutionary chiropractic, health care and personal development educators and very dear friends, Christopher Kent, DC, JD and Patrick Gentempo Jr., DC, continue to impact, inspire, and assist me in better communicating and sharing my evolving theories and practices within the profession and beyond!

In addition to the gift of his friendship, a true visionary, Jacob Liberman, OD, PhD, introduced me to the various aspects of light and its participation in the fields of consciousness and physiology.

Love to my dear friends Richard Kaye, DC, and Amy and Bobby Moberger, who have had my back and held my hand through a wide range of life's happenings these past decades.

Wisdom from the late Ralph Boone, PhD, DC—a trusted friend, my academic tutor and developer of our ambitious and successful interdisciplinary research agenda—paved the way for much that followed on the research front.

Edmond Jonckheere, PhD, at USC has been the senior researcher of the Network Wave since 1997 and has guided graduate students while studying the electrophysiology of Network care. Srideep Musuvathy, PhD, and Roberto Martin Del Campo Vera, PhD, added their discernments and further refinements in the mathematical modeling of the Network Wave and development of novel models and applications. Gratitude to Marissa Ericson, PhD, current director of research in EpiEnergetics. She has been a resource for my journey into the intersection of consciousness, the nervous system, multiple dimensions and **MORE.**

It has been exciting over the years to collaborate with Dan Lemberger, DC, and Simon Senzon, DC, on several academic papers leading up to the EpiEnergetics model. Also, heartfelt thanks for Dan's guidance over the years as an integrator in various aspects of the delivery of my methods.

Continuing on the academic front, thank you to Gerry Clum, DC, who introduced me to the social science model in healing and advised me— personally and politically at critical times. Also to one of chiropractic's larger-than-life personalities, Reginald Gold, DC, whose treatise on the Triune of Life launched me into the relationship between organizing intelligences, energy and their physical manifestations—from which EpiEnergetics has evolved. To Tom Whitehorn, DC, who was my mentor through chiropractic college and one of my largest early professional influences. And to Thom Gelardi, DC, who helped birth, defend and make the non therapeutic model of chiropractic to support the self organizing intelligence viable in the current educational and political environment. To Ron Oberstein, DC, who continues to support the most traditional perspectives of chiropractic which the others I have acknowledged represent and seeks to expand its impact in larger circles of outreach.

A shout out to Nathanial Altman, who in 1994 co-authored my first published book, *The 12 Stages of Healing*. His partnership in articulating the cosmology of the physical, emotional, mental, social and spiritual attributes of healing helped create a matrix for what was to come.

Gratitude to the brilliant Janet Mills, who has assisted in so many ways both during and since the writing of *The 12 Stages of Healing* and *Healing Myths, Healing Magic*.

Namaste to Sri Bhagavan of the Oneness University for his teachings and blessings—and for our times of collaboration for greater impact in the world.

Applause to William Reilly, former EPA administrator, former President and Chairman of the World Wildlife Fund, and Head of the US Delegation to the Earth Summit, and his brilliant and elegant wife, Elizabeth. For decades, Bill shared Next Tier energetic models seeking a more dignified use of energy for the earth and its inhabitants. He strives for the sacred balance between corporate profits, ecological production of service and energy conservation. A valued "old school" gentleman, his respectful and resourceful politics successfully bridge worlds, helping make this Next Tier possible.

So many souls have been involved in my nearly seven-decade journey—with four decades of personal and professional inspiration, perspiration, creation and service—that naming them all would warrant another volume! You know who you are. Please know that you truly are so very appreciated.

And finally...to the hundreds of thousands who have received my gifts in their many forms and led to the awareness that inspired the need for the content in this book...and to you now reading this. *YOU* are an ever-present driving force in my life. Thank you for bringing your personal energetics to a world in need of so much **MORE**.

Printed in Great Britain
by Amazon

29394246R10209